RESPONSIVE REGULATION

Transcending the Deregulation Debate

Ian Ayres
John Braithwaite

New York   Oxford
OXFORD UNIVERSITY PRESS

Oxford University Press

Oxford   New York
Athens   Auckland Bangkok   Bombay
Calcutta   Cape Town   Dar es Salaam   Delhi
Florence   Hong Kong   Istanbul   Karachi
Kuala Lumpur   Madras   Madrid . Melbourne
Mexico City   Nairobi   Paris   Singapore
Taipei   Tokyo   Toronto

and associated companies in
Berlin   Ibadan

First published in 1992 by Oxford University Press, Inc.,
200 Madison Avenue, New York, New York 10016

First issued as an Oxford University Press paperback, 1995

Oxford is a registered trademark of Oxford University Press

Library of Congress Cataloging-in-Publication Data
Ayres, Ian
Responsive Regulation: transcending the deregulation debate/
Ian Ayres, John Braithwaite
p. cm.—(Oxford socio-legal studies)
Includes bibliographical references and index.
ISBN 0-19-507070-4
ISBN 0-19-509376-3 (pbk)
1. Trade regulation. 2. Deregulation. 3. Industry and state.
I. Braithwaite, John. II. Title. III. Series.
K3842.A97 1992 343'.08—dc20 [342.38] 91-17131

9 8 7 6 5 4 3 2 1

Printed in the United States of America
on acid-free paper

Oxford Socio-Legal Studies

Responsive Regulation

GENERAL EDITORS   Donald R. Harris   Keith Hawkins
Sally Lloyd-Bostock   Doreen McBarnet

Oxford Socio-Legal Studies is a series of books published for the Centre for
Socio-Legal Studies, Wolfson College, Oxford. The series is concerned
generally with the relationship between law and society, and is designed to
reflect the increasing interest of lawyers, social scientists and historians in this
field.

Recent titles

Christopher J. Whelan
   SMALL CLAIMS COURTS: A Comparative Study
Paul Rock
   HELPING VICTIMS OF CRIME: The Home Office and the Rise of
   Victim Support in England and Wales
John Eekelaar
   REGULATING DIVORCE
Lenore J. Weitzman and Mavis Maclean
   ECONOMIC CONSEQUENCES OF DIVORCE: The International
   Perspective

To Jay and Karen,
Val, Ben, and Sari.

Acknowledgments

This book represents a collaboration made possible by our relationships with the American Bar Foundation (ABF) and Research School of Social Sciences, Australian National University. Both institutions encourage interdisciplinary forms of social science scholarship of the kind attempted herein.

During the last three years, Ayres has enjoyed a joint appointment with the Foundation and Northwestern University and Braithwaite has benefited from being a regular visiting fellow with the ABF. Our work on responsive regulation flourished during the time we worked at the Foundation and received its generous intellectual and financial support. Ayres was also sponsored by the Australian National University in a visit to Canberra to finish the book.

In several chapters, use has been made of data from Braithwaite's ongoing research on nursing home regulation, to be published with Valerie Braithwaite, Diane Gibson, Toni Makkai, and David Ermann. We thank the Australian Department of Community Services and Health, the Australian Research Council, and the American Bar Foundation for funding this work.

The authors would also like to thank the Michigan Law Review for permission to include in Chapter 4 a revised and expanded version of Braithwaite's "Enforced Self-Regulation: A New Strategy for Corporate Crime Control" (1982).

It would be diffucult to list all of the scholars and practitioners in the regulatory research community who have shaped our thinking on the matters discussed in this book. However, we must express particular thanks to the people whose comments substantially improved our manuscript: Ken Abbott, Ellen Baar, Geoffrey Brennan, John Clifford, Ross Cranston, Patricia Day, Shari Diamond, John Donohue, Brent Fisse, Meyer Freed, Gil Geis, Barbara Glenn, Bob Goodin, Peter Grabosky, Fred Gruen, David Haddock, Alan Hamlin, Rudolph Klein, Errol Meidinger, Joseph Murphy, Philip Pettit, Paul Quirk, Donna Randall, Eric Rasmusen, Joel Rogers, John Scholz, Philip Selznick, Susan Shapiro, Peter Siegelman, Kent Smith, and participants at the 1989 A.N.U Conference on Institutional Design. Presentations at the American Bar Foundation, the American Law and Society Association Meetings; the Australian Law and Society meetings, the University of Sydney, and the University of Illinois also helped us to improve our reasoning and exposition.

Rebecca Mitchells, Miriam Landau, and Robert Wilkin provided excellent research assistance. We thank Audrey Magee, Frances Redrup, Anne Robinson, Lorrie Wessel, and Johanna Womack for their help with the production of the manuscript.

Contents

Oxford Socio-Legal Studies

Responsive Regulation

1

The Politics of an Idea

This book is about the need to transcend the intellectual stalemate between those who favor strong state regulation of business and those who advocate deregulation. It is a debate that has been rerun so many times that to open it up in an audience of regulatory policy makers today is to put them immediately to sleep. The practitioners yawn because they know that in reality regulation occurs in "many rooms" (Galanter, 1981; Nader and Nader, 1985). A free market can mean that private regulation by cartels will defeat competition; detailed state regulation can be a symbolic exercise that is readily side-stepped by minor realignment of the market.

Practical people who are concerned with outcomes seek to understand the intricacies of interplays between state regulation and private orderings (e.g., Rose-Ackerman, 1988). The empirical foundation for their analysis of what is good regulatory policy is acceptance of the inevitability of some sort of symbiosis between state regulation and self-regulation. This is true of the most basic commercial legal forms:

> The drafting of the Uniform Commercial Code was a self-conscious attempt (by Karl Llewellyn) to synthesize formal law and commercial usage: the formal law would incorporate the best commercial practice and would in turn serve as a model for the refinement and development of that practice. The Code's broadly drafted rules would be accessible to businessmen and would provide a framework for self-regulation which would in turn furnish attentive courts with content for the Code's categories. Thus the Code would serve as a vehicle for business communities to evolve law for themselves in dialogue with the courts, operating not as interpreters of imposed law but as articulators and critics of business usage. (Galanter, 1981: 29–30)

Good policy analysis is not about choosing between the free market and government regulation. Nor is it simply deciding what the law should proscribe. If we accept that sound policy analysis is about understanding private regulation—by industry associations, by firms, by peers, and by individual consciences—and how it is interdependent with state regulation, then interesting possibilities open up to steer the mix of private and public regulation. It is this mix, this interplay, that works to assist or impede solution of the policy problem. Participants on both sides frame the deregulation debate as a kind of "Live Free or Die" policy choice.[1] Even lovers of liberty might reasonably ask whether third alternatives do not exist. This book is

3

about proposing such alternatives. We argue that by working more creatively with the interplay between private and public regulation, government and citizens can design better policy solutions.

In this chapter we have three objectives. In the first section, we sketch the notion of responsive regulation. We introduce the specific policy proposals of the following chapters and connect these policies to the thrust of our metaregulatory theory. The second section argues for the book's contemporary relevance. Far from the perception that we live in an era of vast deregulation, we argue that administrative and regulatory practice is in a state of flux in which responsive regulatory innovations are politically feasible. Finally, in the third section, we place our theories of responsive regulation within a republican tradition that is distinct from political theories of (neo-) corporatism, liberalism, or pluralism.

The Idea of Responsive Regulation

Responsive regulation is distinguished (from other strategies of market governance) both in what triggers a regulatory response and what the regulatory response will be. We suggest that regulation be responsive to industry structure in that different structures will be conducive to different degrees and forms of regulation. Government should also be attuned to the differing motivations of regulated actors. Efficacious regulation should speak to the diverse objectives of regulated firms, industry associations, and individuals within them. Regulations themselves can affect structure (e.g., the number of firms in the industry) and can affect motivations of the regulated.

We also conceive that regulation should respond to industry conduct, to how effectively industry is making private regulation work. The very behavior of an industry or the firms therein should channel the regulatory strategy to greater or lesser degrees of government intervention.

Most distinctively, responsiveness implies not only a new view of what triggers regulatory intervention, but leads us to innovative notions of what the response should be. Public regulation can promote private market governance through enlightened delegations of regulatory functions. In the next chapters, we argue in a broad variety of contexts that public policy can effectively delegate government regulation of the marketplace to public interest groups (Chapter 3), to unregulated competitors of the regulated firms (Chapter 5), and even to the regulated firms themselves (Chapter 4).

Such delegation should be neither wholesale nor unconditional. Moreover, one of the things that can be delegated is the monitoring of other delegations. Central to our notion of responsiveness is the idea that escalating forms of government intervention will reinforce and help constitute less intrusive and delegated forms of market regulation. In Chapter 2 we introduce the concept of an enforcement pyramid that we argue can be implemented in multiple ways to the same effect. By credibly asserting a willingness to regulate more intrusively, responsive regulation can channel marketplace transactions to less intrusive and less centralized forms of government intervention. Escalating forms of responsive regulation can thereby retain many of the benefits of laissez-faire governance without abdicating government's responsibility to correct market failure.

Responsive regulation is not a clearly defined program or a set of prescriptions concerning the best way to regulate. On the contrary, the best strategy is shown to depend on context, regulatory culture, and history. Responsiveness is rather an attitude that enables the blossoming of a wide variety of regulatory approaches, only some of which are canvased here. Although our ideas for responsive regulation bear many of the marks of Nonet and Selznick's (1978) "responsive law" concept— flexibility, a purposive focus on competence, participatory citizenship, negotiation— we are skeptical about repressive, autonomous, and responsive law being evolutionary stages in legal development. Indeed Nonet and Selznick (1978:23) themselves are careful to limit their claims that responsive law is a developmental response to the stresses inherent in the functioning of autonomous law. Our attempt to sensitize readers to innovative regulatory possibilities thrown up by thinking responsively is devoid of any grand theoretical aspirations.

The attitude of responsiveness is very similar to the attitude of interactiveness that Sigler and Murphy (1988) advocate in *Interactive Corporate Compliance*, although there are important differences in the models we develop from those of Sigler and Murphy. Responsiveness, like interactiveness, is not one of those notions such that if two people know what responsiveness is, they will come up with the same solution for the responsive regulator to implement in a particular situation. An attitude of responsiveness does generate different policy ideas that do transcend the divide between regulatory and deregulatory solutions. But for the responsive regulator, there are no optimal or best regulatory solutions, just solutions that respond better than others to the plural configurations of support and opposition that exist at a particular moment in history.

With this as an introduction, let us review more specifically the key policy ideas of this book. Chapters 2 to 4 develop four separate and rather different ideas for making regulation responsive. They are designed as self-contained chapters so readers can approach the book by dipping into just one of them. However, the reader who takes in the whole book will find that some of the problems left unsolved by the idea in one chapter will be addressed by the idea in another. Although some reference is made to these connections within each chapter, they are more fully drawn together in Chapter 6. Each chapter represents a different exemplification of how to think responsively. None represents an idea that is conceived as universally applicable; responsiveness, after all, implies that there are no universal solutions.

Chapter 2 seeks to solve the policy problem that regulatory styles which are cooperative on the one hand or punitive on the other "may operate at cross-purposes because the strategies fit uneasily with each other as a result of conflicting imperatives" (Rees, 1988: 12). It is contended that both an economic analysis and a social analysis converge on the need to avoid policies of consistent reliance on either punishment or persuasion as the means of securing regulatory objectives. From both analytical viewpoints, tit-for-tat is the strategy of mixing punishment and persuasion that is most likely to be effective. Tit-for-tat is a regulatory strategy that is provokable but forgiving.

Furthermore, it is contended that the achievement of regulatory objectives is more likely when agencies display both a hierarchy of sanctions and a hierarchy of regulatory strategies of varying degrees of interventionism. The regulatory design requirement we describe is for agencies to display two enforcement pyramids with a range of interventions of ever-increasing intrusiveness (matched by ever-decreasing frequency of use). Regulators will do best by indicating a willingness to escalate intervention up those pyramids or to deregulate down the pyramids in response to the industry's performance in securing regulatory objectives.

Finally, it is argued that the greater the heights of tough enforcement to which the agency can escalate (at the apex of its enforcement pyramid), the more effective the agency will be at securing compliance and the less likely that it will have to resort to tough enforcement. Regulatory agencies will be able to speak more softly when they are perceived as carrying big sticks.

Chapter 3 addresses the problem that policies that secure the advantages of an evolution of cooperation between regulatory agencies and industry are policies that also run the risk of an evolution of capture and corruption. Tripartism—empowering citizen associations—is advanced as a way of solving this dilemma. We develop a game–theoretic model of regulatory capture in which firms lobby to win the hearts and minds of agencies. We distinguish between three different forms of capture that have sharply different welfare consequences. In some circumstances, tripartism can foster a form of welfare-enhancing capture without forfeiting the agency's role in protecting the public interest. Again, there is convergence between an economic analysis of capture and a social analysis concerned with citizen empowerment. A case is made that a republican regulatory tripartism may facilitate the attainment of regulatory goals, prevent corruption, prevent harmful capture, encourage certain forms of capture that we find to be beneficial, and nurture democracy.

Chapter 4 illustrates one of the creative options available to escalate the interventionism of regulatory strategy to a middle path between self-regulation and command and control government regulation. This option is enforced self-regulation. It means that firms are required to write their own set of corporate rules, which are then publicly ratified. And when there is a failure of private enforcement of these privately written (and publicly ratified) rules, the rules are then publicly enforced.

The thesis of Chapter 5 is that in some regulatory settings, regulating only an individual firm (or a subset of the firms) in an industry can promote efficiency by avoiding the costs associated with industry-wide intervention or laissez-faire. The existence of a single (or a few) competitive firm can have a dramatic effect on the competitive conduct and performance of an entire industry. Indeed, the willingness of concentrated private consumers to subsidize second sources of competition among their suppliers provides strong empirical support for government intervention on behalf of more diffuse consumers.

Far from denying the powerful effect of competition, partial-industry regulation uses the spur of competition to affect the unregulated portion of the market. But unlike across-the-board industry regulation, if government decisions go awry, the mistakes do not need to affect adversely the unregulated firms. Instead of completely displacing the market, partial-industry regulation creates a system of "checks and balances" between the two regulatory extremes. The regulated portion of the industry mitigates the prospect of private collusion. And the unregulated portion of the industry mitigates the risk that captured or benighted regulation will harm the public.

In advancing these ideas we rely heavily on illustrative material from the United States, Australia, and to a lesser extent Britain. Yet, we advance them as ideas that might be given life in any country, although of course, the institutional embodiment of the ideas would be radically different in other cultures. Indeed, one of our fondest hopes for this book is that some might read it in the Soviet Union and Eastern Europe. As these nations address their problems of paralyzing overregulation, it seems to us important that they learn some lessons from the painful mistakes of the West, that they do not fall prey to a jingoistic libertarianism that seeks to sweep away all regulation as automatically bad. Although Eastern Europe and the Soviet Republics need a large dose of deregulation, they also need to create new regulatory orders almost from the ground up if their new market economies are to work and survive—securities regulation, antitrust, environmental, and consumer protection enforcement. It seems to us an important task to persuade the newly emerging consumer and environmental movements of Eastern Europe to press for responsive processes of deregulation and regulation.

In the next section, we argue that in today's environment of regulatory flux responsive regulatory strategies are politically feasible. We show that a number of the responsive strategies that we propose have already been put in place in a variety of contexts. To that extent we provide the beginnings of a theoretical justification for these nascent applications of responsive regulation and normatively argue for their proliferation.

Contemporary Relevance

The Era of Deregulation?

It is a commonly held view that we live in an era of deregulation in the Western world. Business is said to be fighting back against overbearing state intervention; the values of the market are reasserting their ascendancy. We think this is not a very perceptive account of what is happening in the capitalist democracies. We have not, and are not, experiencing an era of deregulation so much as an era of regulatory flux—an era when dramatic regulatory, deregulatory, and re-regulatory shifts are occurring simultaneously.

Even the United States, after 8 years of an administration with a stronger ideological commitment to deregulation than any in the history of the Western world (the only competitor for this title being the Thatcher government), has hardly shifted the balance away from state regulation. Unfortunately, we have to labor this point with quite a bit of evidence, as our experience is that both supporters and opponents of the Reagan presidency are inclined to dismiss such an assertion. We consider in turn regulation of the environment, occupational health and safety, nursing homes, financial institutions, securities and futures markets, defense contracting, tax enforcement, antitrust, consumer product safety, and food standards (see also Meiners and Yandle, 1989).

In the early years of the Reagan administration, there was certainly fierce deregulation of environmental protection. In 1982, the General Accounting Office found the Environmental Protection Agency (EPA) enforcement actions under the Clean Water Act to have dropped to 27 percent of its 1977 peak (General Accounting Office, 1983: 58). But the deregulation produced a backlash, to the point where 1984 enforcement *exceeded* the 1977 level by 30 percent (Andreen, 1987: 207). In the following years, enforcement, particularly criminal enforcement, underwent further dramatic acceleration. Jail terms for federal environmental crimes during financial years 1986–1989 were more than nine times their level for 1983–1985 (*Corporate Crime Reporter,* 15 May, 1989: 18). EPA referrals of civil cases to the Department of Justice in 1986–1989 were also running at more than twice the level of 1981–1985, and indeed of the Carter years (*Corporate Crime Reporter,* 2 April, 1990: 21).

The Occupational Health and Safety Administration (OHSA) experimented with self-regulatory innovations between 1982 and 1984 (Rees, 1988). However, the experiments were never expanded into programs. OHSA has always been a weak regulatory presence, even if its tiny band of rulebook-oriented inspectors were at times an irritation to American business. There were no cases of OSHA civil penalty assessments of over $100,000 under the Nixon or Ford administrations. Under Carter, there were four that were well in excess of this threshold ($804,190; $515,917; $462,300; $366,800). Again in the first Reagan term, this fell back to zero assessments in excess of $100,000. But in the second Reagan term this rose to fifty-seven, fourteen of them exceeding $1 million (*Corporate Crime Reporter,* 10 April, 1989). The self-regulation innovations had fizzled and as Vice-President Quayle proudly announced during his preelection debate with Senator Bentsen, the agency was being a tougher enforcer than it ever had been. It remains true, however, that under Reagan OSHA suffered severe cuts in staffing.

Funding for Department of Energy environmental, health, and safety programs was cut from $61 million in 1981 to $39 million in 1985. Scandal and backlash ensued here too, particularly concerning safety in the nuclear weapons industry. For 1989, the budget appropriation was up to $90 million (*New York Times,* 7 November, 1988).

The new Reagan administration also sought to deregulate nursing home standards by replacing annual government inspections with triennial inspections by the American Council on Hospital Standards, a move that was unsuccessful (Jost, 1983, 1988). The administration did cut the number of health facility inspectors (mostly nursing home inspectors) that it funded in the states from 2,400 to 1,800 in 1982. By the end of Reagan's second term the number of these inspectors exceeded 4,000. Moreover, during the Reagan era, the federal policy of support for a "consultative" approach to nursing home regulation was sharply reversed and replaced with a law enforcement policy. Nursing home enforcement did in fact substantially increase during the Reagan era, and a variety of new and tougher standards were passed by the Congress in 1987.

The rash of Savings and Loans crashes between 1984 and 1987 ushered in a tightening of prudential regulation of financial institutions. As of February 1988, 357 financial institutions were under investigation for criminal misconduct—a 100 percent increase in 2 years (Wells, 1988: 7). State and federal legislators found themselves under attack in 1990 if they could be portrayed in election advertisements as supporters of the 1980s deregulation of the Savings and Loans industry. Finance and banking regulation generally enjoyed a 130 percent budget increase and a 44 percent staffing increase during the Reagan years (Tramontozzi and Chilton, 1987; 4–5). It was during the Reagan administration that handcuffs and wired undercover operatives first appeared on Wall Street and in the Chicago futures exchanges. It was the Reagan Securities and Exchange Commission that was the first to take seriously insider trading as a crime. Scandals during the Reagan era led for the first time to a half credible enforcement program against the longstanding problem of defense contracting fraud. The federal government also got much tougher with corrupt government officials who benefited from the largesse of corrupt industries. Indictments of corrupt federal officials were more than twice as high in each of the years 1983 to 1986 as in all the years 1977 to 1982.[2]

Tax offenders did not exactly get an easier run under the Reagan Administration. Between 1980 and 1985 the percentage of federal tax convictions that resulted in a prison term increased from 34 percent to 48 percent and average prison terms doubled in length (*Corporate Crime Reporter*, 26 October, 1987: 15–16).

With antitrust, the picture is mixed. The Reagan administration, like many Western governments during this period, became much less interventionist in its approach to mergers. Although the Carter Federal Trade Commission brought twenty-two merger cases in 4 years, there were only thirteen merger cases in the first 7 years of the Reagan administration (*Corporate Crime Reporter*, 14 November, 1988: 3). On the other hand, overall the antitrust enforcement of the Department of Justice got tougher with more than twice as many criminal cases a year being run under Reagan than under Carter; yet with fewer civil cases going to court (*Corporate Crime Reporter*, 5 October, 1987: 1; 18 April, 1988: 8; 24 July, 1989: 19). Days served in jail and fines paid by antitrust offenders also jumped sharply after the Reagan administration took over (*Corporate Crime Reporter*, 25 May, 1987: 20). Antitrust shows every sign of getting tougher under Bush, with huge increases in maximum corporate penalties and increased prison terms being recommended by the U.S. Sentencing Commission.

Regulatory cuts were made and maintained at the Consumer Product Safety Commission, the Food Safety and Inspection Service in the Agriculture Department, and the National Highway Traffic Safety Administration (Tramontozzi and Chilton, 1987). But the biggest cuts in regulatory expenditure were the total demise of the Civil Aeronautics Board and a 51 percent expenditure reduction at the Interstate Commerce Commission pursuant to the deregulation of trucks, buses, and railroads. Both of these cutbacks were decisions of the Carter Administration. In spite of this, real regulatory spending increased by 10 percent during the Reagan years (Tramontozzi and Chilton, 1987).

Overall, it is difficult to conclude that the Reagan presidency was an era of deregulation. There is nothing to match the initiatives of the Carter administration in deregulating airlines, the trucking industry, rail, financial institutions, and decontrolling oil and natural gas prices. The Carter deregulatory accomplishments appear more durable because they were focused on areas of economic regulation (to the exclusion of "social" regulation) where there was a broad coalition of both conservative and liberal support (Derthick and Quirk, 1985: 218). If there has been an era of deregulation in the United States, it is over. There has certainly been an era of deregulatory rhetoric and, like Sigler and Murphy (1988: 42–43), we wonder if this has produced a backlash:

> The invitation to non-compliance inherent in the stance of deregulation has not been misread by the managers of many businesses. Deregulation as a policy contains the seeds of its own destruction. Widespread non-compliance, encouraged during the Reagan years by the mood of the national administration, could lead to reregulation on a massive scale, in reaction to the need to protect the public against business.

Harris and Milkis (1989) argue that the expansion of presidential control over the administration of regulatory agencies under Reagan ironically may have been the very kind of centralization of control that will be a boon to future administrations that seek to re-regulate. In this regard they cite the prophesy of the *National Journal:*

> One popular image of President Reagan's first term portrays him successfully pulling the fangs out of government regulation. But a more realistic portrait would show Reagan as tamer, using whip and stool to hold the regulatory process at bay. When Reagan folds his whip four years from now, most of the regulatory restraints he imposed could be reversed by a new Administration. (*National Journal,* December 1, 1984: 2284)

In fact, Harris and Milkis point out that by 1984, Reagan was already beginning to fold his whip, that the early deregulatory successes appeared to be ''temporary regulatory relief rather than lasting regulatory change,'' and that this relief came at a serious political cost for the administration. Ultimately then, Harris and Milkis (1989: 275) lament, ''deregulation failed.'' It failed because there was no real strategy that took seriously the political appeal that public interest groups supporting regulation could bring to bear. There was no strategy to counter the option that the public interest groups had in a federal system of securing tougher state enforcement when federal enforcement withered (Harris and Milkis, 1989: 292). Nixon, too, was wrong in his political judgment that environmentalism was a fad that would pass (Marcus, 1980: 87). The social forces that gave rise to the growth of public interest movements in the 1970s have not disappeared (McFarland, 1976: 4–5).

We are at a political crossroads today where sophisticated strategists of the right can see that they have as great a need to engage politically with public interest movements as the public interest groups have a need to engage with business and the state. Hence, there is political relevance to all sides of options, such as those we discuss in Chapter 3, concerning the more systematic involvement of public interest groups in regulatory negotiation. Many observers on both the right and the left can agree with Boyer's (1989: 125) assessment of the history of the U.S. Federal Trade commission of the last 20 years as ''alternating between the regulatory extremes of mindless activism and enforced torpor.'' Those who prefer torpor and those who prefer boots-and-all activism might be able to agree that the worst possible compromise is to seesaw between the two. There has to be space for agreement between the left and right that matters, such as our economic future and our environmental future, are too important to seesaw them away.

Therefore, although Reagan had stronger rhetoric than Carter about getting government off the back of business, it was Carter who was a better ally for the deregulators. And this just repeats a familiar postwar pattern of conservative administrations letting business down on this score (more generally, see Goodin, 1983; but also see Scholz and Wei, 1986). Nixon was the greater presider over new regulations and entire new regulatory agencies such as the Occupational Safety and Health Administration, the Nuclear Regulatory Commission, the Environmental Protection Agency, the Mine Safety and Health Administration, the National Highway Transport Safety Administration, and the Consumer Product Safety Commission. For the period 1953 to 1975, Republican administrations gave the "big six" regulatory Commissions more budgetary support than the Democratic administrations (Stewart et al., 1982). The same story is true of Australia since the 1950s. The deregulatory accomplishments of conservative governments have been less than those of the Hawke Labor governments (see also Grabosky and Braithwaite, 1986: 205).

Some might say that Margaret Thatcher's Britain is another story, the story of a conservative government delivering the goods on deregulation. It remains to be seen how much of Margaret Thatcher's deregulation will endure the reigns of future Labor governments. We suspect that history might not judge her as having effected a substantial deregulation of the British economy. Her major conservative accomplishments have been in the fields of privatization and increasing inequality rather than deregulation. There is a tendency to confuse privatization and deregulation as the same issue when indeed privatization is often accompanied by an increase in regulation. Hence, when the Thatcher government privatized telecommunications, it set up a new regulatory agency to oversee the new private companies. When the Thatcher government instituted policies that shifted radically the provision of nursing home beds from the public sector to the private nursing home industry (Day and Klein, 1987), 200 little nursing home inspectorates were set up in the district health authorities around the country to upgrade the casual public oversight of this industry that existed previously. Ironically, these inspectorates have not only stepped up regulatory scrutiny of the new private sector homes, but of the public sector and charitable providers as well. These developments have been of such profound significance in Britain that Rudolf Klein and Patricia Day of the University of Bath speak of the emergence of a new regulatory state. An example of radical privatization seriously mooted in the United States, which would be bound to increase regulation, is the proposal to give all school students a voucher with which they could purchase education from any school of their choice—public or private. If such a policy were implemented, it would inevitably be accompanied by substantial resourcing of inspectorates to ensure that all schools meet minimum certification standards. Privatization and deregulation can be negatively correlated social trends.

In his important book on financial, insurance, securities, and antitrust regulation in Britain during the Thatcher era Michael Clark concludes that "the changes now in progress amount to the almost complete abandonment of the exclusive, informal gentleman's club model of self-regulation and the establishment of formal, public and bureaucratic regulation with a large measure of formal supervision." (Clark, 1986: 4). Clark explains this regulatory growth (under a government with a deregulatory ideology) by the internationalization of markets and the political program of creating a mass shareholding democracy—both bringing outsiders into the gentlemen's club who want formal assurances that the gentlemen will play by the rules. Whatever country one examines, the mixed and somewhat Pyrrhic victories conservatives have won on the question of deregulation can give cause for gloom on the right.

Gloom on the Left

By and large, we support spending more of the community's scarce resources on protecting the environment, protecting its workers from industrial accidents and disease, guaranteeing that consumer products are safe, enforcing antitrust laws, protecting vulnerable people who are cared for by large organizations that run nursing homes, hospitals, hostels, and prisons, and running affirmative action programs. Many on the left believe that a book like this is a naive sort of enterprise for folk who have such beliefs. Some of them think this *is* the era of deregulation, that business, even more so than usual, is winning. When business does not seem to win, some critics think that it is only because protecting citizens in this way is ultimately functional for the survival of capitalism, for example, by defending its legitimacy. Gloomy left scholars subscribe to what Hindess (1982) calls "capacity-outcome" approaches to understanding struggles. They assume that all one needs do to determine the likely outcome of struggles is to identify the resources or capacities available to the conflicting interests; the outcome of the struggle can then be read off in an a priori fashion.

How do we reply to scholars of the gloomy left school who see capital as structurally impregnable? Our answer returns us to why we think it is not very accurate to describe the present as an era of deregulation. Even when the business community fills key state posts with its ideological sympathizers, it turns out that deregulation is not ubiquitous. The sources of power are diffuse in modern societies. It is this diffuseness we must understand if we are to develop a more sophisticated and predictive theory of regulation than the crude "capture" theories of the left and right, which conceive of regulation as solely benefiting the regulated. In this regard, we find useful the neo-corporatist work of Streeck and Schmitter (1985) on the shifting balances between the key institutions for securing social order—the community, the market, the state, and the associations.

The nineteenth century saw an expansion of markets into traditional domains of preexisting communities. In the twentieth century, the state asserted itself over domains that had become the prerogative of the market during the nineteenth century. By the late twentieth century, however, strong countercurrents had developed. One was the deregulation push to win back some of the encroachment the state had made on the market. Another was a reassertion of community—the rapid rise of the consumer movement, the environmental movement, and the women's movement, among others since the 1960s (McFarland, 1976; Handler, 1978; Marcus, 1980; Berry, 1984; Derthick and Quirk, 1985; Vogel, 1986; Harris and Milkis, 1989). Interconnected with this is the increasing importance of peak associations in the polity, especially in the neocorporatist states (e.g., Norway, Sweden, Austria); these are intermediate orders between the individual and the state. Although the community I once may have shared with my fellow villagers may have been destroyed by capitalist markets, as a law and society teacher, I find a community in the Law and Society Association; as a lawyer, on an American Bar Association Committee; as a teacher, with the colleagues on my university faculty; as a bridge player, in my bridge club; and still in my geographically extended family. These communities matter in that they can all make demands that trouble my conscience; I enjoy pride or suffer shame according to the regard I am held within them (Scheff, 1989).

The neocorporatists are right to direct our attention to the associational order not only as something that fosters a new kind of community, but also as a politically significant institutional order in its own right. Streeck and Schmitter (1985) argue that the associational order has increased in influence to the point where we should put it alongside community, market, and state as institutionally fundamental in making order possible in modern capitalist states.

Where one institutional order is weak in a society, massive and often unsuccessful efforts are made to compensate through the other institutions. To deal with the problem of crime control, for example, the key institutional order that must be effective is community (Braithwaite, 1989a). But this institution is weak in the United States (Bellah et al., 1985). Consequently, massively expensive, ineffective, and oppressive crime control efforts are mounted in the state and market (the private security industry) institutional arenas.

The postwar, pre-coup Soviet Union, in contrast, could rely more heavily on community in some important senses—from the beginning of school Soviet children were socialized to commit to collective obligation, with consequent benefits for crime control (Bronfenbrenner, 1972). However, market and state institutions were weak. Although obviously the Soviet state has been strong in its coercive power, it has been weaker than the democracies at commanding voluntary consent from its citizens. Crucial to this weakness has been the failure of the state to use its authority to secure the rule of law; the law is not respected because it has been little more than an extension of the power of party functionaries (Tay, 1990). These weak Soviet institutions are responsible for severe economic problems. Inefficient or corrupt enterprises have not been put out of business by competitors, by criticism from opposition political parties, or by a free press. A major part of the Soviet response was to recruit a massive army of volunteer-citizen inspectors to blow the whistle on inefficiency, fraud, and waste. The most important citizen inspectorates were the People's Control Committee (9.5 million volunteers) and the trade union inspectors (10 million) (Adams, 1977: 139; see also Lampert, 1985). In effect, this was a hybrid community–association compensatory response. In 1975, 22 percent of the adult population of the Soviet Union was involved as volunteer inspectors, a remarkable accomplishment in itself, regardless of their questionable effectiveness and political capture (Adams, 1977: 139). There is no shortage of specific cases where citizen inspectors were demonstrably effective in exposing corruption and waste. However, the bottom line of the Soviet economy equally demonstrates that any such success did not begin to compensate for the institutional malaise of the Soviet market and state. Hence perestroika and the coup.

Although it is true that the failings of one institutional order can rarely be fully compensated for by the others, it is also true that the institutions of community, market, state, and associational order are to some extent both mutually constituting and mutually constraining. We have already mentioned how community has been reconstituted in certain important ways by the rising associational order. We have much to say in Chapter 3 about how the virtues of community, particularly trust, make effective markets possible. A strong state also constitutes markets—through laws of contract, through antitrust laws that brought markets into existence when cartels were dismantled (something that could not be achieved when the state was weak), and through other indispensable infrastructure such as roads and bridges. Historically, advanced capitalism was not possible until central states acquired considerable authority.

Just as there is some truth in the claim that state regulation constitutes markets, so there is something to the claim that the wealth generated by the market enables regulation. We hear this claim when conservative politicians berate antigrowth Greens with the assertion that only wealthy market economies can afford pollution control or regulation of pharmaceuticals. With some justification, they say go to Mexico City and see the pollution and the poisons you will be served in a pharmacy without a prescription; or go to the Silesian conurbation in Poland and breathe the air, take their medicines.

In the modern world, it is also true that associational self-regulation constitutes markets. The self-regulation of stock exchanges (associations of brokers) constitutes this most central institution of the capitalist economy (Stenning et al., 1987);[3] the self-regulation of the legal (Halliday, 1987) and accountancy (Willmott, 1985) professions is vital to constituting the legal and accounting framework without which markets would collapse into disorder.

Finally, we argue in Chapter 3 that the state can and should have a vital role in constituting the associational order. There it will be argued that a state policy of empowering citizen groups in regulatory deliberations will strengthen such groups and bring new organizations into existence.

All of this leads us to view assertions that business is all-powerful against the regulatory demands of the community, the state, and the associational order as an unsophisticated basis for unbridled pessimism. Our view is that the community, market, state, and associational order each are important in both challenging and constituting the power of the other. In an era of regulatory flux, all domains of institutional power are unusually vulnerable. Yes, the regulatory power of the state is vulnerable to the deregulatory reassertion of the market by business. But business is also vulnerable to the associational order of trade unions, environmental groups, and the like. And the state is vulnerable when accused of regulatory failure by the community (witness the Bush–Dukakis election advertisements on their opponents' environmental protection failures and contemporary mutual recriminations over responsibility for Savings and Loans deregulation). The countercurrents do mean that we are in an era of regulatory flux rather than an era of deregulation (see also Sigler and Murphy, 1988).

This means that the time is ripe for creative options to bridge the abyss between deregulatory and proregulatory rhetoric, to drag this lagging rhetoric toward the new reality of regulatory flux. There is no inevitability that creative options, which transcend the dichotomy of deregulation versus intensified state control, will be crushed by business. There is no inevitability that business will see it as in its interest to crush them. One should be neither optimistic nor pessimistic about change, simply open to the contingent opportunities for reform that arise in a world of institutional flux.

Limited Progress in the Face of Gloom—An Illustration

Earlier we pointed to the importance of professional self-regulation in constituting markets. An example of the countercurrents in an era of regulatory flux is that one of the authors finds himself in the early 1990s involved as a part-time Commissioner with the Australian Trade Practices Commission (TPC)[4] to urge self-deregulation on some professions. This means, for example, urging the professions to dismantle restrictions on advertising, fee setting, and barriers to entry so that markets for professional services might become more competitive. Should the appeals for self-deregulation fail, perhaps a more litigious state-enforced deregulation (regulated deregulation!) will ensue.

The trend of Australian antitrust and consumer protection is very much in the direction urged in this book (more generally, see Grabosky and Braithwaite, 1986: 227–229). Business journal stories appear with a photograph of the chairman of the Trade Practices Commission peering from under a banner that reads "Self-regulate or else, TPC chairman says" (*Money Management,* 17 August, 1989: 1). On appeal from the Australian Consumers' Association, the Trade Practices Tribunal overturns the Commission's authorization of the Media Council of Australia's self-regulatory codes for advertising because of inadequate provision for community involvement in the self-regulation scheme.[5] As telecommunications, airlines, international cargo shipping, and the waterfront are deregulated, the Commission, with support from business, the conservative opposition (Liberal Party), and the consumer movement, pleads (with only limited success) to a Labor government for more resources so it can more effectively regulate compliance with antitrust laws in the deregulated industries and so it can foster voluntary trade practices compliance programs in these industries.[6]

This shift in direction for the TPC—from legalistic enforcer to facilitator of deregulation and self-regulation (and law enforcer when these approaches fail)—is met with suspicion. Some in the consumer movement believe that those appointed to the Commission from the consumer movement have sold out to placating business with soft options. Some in the business community believe that the new direction is a conspiracy by these very same people to impose more onerous consumer protection standards on business by the back door, without having to fight the business lobbies in the corridors of parliament. The new approach puts a cloak of reasonableness around proposals that are designed to do business in.

The reforms discussed in this book are proposed with the goal of selling out neither consumers nor business. Rightly or wrongly, we believe that they have the potential to deliver a regulatory system that at the same time is less costly for business and improves the protection of consumers. And it is interesting that the TPC has not always found it difficult to persuade both business and consumer groups, both conservative and social democratic parties, that this is the case with the reform directions discussed earlier. Indeed, at the time of writing, it is having some problems keeping up with the proposals coming from industry associations, sometimes joined by consumer and other community groups who wish to cooperate with them, seeking the Commission's approval for or evaluation of coregulatory schemes.

This is not to say that all of these responsive regulatory programs will ultimately be evaluated as successes. Nor is it to deny the existence of voices who cry cooptation and overstepping of the Commission's statutory mandate through these innovations.[7] Nor do we wish to enter the debate on the side of saying that these latter voices are wrong. It is simply to say that there is nothing necessarily unreal about the prospect of business and consumer associations being simultaneously persuaded of the value of the reform directions discussed in this book. Nor is there anything necessarily unreal about business and trade unions, business and environmental groups, professions and women's groups, farmers and animal welfare groups being simultaneously so persuaded. Increasingly, in the era of regulatory flux that we perceive in the Western world, this is a possibility and a reality. Now is an historical period with unusually rich opportunities for transcending the entrenched positions of government regulators and deregulators in this old debate.

The immediate influence in Australia of a book by Reagan administration economic advisor, Michael Porter (1990), *The Competitive Advantage of Nations,* illustrates the crumbling of old battle lines underway. Porter argues for sophisticated and credible antitrust enforcement to preserve the clusters of competing firms in a home market that are the key to international success. More intriguingly, Porter contends that there is a commonality of interest between business on the one hand and environmental and consumer groups on the other in supporting tough product standards regulation.

> Stringent standards for product performance, product safety, and environmental impact contribute to creating and upgrading competitive advantage. They pressure firms to improve quality, upgrade technology, and provide features in areas of important customer (and social) concern. . .
> Firms, like governments, are often prone to see the short-term cost of dealing with tough standards and not their longer-term benefits in terms of innovation. Firms point to foreign rivals without such standards as having a cost advantage. Such thinking is based on an incomplete view on how competitive advantage is created and sustained. Selling poorly performing, unsafe, or environmentally damaging products is not a route to real competitive advantage in sophisticated industries and industry segments, especially in a world where environmental sensitivity and concern for social welfare are rising in all advanced nations. Sophisticated buyers will usually appreciate safer, cleaner, quieter products before governments do. Firms with the skills to produce such products will have an important lever to enter foreign markets, and can often accelerate the process by which foreign regulations are toughened (Porter, 1990: 647, 648–9).

Western buyers will not be jostling to purchase pharmaceuticals manufactured in the Soviet Republics because state regulators and consumer movements there continue to be undemanding of high product standards. Competitive advantage will continue to rest with the nations that have aggressive consumer movements (e.g. Sweden, the United States, perhaps Australia) and consequently, credible regulation.

Not Corporatism, Not Liberalism, Not Pluralism

The policy ideas in this book can and do win some sympathy from citizens at diverse points on the political spectrum because they are in a sense no more than methodologies for constituting win–win solutions in the regulation game. Readers need not buy our politics to buy our ideas. Nevertheless, we would be less than candid if we did not explain how we would defend responsive regulation from the standpoint of our more general normative theory of politics. As republicans, we cannot be sympathetic to the libertarian view that the state should be kept weak because it poses a threat to freedom; we are unsympathetic to the socialist view that the market order should be weakened because it is exploitative; we are unsympathetic to the liberal view that the community and associational orders should be kept weak because they threaten individualism with a range of communitarian pathologies—vigilantism, disrespect for privacy, intolerance of diversity, oligarchy.[8] Instead we agree with those neocorporatists who advocate a mixed institutional order (Streeck and Schmitter, 1985), one where markets, community, state, and associations[9] each exercise countervailing power over the others and check the grave dangers when any one of these institutional orders dominates.[10] Although we share this common ground with the neocorporatists, our analysis is in the republican rather than in the corporatist tradition of political theory because of the emphasis we place on direct citizen participation in the regulatory game, often at a very local level (e.g., the workplace, the nursing home). In Chapter 3, it becomes clear that our advocacy of contestability for public interest group power does not fit Schmitter's (1979: 13) defining characteristic of corporatism as "a system of interest representation in which constituent units are organized into a limited number of singular, compulsory, noncompetitive, hierarchically ordered and functionally differentiated categories . . . granted a deliberate representational monopoly" (see also Streeck et al., 1981).

We also place greater emphasis on communitarian sources of order in the regulatory arena than corporatist scholars who analyzse the interplay between purely self-interested associations that do deals to maximize the economic returns of their constituents. In short, we see public-regarding aspirations to be a responsible citizen, to be law abiding, as important in both a normative and an explanatory sense in the regulatory arena.

Our regulatory program of transcending regulation versus deregulation is articulated to a multidimensional conception of an effectively working democracy wherein citizens are increasingly empowered by: (1) choices to vote with their feet in the marketplace; (2) voting rights in a representative democracy; (3) opportunities and resources to participate directly in any local area of collective decision making that has an important effect on their lives—in their workplace, school, local planning authority, nursing home, etc. (Handler, 1990); and (4) opportunities to stand for office, vote, and collectively participate in special-interest and public-interest associations that are genuinely empowered right up to the national level of the democracy. The deeper ideological dimension of the program is a resistance to unidimensional étatisme or market visions of democracy or freedom, a replacement of the liberal conception of the atomized free individual with a republican conception of communitarian empowerment.

Just as the principles of institutional design we consider deviate from the neocorporatist model, so they do from pluralism. Schmitter's (1979: 15) influential distinguishing of corporatism and pluralism specifies that under pluralism, interest groups "are not specially licensed, recognized, subsidized, [or] created . . . by the state." The pluralist ideal is of interest groups that spontaneously arise. In Chapter 3 we advocate state and community empowerment of inherently weaker interests that enables the organization of the disorganized. We argue, therefore, for an interventionist state that redistributes power through enforcing participation rights for powerless groups and providing resources for them. This is a social democratic state rather than a liberal pluralist state—a state that actively redistributes both the wealth that enables market power and the participation rights that enable democratic power.[11]

It can be seen that we favor a republican version of social democracy over a neocorporatist social democracy. Those definitions of neocorporatism which restrict representation to "producer groups" (unions and business) (e.g., Pantich, 1979, 1980) are especially at odds with the vision of democracy we explore. We suggest empowering consumer groups as well as producer groups. Furthermore, state intervention to empower the powerless implies less attention to producers who generally gain recognition through the market, and more attention to those excluded from market power—those who work at home caring for children, the aged, the disabled, those who fight for the claims of trees and animals. Republican social democracy is our greatest hope for averting both the oligarchic tendencies of neocorporatism and the crises of ungovernability engendered by pluralism. If, as suggested in Chapter 3, as few as one representative from each relevant interest is empowered by the state to sit at the regulatory negotiating table, then there need be no crisis of ungovernability. We can thereby avoid a babble of voices so chaotic that it is difficult to ever get anything settled. And if the state allows and encourages incumbency of each seat at the negotiating table to be contested in the way described in Chapter 3, then the spectre of corporatist oligarchy might also be addressed.

Therefore we subscribe to a version of republicanism that has been admirably summarized by Sunstein (1988) as involving four basic commitments: (1) deliberation in government that shapes as well as balances interests (as opposed to simply doing deals between prepolitical interests); (2) political equality (which we read as requiring the organizational empowerment of disorganized constituencies); (3) universality, or debate to reconcile competing views, as a regulative ideal; and (4) citizenship, community participation in public life.[12]

Although it is important to clarify our ideological position to distinguish it from liberalism, pluralism, and neocorporatism, it is by no means necessary to accept this position to think that the ideas we advance may be desirable or practical. Indeed, we are amazed when we present these ideas at the breadth of ideological positions among both the supporters who praise us and the opponents who condemn us.

Perhaps the motley political color of the supporters is only because our advocacy is of a method of regulation rather than of the ends of regulation, a method that is negotiated and flexible. People with radically different interests can agree on a fair way of negotiating. In the same way, people of different ideologies can agree on a method of resolving regulatory conflict that seems a practical means to a world that is better from all of their points of view, even if it is not their ideal world.

2

The Benign Big Gun

In this chapter, we show a convergence between a rational choice analysis of what works in securing compliance with regulatory laws and some sociological analyses that reject the assumptions of the rational choice model. The convergence is about the efficacy of tit-for-tat (TFT) enforcement—regulation that is contingently provokable and forgiving. Building on this convergence, we argue that regulatory agencies are often best able to secure compliance when they are benign big guns. That is, regulators will be more able to speak softly when they carry big sticks (and crucially, a hierarchy of lesser sanctions).[1] Paradoxically, the bigger and the more various are the sticks, the greater the success regulators will achieve by speaking softly.

We argue for a minimal sufficiency principle in the deployment of the big and smaller sticks: the more sanctions can be kept in the background, the more regulation can be transacted through moral suasion, the more effective regulation will be. The key conclusions are derived from qualifying the assumptions that the regulatory behavior of firms is rational and unitary. Among the alternative claims advanced are the following:

1. To understand regulation, we need to aggregate firms into industry associations and disaggregate firms into corporate subunits, subunits into individual corporate actors, and individuals into multiple selves. Regulatory agencies advance their objectives in games at each of these levels of aggregation by moves in games at other levels of aggregation.

2. Some corporate actors will only comply with the law if it is economically rational for them to do so; most corporate actors will comply with the law most of the time simply because it is the law; all corporate actors are bundles of contradictory commitments to values about economic rationality, law abidingness, and business responsibility. Business executives have profit-maximizing selves and law-abiding selves, at different moments, in different contexts, the different selves prevail.

3. A strategy based totally on persuasion and self-regulation will be exploited when actors are motivated by economic rationality.

4. A strategy based mostly on punishment will undermine the good will of actors when they are motivated by a sense of responsibility.

5. Punishment is expensive; persuasion is cheap. A strategy based mostly on punishment wastes resources on litigation that would be better spent on monitor-

ing and persuasion. (A highly punitive mining inspectorate will spend more time in court than in mines).

6. A strategy based mostly on punishment fosters an organized business subculture of resistance to regulation wherein methods of legal resistance and counterattack are incorporated into industry socialization (Bardach and Kagan, 1982). Punitive enforcement engenders a game of regulatory cat-and-mouse whereby firms defy the spirit of the law by exploiting loopholes, and the state writes more and more specific rules to cover the loopholes.

This chapter is divided into two parts. In the first part we explore the multiple motivations and objectives of the regulated. We argue that firms and the decision makers within them are actuated by different motives. Our larger argument is that sound public policy must and can speak to the diverse motivations of the regulated public. We suggest that TFT regulatory strategies may work well not only in constraining noncompliance of purely economic actors, but also in engendering the inculcation of trust and civic virtue.

In the second part, we build on these insights to argue that pyramids of increasingly stringent enforcement measures are needed to respond to the diverse objectives of the regulated firms. An enforcement pyramid subjects regulated firms to escalating forms of regulatory intervention if they continually refuse to respond to regulatory demands.

Mixed Motives and Tit-for-Tat

Deterrence Versus Compliance Models of Regulation

The first step on the road to our conclusions is to understand that there is a long history of barren disputation within regulatory agencies, and more recently among scholars of regulation, between those who think that corporations will comply with the law only when confronted with tough sanctions and those who believe that gentle persuasion works in securing business compliance with the law. Reiss (1980) has dubbed these two competing models of regulation "deterrence" versus "compliance." Justice Holmes long ago adopted the deterrence model in arguing that the law needed to be tailored with a mind not toward "good men" (who would look to law as a guide for proper action), but with a mind toward "bad men" (who would try to evade the legal strictures of society).[2] Today most, although by no means all, regulators are in the compliance camp (see the studies cited by Hawkins, 1984: 3; Grabosky and Braithwaite, 1986), whereas most regulation scholars are in the deterrence camp.

Many of the academics, be they conservative economists or radical criminologists, interpret this state of affairs as evidence of how captured the regulators are in their analysis, in contrast to the independence and worldly wise cynicism of their own position. The regulators, on the other hand, are often inclined to construe the disagreement as evidence of how out of touch academics are with how to achieve results in the real world.

Happily, this era of crude polarization of the regulatory enforcement debate between staunch advocates of deterrence and defenders of the compliance model is beginning to pass. Increasingly within both scholarly and regulatory communities there is a feeling that the regulatory agencies that do best at achieving their goals are those that strike some sort of sophisticated balance between the two models. The crucial question has become: When to punish; when to persuade?

The Game Theorist's Answer

The game theory literature stood ready with some answers to this question. It was John Scholz (1984a, b) who made the great contribution of translating this work into the regulatory arena. In the next chapter a more detailed treatment of this contribution lays the foundations for the game theoretic analysis of capture and tripartism therein. For the moment, we just overview its conclusions.

Scholz models regulation as a prisoner's dilemma game wherein the motivation of the firm is to minimize regulatory costs and the motivation of the regulator is to maximize compliance outcomes. He shows that a TFT enforcement strategy will most likely establish mutually beneficial cooperation, under assumptions he believes will be met in many regulatory contexts. TFT means that the regulator refrains from a deterrent response as long as the firm is cooperating; but when the firm yields to the temptation to exploit the cooperative posture of the regulator and cheats on compliance, then the regulator shifts from a cooperative to a deterrent response. Confronted with the matrix of payoffs typical in the enforcement dilemma, the optimal strategy is for both the firm and the regulator to cooperate until the other defects from cooperation. Then the rational player should retaliate (the state to deterrence regulation; the firm to a law evasion strategy). If and only if the retaliation secures a return to cooperation by the other player, then the retaliator should be forgiving, restoring the benefits of mutual cooperation in place of the lower payoffs of mutual defection. Drawing on the work of Axelrod (1984), Scholz contends that in the prisoner's dilemma game TFT has been pitted against other strategies to demonstrate mathematically, experimentally, and through the use of computer-simulation tournaments that TFT will often maximize the payoffs of players.

> As a "nice" strategy (one that does not use deterrence until after the firm defects), TFT gains the full advantage of mutual cooperation with all firms pursuing nice strategies. As a vengeful strategy which retaliates immediately, it gets stuck with the sucker payoff only once against firms that evade in every round. Yet as a forgiving strategy it responds almost immediately if a previous evader begins to comply, thereby restoring the benefit of mutual cooperation rather than the lower payoffs of mutual defection. Furthermore, the simplicity of TFT makes it easily recognized by an opponent. (Scholz, 1984a: 192)

Alternative Motivational Accounts

The TFT policy prescription is for the regulator to try cooperation first. This conclusion is not grounded in any assumption that business people are cooperative in nature; rather, the payoffs in the regulation game make cooperation rational until the other player defects from cooperation. The motivational account of the firm is of a unitary actor concerned only with maximizing profit.

Braithwaite's empirical work on corporate offending has led him to posit some alternative motivational accounts. Throughout this chapter, data from this work will be used to illustrate these alternative accounts. The fieldwork on the impact of adverse publicity on corporations is summarized in Fisse and Braithwaite (1983), on pharmaceutical companies in Braithwaite (1984), on coal mining companies in Braithwaite (1985), on Australian regulatory agencies in Grabosky and Braithwaite (1986), and a very preliminary report on the work on nursing home regulation is provided in Braithwaite et al. (1990). The data consists of interviews with executives, observation of corporate decision making, and observation of regulatory encounters. We argue that a strong case for TFT can be made from the alternative motivational accounts revealed from these studies. The first stage of our argument is, therefore, that TFT is an unusually robust policy idea because radically divergent accounts of regulation converge on the efficacy of TFT. First, however, we must go to the conclusions from Braithwaite's empirical work.

The first strand of this work is the research with Brent Fisse in *The Impact of Publicity on Corporate Offenders*. Interviews with executives of large corporations that had been through adverse publicity crises concerning allegations of corporate wrongdoing showed that both individual executives and the corporation collectively generally valued a good reputation for its own sake. There was some concern that adverse corporate publicity might do serious damage to profits, but neither this subjective concern nor the objective fact of economic damage to the corporation from adverse publicity was widespread. Nevertheless, the informants cared deeply about the adverse publicity; they viewed both their personal reputation in the community and their corporate reputation as priceless assets.

The implications of this first empirical questioning of the pure economic rationality model of regulatory encounters do not seem too profound. If individual and corporate actors are deterred not only by economic losses but also by reputational losses, then consideration can be given to adverse publicity sanctions for regulatory offenders. These are precisely the policy solutions considered by Fisse and Braithwaite (1983). TFT can operate perfectly well with adverse publicity supplying the punishment payoff.

Other data suggest, however, that we need to delve deeper into the limitations of a rational calculus (see Yeager [1990] on deontological reasoning in business organizations). Corporate actors are not just value maximizers—of profits or of reputation. They are also often concerned to do what is right, to be faithful to their identity as a law abiding citizen, and to sustain a self-concept of social responsibility. During Braithwaite's fieldwork, business informants repeatedly argued that the common characterization of them as motivated only by money was a simplistic stereotype. Conceding that their primary motivations were economic, they claimed that they and their colleagues took seriously business responsibility, ethics, and obligations to abide by the law and to be responsive to nonshareholding stakeholders in the corporation. This was true even of respondents who admitted widespread law breaking in their company or their industry.

Some economists will read all such claims as humbug, and there are many instances where Braithwaite would not want to disagree with such a reading of his fieldwork notes. The problem is, however, that to discount every incident of nonutilitarian reasoning as a delusion or a smokescreen to conceal some deeper rational pursuit of interests is to be tautological about the proposition that human beings always pursue their economic interests or their reputational interests, or whatever conception of interest is advanced as self-evident. It is one thing to analyze these fieldwork notes and observe that there is other evidence that this actor is not sincere in a belief about doing what is right whatever the cost. It is another to insist that business executives are motivated only by money when they say otherwise, and when there is evidence of economically irrational compliance with the law. Such insistence will build a science on foundations immune from empirical refutation. We should not scoff at a top pharmaceutical executive who says that concern for improving human health motivates her and her staff to maintain high standards more than the fear of regulatory sanctions, where this is a company that can be observed to maintain fairly high standards in a Third World country that effectively has no pharmaceuticals regulation.

Nor should we scoff at the Director of Nursing at a large nursing home who said to one of Braithwaite's co-fieldworkers: "You become family to them. You are their mother, their sister." The reason the fieldworkers took this account seriously is that they talked to residents who agreed with the assessment; they observed the Director of Nursing interacting lovingly with residents; and inspectors reported that they too had always observed this.

There is another path this debate can take. Smith says one reason he pays the taxes he owes the government is that he believes it is right to do so. The reader accepts that Smith is sincere in this belief. Furthermore Smith asserts that it is economically irrational for him not to seize a variety of opportunities to cheat that he chooses not to exploit. For example, Smith, an Australian citizen, says he travels to the United States every year, with the American Bar Foundation meeting his expenses. If he were to present his airline ticket and other receipts to the Australian Taxation Office as tax deductible research expenses, he could collect payment twice with little risk of detection. Yes, the reader accepts that Smith is both sincere in his commitment to being an honest taxpayer and is also irrational not to seize certain opportunities to be dishonest that are known to him.[3]

The cynic says, however, if we go back far enough into Smith's life, we will understand the psychic rewards he has been given for honesty. We might be able to see the praise that his mother heaped on him when he returned the money he had taken from her purse, and a learning theory analysis of such incidents would enable us to understand why Smith will continue to derive satisfaction from being honest for the rest of his life. Ultimately, the cynic alleges, Smith only chooses honesty because of his self-interested approach to reaping those psychic rewards on his mother's knee?[4] Smith concedes the cynic may be right in this diagnosis. Even though he may be right such speculative reduction to ultimate interest pursuit makes for an unilluminating social science. If we expand backward with self-interest as an explanation until it absorbs everything, including even altruism, then it signifies nothing—it lacks explanatory specificity or power.

What matters in understanding what Smith does today is the motivational structure that is in place in Smith today. If Smith's motivation is substantially about rejecting the appeal of self-interested reasoning in favor of deontological reasoning,[5] seeking to change his behavior by strengthening the appeal to this self-interest will not work. It might even insult him, provoking him to dig in deeper with his principles. This empirical fact about the here and now is quite unaffected by the other fact—that ultimately it was self-interested motivations in Smith's past that explain his contemporary spurning of economic self-interest. To do good social science, we are best to be informed by empirical evidence about what motivates actors at a particular moment in history so that we can understand the choices those actors make at that moment. If Smith is more strongly motivated by honesty than by money in a particular context, then in that context appeals to honesty are more likely to move him than opportunities for more money, or indeed appeals to what a self-interested little brat he was when on his mother's knee.

So we think it important to know empirically that in the context of regulatory choices, business executives, with varying degrees of apparent sincerity of commitment to action, explain their motivation in the discourse of social responsibility. The variants of that elevation of social responsibility above economic interest are many. It can be the responsibility to obey the law whatever the cost, the responsibility to scientific integrity for pharmaceutical industry scientists, the responsibility to patients for nurses working for a nursing home corporation, the responsibility to professional ethics for company lawyers, or the responsibility a coal mining executive says he has to never put profit ahead of the lives of his workers. There is something about the context of social encounters concerning choices to comply with regulatory laws that makes social responsibility discourse of one sort or another rather prominent, at least in the diverse regulatory arenas that Braithwaite has studied.

Quite often in this research, the rhetoric about putting social responsibility ahead of profits is not matched by responsible action. But, also quite often, the nursing home manager, for example, will be observed to do what she sees as responsible even when she knows that it is costly and when the legal risks from not doing it are perceived as zero, and in fact *are* near zero. Go out with nursing home inspectors in a jurisdiction that never prosecutes, never takes legal action for noncompliance with a standard, and you may be surprised at how frequently profit-making organizations agree to do costly things to comply with the law. When you ask them why, they say: "because it is the law" or "because I agree with the lady from the Health Authority when she says that this is in the best interests of the residents."

So Braithwaite concluded in *To Punish or Persuade* that you could not develop a sound regulatory enforcement policy unless you understood the fact that sometimes business actors were powerfully motivated by making money and sometimes they were powerfully motivated by a sense of social responsibility. He, therefore, rejected a regulatory strategy based totally on persuasion and a strategy based totally on punishment. He concluded that business actors exploit a strategy of persuasion and self-regulation when they are motivated by economic rationality. But a strategy based mostly on punishment will undermine the good will of actors when they are motivated by a sense of responsibility. This will be true of any version of responsibility that is construed by actors as a more noble calling than making money. When actors see themselves as pursuing a higher calling, to treat them as driven by what they see as baser motivation insults them, demotivates them:

ADMINISTRATOR: We don't do anything right. The industry is like a bad girl. . . . Why can't you put down something we do right. . . . People don't go into this industry unless they have some compassion. . . . Nurses are not machines. . . . They get burnt out by inspectors criticizing them. . . . All these psychologists with books on praise—from Dr. Spock up—praise children and they do the right thing. But no one thinks to apply that to us.

* * *

INSPECTOR TO ADMINISTRATOR: Your staff were real nice to work with.
ADMINISTRATOR: So were you. Not like Public Aid [another regulatory agency]. They're so demoralizing.
BRAITHWAITE: What's the difference?
ADMINISTRATOR: Public Aid nurses always assume the worst. They treat you as if you are doing something wrong. . . .

A crucial danger of a punitive posture that projects negative expectations of the regulated actor is that it inhibits self-regulation. This is not something peculiar to business regulatory encounters. Lansky (1984) makes the same point about the dangers of treating violence in patients as an eruption that must be held down by regulation of movement, physical or chemical restraint. A model of "holding-down" both inhibits dialogue about the interpersonal vulnerabilities that lead to the violence and justifies "a type of overregulation that humiliates the patient and complicates the return of self-regulation" (Lansky, 1984: 23). When punishment rather than dialogue is in the foreground of regulatory encounters, it is basic to human psychology that people will find this humiliating, will resent and resist in ways that include abandoning self-regulation. The point is not new; it is made in a passage from Confucius that every educated Chinese used to know by heart: "If people be led by laws and uniformity is sought to be given them by punishments, they will try to avoid punishments but have no sense of shame" (Tay, 1990: 160–61).

Individual rebellion against being stigmatized as controllable only by punishment is aggregated within business communities into collective forms of resistance. Bardach and Kagan (1982) identify one of the problems of a mostly punitive policy is that it fosters an organized business subculture of resistance to regulation—a subculture that facilitates the sharing of knowledge about methods of legal resistance and counterattack. When regulators wade in with a punitive model of human beings as essentially bad, they dissipate the will of well-intentioned actors to comply when they treat them as if they are ill intentioned. The problem with the persuasion model, however, based as it is on a typification of people as basically good—reasonable, of good faith, motivated to abide by the law—is that it fails to recognize that there are some who are not good, and who will take advantage of being presumed to be so.

To reject punitive regulation is naive; to be totally committed to it is to lead a charge of the Light Brigade. The trick of successful regulation is to establish a synergy between punishment and persuasion. Strategic punishment underwrites regulatory persuasion as something that ought to be attended to. Persuasion legitimates punishment as reasonable, fair, and even something that might elicit remorse or repentance.

We reject Holmes' notion that the law should solely adopt a "bad man" perspective. Going in with punishment as a strategy of first choice is counterproductive in a number of ways. First, punishment is expensive; persuasion is cheap. Therefore, if persuasion is tried first and works, more resources are left to expand regulatory coverage. In contrast, a mining inspectorate with a first preference for punitive enforcement will spend more time in court than in mines. Second, punitive enforcement engenders a game of regulatory cat-and-mouse whereby firms defy the spirit of the law by exploiting loopholes, and the state writes more and more specific rules to cover the loopholes. The result can be: (1) rule making by accretion that gives no coherence to the rules as a package, and (2) a barren legalism concentrating on specific, simple, visible violations to the neglect of underlying systemic problems (Bardach and Kagan, 1982; Braithwaite, 1985). Third, heavy reliance must be placed on persuasion rather than on punishment in industries where technological and environmental realities change so quickly that the regulations that give detailed content to the law cannot keep up to date.

Given these problems of punitive enforcement, and given that large numbers of corporate actors in many contexts do fit the responsible citizen model, *To Punish or Persuade* argued that persuasion is preferable to punishment as the strategy of first choice. To adopt punishment as a strategy of first choice is unaffordable, unworkable, and counterproductive in undermining the good will of those with a commitment to compliance. However, when firms which are not responsible corporate citizens exploit the privilege of persuasion, the regulator should switch to a tough punitive response.

By a very different route from the economic rationality calculus in the work of Scholz and Axelrod, *To Punish or Persuade* came to essentially the same conclusion—that TFT was the best strategy. Regulator defection to a punitive strategy with recalcitrant companies, or companies that defied the spirit of the law by exploiting loopholes, would underwrite the authority of the regulator through victories in court. It would also support the sense of fairness of responsible companies who eschewed the temptations of regulatory cat and mouse. Preserving that perception of fairness is important to nurturing voluntary compliance. Chester Bowles (1971) concluded from his experience with the U.S. Office of Price Administration during World War II that 20 percent of all firms would comply unconditionally with any rule, 5 percent would attempt to evade it, and the remaining 75 percent are also likely to comply, but only if the punitive threat to the dishonest 5 percent is credible (Bardach and Kagan, 1982: 65–66; see also Levi, 1987).

TFT is the best strategy for Scholz because, in maximizing the difference between the punishment payoff and the cooperation payoff, it makes cooperation the most economically rational response. TFT is the best strategy in *To Punish or Persuade* because it holds out the best hope of nurturing the noneconomic motivations of firms to be responsible and law abiding. Paradoxically, diametrically opposed motivational accounts of business can converge on the same enforcement prescription.

TFT resolves the contradictions of punishment versus persuasion outlined earlier. By cooperating with firms until they cheat, regulators avert the counterproductivity of undermining the good faith of socially responsible actors. By getting tough with cheaters, actors are made to suffer when they are motivated by money alone; they are given reason to favor their socially responsible, law-abiding selves over their venal selves. In short, they are given reason to reform, more so because when they do reform they find the regulator forgiving. When they put reforms in place, they find that the forgiving regulator treats them as if their socially responsible self was always their "real" self. For Scholz, forgiveness for firms planning to cooperate in the future is part of maximizing the difference between the cooperation and punishment payoffs. In *To Punish or Persuade,* forgiveness is advocated more for its importance in building a commitment to comply in future.

By nurturing expectations of responsibility and cooperation, the regulator can coax and caress fidelity to the spirit of the law even in contexts where the law is riddled with gaps or loopholes. In this way TFT resolves the loophole-opening contradiction of punitive regulation.

In all of these ways analyses of what makes compliance rational and what builds business cultures of social responsibility can converge on the conclusion that compliance is optimized by regulation that is contingently ferocious and forgiving.

The Lexical Ordering of Money and Responsibility

Braithwaite and his colleagues came to realize during their fieldwork on nursing home regulation that another distinction apparent in the modes of economic reasoning about regulatory compliance is recognized in philosophical discourse. This is the idea of two principles being lexically ordered. A lexical order is one "which requires us to satisfy the first principle in the ordering before we can move on to the second" (Rawls, 1973: 43). Some of our subjects were remarkably explicit in their attachment to the idea of lexical ordering:

> The advice I give to the Directors of Nursing in my nursing homes is to list their priorities under the following headings: 'Must do. Should do. Could do. Won't do.'
> Then they should start at the top of the list and work down until the money runs out.

In the nursing home fieldwork, the goals of making money and caring for residents have been found to be differently lexically ordered between different actors. Before moving on to these cases, however, we first consider actors more singlemindedly motivated by either profits or what they define as caring for the patients.

There are actors, individual and corporate, whose behavior can reasonably be modeled as a rational pursuit of profit without any concern for resident care except insofar as improving resident care will contribute to profit. In contrast, there are many individual actors in the nursing home industry whose motivation can reasonably be modeled as the pursuit of what is best for the care of the residents without any concern for maximizing profits: economic considerations are viewed as obstacles that less caring others put in the way of those concerned to do best by the residents.

No examples have been discovered of organizations that could be modeled as seeking to maximize the care of residents without any concern for profits. However, one case was encountered of an unusually profitable American nursing home corporation where several senior executives espoused the philosophy that the way for this corporation to make profits was for its middle managers and staff not to be concerned about money. Attracting wealthy private-pay residents (as opposed to Medicaid–Medicare residents) was seen as necessary for high profits. The best way to attract them was to engender an atmosphere within the nursing home that whatever was needed for the resident to be comfortable and happy would be done, regardless of cost. One head office executive made the analogy to a 5-star hotel, in which "when you want something, you're likely to get it." So there was a conscious effort to tell staff and middle managers that it was not their job to worry about money; it was their job to provide the best possible care for those residents. The senior managers believed that if they succeeded in engendering this attitude, "the profits automatically follow." As soon as you have staff who are calculating over the need to cut corners on care to save cost, the ideology of excellence, of doing whatever it takes to provide the best quality care possible is threatened. In the view of these senior executives, profit was the goal, but paradoxically the best way to achieve that goal was to have staff who were constrained not to care about it (see generally, Pettit and Brennan, 1986; Pettit, 1988).

A more common type of nursing home management is intensely concerned with profits but sets itself a minimum standard of basic care that must be met for each resident before the pursuit of maximum profits is countenanced. This minimum standard of care on the one hand, and profit on the other, are lexically ordered. Different nursing homes of this type set very different levels of minimum standards of acceptable care that they are first constrained to meet. Some nursing homes in Australia and the United States will not tolerate physically restraining any of their residents. For them, it is unacceptable to cut costs by applying a restraint to a resident. This can be quite a sacrifice because a good way of reducing the hours of staffing needed to run a nursing home smoothly can be to tie up all the residents who might fall, annoy other residents, tear off their dressings, or cause disruption by tugging at furniture or curtains. At the other extreme, U.S. Health Care Financing Administration survey data for 1986 showed that 77 percent of nursing home residents in Nevada were physically restrained.

Other nursing homes that have minimum standards of care and profits in this lexical order set the minima very low: "We provide basic medical care. We give them enough food. We shovel it in one end and keep their bums clean when it comes out the other end." Such nursing homes can be horrible places, lacking joy, activity, love, and any spark of what it is to be human. But impeccable basic care may be provided and healthy profits made. And depressing as these nursing homes are, low as the minimum care standards are, these standards are minimum requirements on the responsible conduct of the business that are taken seriously. Braithwaite encountered two cases of depressing homes of this sort that had residents who could no longer pay their fees. Their savings were gone and, although destitute, they had no entitlement to nursing home benefits. For example, one was a recent Vietnamese boat person who was not entitled to Australian retirement benefits. In both cases, the proprietors of these nursing homes of otherwise quite low standards continued to care for these residents, at a substantial loss. The minimum standard of responsible business conduct for those proprietors did not sink to putting "residents of mine in need of care out on the street."

Instead of nursing home management feeling constrained to meet a minimum standard of care and then maximizing profits, other nursing homes seek to maximize the quality of care up to the point where they run up against a financial constraint. Many church and charitable nursing homes are like this. They see their goal as providing the best possible care for their residents, constrained only by the need to stay in business. The financial constraint can be to break even, or to make a loss no greater than they can manage to make up through the annual fete, to make a "steady profit," or to meet loan repayments.

What strategy can the regulator implement to deal with actors some of whom are: (1) exclusively motivated by money, (2) exclusively motivated by caring goals, (3) virtually exclusively oriented to caring because they think this is the best way to make money, (4) lexically ordered—minimum care constraint/maximum money, and (5) lexically ordered minimum money constraint/maximum care? We argue that the best strategy to deal with such motivational diversity is TFT.

We have already argued that if an actor is motivated by social responsibility goals—in this context, resident care goals—then persuasion rather than punishment is the best strategy to further cultivate that motivation. This will be true irrespective of whether the caring motivation is itself motivated by profit seeking, nursing professionalism, love, religion, or what the carer learnt on his mother's knee. In the case where the commitment to caring is up to only a depressingly low minimum, the regulator will still do best to build on that minimum, to seek to define the requirements of the law as part of that minimum level of care that the actor feels responsible to meet. Only when it fails in getting the acceptance of such a definition should it shift to the tough enforcement response.

In the obverse case where the organization pursues maximum quality of care until a financial constraint is struck, in most cases the regulator will be rewarded by a presumption that persuasion will be positively responded to. However, such organizations will at times confront financial crises that constrain their maximizing of care below a level acceptable to the regulator. Then, even with this type of caring organization, the regulator must defect to punishment to defend the integrity of the standards in the law.

What then of the uncaring actor concerned only to maximize profits? The reasons for playing the regulatory game TFT even here are supplied by the economic rationalist analysis in the work of Axelrod and Scholz. By sustaining the rewards that the compliant profit-maximizer gets from repeated cooperation, TFT can be the best strategy here too.

A final type of actor we must consider is neither totally committed to money or responsibility goals, nor committed to any lexical ordering of the two. Rather, these actors have a trade-off function for choosing between being responsible and making money; when the money involved passes a certain threshhold, responsibility is forgotten. Up to a certain point on the trade-off function, these actors behave the same as one totally motivated by responsibility. Beyond that point, they behave the same as actors totally motivated by money. Since we have shown that TFT is the best strategy for actors totally motivated by social responsibility and for actors totally motivated by money, it follows that TFT is the best strategy for actors who trade off the two concerns.

It may be that there are two types of cases that challenge this general conclusion that TFT is the best way to go. The first is a type of case that Braithwaite and his colleagues have not encountered in their nursing home fieldwork—an organization that is concerned neither about being socially responsible in caring for residents nor about behaving in an economically rational way in its dealings with the regulatory agency. Let us call this the pathological irrational organization. Although Braithwaite did not encounter them, some of his regulatory informants claimed that they had— these were nursing homes that the regulators had been forced to close down. Their proprietors resented the government telling them what to do to care for their residents, so much so that they allowed themselves to be put out of business rather than toe the line. It may be that such irrationally unresponsive organizations that are still in business are so rare, and so difficult to identify in advance of the making of regulatory requests, that TFT will not necessarily cause substantial regulatory failure. The costs of falsely identifying organizations as pathological may be so great that the ''suck it and see'' quality of TFT may still be the best option.

But TFT will certainly cause regulatory failure here if its sanctions are limited to purely deterrent sanctions (e.g., fines). To deal with irrational actors, incapacitive sanctions are needed (e.g., license or charter revocation; removal of nursing home residents). The law must have sanctions designed to cope with irrational actors as well as rational actors, because where irrational actors exist they are likely to be the loose cannons on the deck that can do the greatest damage.[6] Just as it is a minor change to TFT based on economic deterrence to accommodate reputational deterrence, so it is a minor change to provide for sanctions that supply incapacitation rather than deterrence.

The second case where trying persuasion first will fail is with the determinedly profit-maximizing actor in a regulatory context where, unlike the nursing home case, the regulator and the firm are in a single-round regulatory encounter, the one-off customs offender in a foreign country. Handler (1986: 4) may be right that ''continuity of relation is probably the norm in the modern state.'' Nevertheless, there are certainly many areas where regulatory encounters are not continuous, but one-off (for example, the regulation of many types of fraud). Persuasion will clearly fail here because the economically rational firm that does not feel constrained to be law abiding will cheat every time. Because persuasion will fail here, it does not follow that automatic recourse to punishment will succeed. The fiscal costs of such a policy are so high that the state can only afford it with the most serious types of offending; for less serious offenses, the state may still do better by seeking voluntary remediation from those actors who do have a commitment to being law abiding.

Braithwaite's nursing home data are adequate to show that the disparate orderings of concerns about money and social responsibility discussed in this section do exist. However, the data do not estimate their respective frequency or even which is the most common. In the next section we see why any such estimation might in any case be misguided positivism. For the purposes of the present analysis, moreover, the relative frequency of different orderings of profit and people concerns does not matter, as our hypothesis is that TFT is the wisest strategy, whatever the ordering.

Disorder in the Multiple Self

In the previous section, we considered different forms of lexical ordering of concern about money and responsibility that are manifest in different regulatory encounters.

What is also manifest, however, is a great deal of disorder. The corporation that the regulator feels should be dealt with as an unscrupulous profit maker this month will be dealt with as a socially responsible corporate citizen the next month. Part of the explanation for this lies in the fact that the corporation is not a monolith: "When it is 'Fred' you have to deal with, steel yourself for the worst. But when 'Harry' is on duty on the other side of the desk, you can work things out without any need to act tough."

However, more than this, the disorder we observe in regulatory typifications even of individual business actors arises because most business actors are bundles of contradictory commitments to values of economic rationality, law abidingness, and business responsibility. Business executives have profit-maximizing selves and law-abiding selves; at different moments, in different contexts, the different selves prevail.

> INSPECTOR 1: She (the administrator) cried at the exit conference when we had some adverse findings. She's crying saying: 'I give good care to my patients. I care about them.'
> INSPECTOR 2: And she does. She does care.
> INSPECTOR 3: [unconvinced] In her own way.
> INSPECTOR 4: [aside to Braithwaite]: She was in Dachau in the war and some of the surveyors call her nursing home Dachau.

Later Braithwaite spent 3 days observing this administrator interacting with another nursing home inspection team and talking with her staff and residents. He saw her caring self, her dictatorial self, and her economically rational self. She was a woman motivated both by her deep concern for her residents and by power. She enjoyed having control over an institution and its people and she bridled at any questioning of her commands. Although the inspectors sought to effect change by appealing to her caring self, they were constantly on guard against an explosive encounter with her dictatorial self.

Situations arise when the money-making self and the responsible self are forced to stare each other in the face. The following incident illustrates two devices used to dissolve such a showdown: (1) laughter—the two selves discover humor in their contradictory predicament, and (2) timing—the selves take turns in prevailing. The incident occurred during an in-house Quality Assurance Committee meeting where the nursing home administrator was alluding to the fact that Medicaid reimbursement is graduated according to the care needs of residents:

> ADMINISTRATOR: If we get 'Mr. Jones' independent on this program, we lose money. They punish us for being successful. So don't be successful in a hurry [general laughter around the table].

Regulatory actors also have multiple selves: they can be nice guys or tough guys, self-interested or public-spirited, professional or unprofessional, diligent or lazy, intelligent or confused. The stuff of regulatory disasters is where the tough, unprofessional, confused self of the regulator encounters the irresponsible profit-driven self of the business executive. Such disasters come to everyone's attention—the head of the regulatory agency cops flak from them, the industry association publicizes them as evidence of the unreasonableness of regulatory demands, the public interest group publicizes them as evidence of industry rapaciousness and irresponsibility, and scholars write books about them. Compound this with the fact that many regulators are not well qualified to do their jobs—they are not the cream of the labor market—and there are good reasons to be cynical that good can come of regulatory encounters.

But this pessimistic analysis misses one important observation that is inescapable if you spend time actually watching regulatory interactions. It is that mediocre people of middling morality and intelligence tend to put their best foot forward when they enter a regulatory encounter. Rather, they have multiple selves, referred to above, and they put their best self forward. The tense, inherently conflictual nature of a regulatory transaction means that the agent of the firm is likely to confront a regulatory agent who has psyched himself to be as professional, intelligent, compassionate, and empathic as he is capable of being. Have a drink with him afterward and he may slip into the unprofessional name-calling mode that is his more relaxed self. But when it matters, when the deal is done, he will amaze at how he can put his best self forward. Obversely, the agent of the firm is likely to put aside his economic self. He will not say "Greed is good," as in Hollywood's portrayal of "Wall Street." He does say:

> NURSING HOME PROPRIETOR TO INSPECTION TEAM: We're pleased to have you here. We've been doing this for such a long time. There are probably some ways that, because we have been at it for so long, that we can't see the wood for the trees. If you find things we are doing wrong, we'll play the game.

The emergence of the business executive's socially responsible self just when it is most needed—at the point where the regulatory deals are done—is not just a matter of the executive choosing alone to put his best self forward. Regulatory agents actively work at encouraging business agents to put their best self forward.

> INSPECTOR TO NURSING HOME ADMINISTRATOR: What you want and what we want more than anything else is to improve the quality of care your residents are getting . . .
> (later) INSPECTOR TO BRAITHWAITE: When you say to them that we all agree that the care of the resident is what we are all concerned about, you know that's not true, that they're concerned about making money. But what are they going to say? They can't turn around and say, 'Hell no, I don't care about the residents; all I care about is profits so I'm not going to do it.'

Sophisticated regulators are practitioners of achieving their goals by manipulating vocabularies of motive (Sarat and Felstiner, 1988). C. Wright Mills has explained how a key research challenge is the understanding of how power can be grounded in the sophisticated deployment of vocabularies of motive:

> Men discern situations with particular vocabularies, and it is in terms of some delimited vocabulary that they anticipate consequences of conduct . . . In a societal situation, implicit in the names for consequences is the social dimension of motives. . . . We influence a man by naming his acts or imputing motives to them or to "him." . . . The research task is the locating of particular types of action within typal frames of normative actions and socially situated clusters of motive. (Mills, 1940: 908,913)

Even without such manipulation, our empirical claim is that business actors are likely to put forward a self that they, the regulator and the researcher observing them, are all likely to view as their socially responsible self. There is an obvious explanation for this. It is good for your survival in the regulatory game, both emotionally and economically (firms often fire employees who upset working relationships with regulatory agencies), to learn how to put your best self forward and how to encourage the other players to put their best self forward. At the end of a day's regulatory negotiation, inspectors sometimes say: "I'm so sick of being nice to people." Even though keeping your guard up by being nice, being empathic, is exhausting, it is less so than the consequences of letting that guard down and unleashing an emotional blood-letting.

Perhaps when the tension abates, when the regulator goes home, the executive's profit-maximizing self will be reasserted to frustrate the achievement of the regulatory goals. But perhaps that profit-maximizing self will think it best to stick with the deal once it is done because this will create a better negotiating position next time. And sometimes, actually quite often, executives will be sincerely persuaded that the inspector has asked them to do something that they should do. At the very least, the tendency to put the best self forward should temper the standard pessimism about the possibility of good coming of regulatory encounters.

What is the implication of all of this for the question of TFT? It is again that TFT is the right way to go. The lesson from the experience of regulators who are sophisticated manipulators of vocabularies of motive is that lurking even within business executives who most of us would typify as ruthless, there is a glimmer of a socially responsible self that can be drawn to the fore in a regulatory encounter.[7] Therefore, we should not succumb too readily to an analysis that says that we can identify certain actors as bound to be recalcitrant, and for whom it would be a waste of time to use persuasion as a strategy of first choice. Furthermore, we should avoid a premature assumption that certain offenders are incorrigible, an assumption that a strategy that is forgiving will only be exploited. Forgiveness, giving the wrongdoer a second chance, can bring out the best in the worst of us—an idea prominent in Christian teaching and in the common sense of those schoolteachers who are competent disciplinarians. So we should be cooperative at first to give others a chance to put their cooperative self forward; we should be tough with cheaters to give them reason to favor their cooperative selves; and we should extend forgiveness to those who show sign of abandoning cheating in favor of cooperation.

Many Players, Many Selves, Many Games

We have argued that firms are not monolithic. Not all of the relevant actors have the same interest in profit maximization as those at the top may have. Regulators do not have their greatest effects by directly sanctioning law breakers; more important is the indirect effect of lending authoritative support to law-abiding constituencies within the organization.

ADMINISTRATOR: Regulation keeps the proprietor on his toes. They know the inspectors are going to come. It helps us. Without them we'd have no power with the proprietor.

Moreover, it has become clear that not only do we need to disaggregate the organization, but also to disaggregate individuals within it who have multiple selves. Furthermore, it should be clear that we need to think about the regulatory game as something played at even higher levels of aggregation than the firm (with the industry association) and at intermediate levels of aggregation between the individual and the firm (the subunit, the subsidiary, the Australian environmental protection division). Although it may be sensible to model the pharmaceutical company as motivated by profit, it may be better to model its research division as motivated by scientific glory, and the industry association lobbyists who work for it as motivated by a desire to sustain a reputation among the political elite as formidable but principled lobbyists.

Cooperative, tough, and forgiving regulatory routines might, therefore, be played *simultaneously* with different audiences in mind as much as *sequentially* as the TFT account implies.[8] Really, however, all of the foregoing recommends that the regulator is best to play TFT in a number of simultaneous games. Thus, the regulatory agency may be in confrontation mode with an industry association that is urging its members to resist a new regulation. At the same time, it is in cooperative mode with one of the member firms of that association that believes the regulation is right. This is a firm that already has corporate policies in place to require compliance. Still at the same time, the agency may be confronting the manager of a particular plant belonging to that firm who has been a recalcitrant offender against the new regulation. The agency may then seek to conspire with the cooperative corporation to sacrifice that plant manager on the altar of an individual criminal prosecution (in which the corporation is not charged). Or the regulator may hint at the desirability of the cooperative firm dismissing the uncooperative manager.

It is in fact very common to observe cooperative games being played at one level to advance imposition of a punishment payoff in a game being played at another level. Braithwaite has observed many encounters where coal mine safety directors or directors of nursing take the inspector aside to say: ''I'm concerned about the lack of safety involved in [these company practices]. I've raised it with head office. They say it will cost too much. But if you look into it and insist that they fix it, they'll spend the money.'' The manager will then direct the inspector to the site of the problem and to the files where failure to address it is documented. With nursing home inspections in the United States and Australia, it is rare for an inspection to take place without one staff member or another giving the inspection team a tip-off of some value.

The irony here is that playing of the game in a cooperative way can generate the information to play the game in a punitive way at another level. Where inspectors walk into a workplace with the demeanor of a tough law enforcer, they get little information. Where they walk in with the demeanor of a friendly persuader, they get the information that can empower them as tough enforcers. TFT is, therefore, better than consistent punitiveness. But it is also better than consistent persuasion at getting information. One reason that actors feed information to regulators about the crimes of other actors is that they fear punishment themselves; they correctly calculate that if they enter into a cooperative game with the regulator, they will be the players least likely to be punished. They would have no reason to make this calculation, however, if they were dealing with a regulatory agency that never punishes. They have maximum reason to do so with an organization that plays TFT with informers. In the whistle-blowing game, as in the other games, players often have mixed motives: they can supply information partly because they think this is right, partly because they fear punishment.

Pyramid Strategies of Responsive Regulation

The Enforcement Pyramid

The more we consider the motivational complexity in regulatory encounters, the more we disaggregate and aggregate to unpack the complexity of agency and action, the more attractive TFT looks. Still we have qualified TFT as it appears in classic economic rationalist formulations. In this classical form, sanctions are conceived only as deterrents, usually monetary deterrents. We have stressed the importance of reputational deterrents; in the next chapter we argue further that the importance of adverse publicity directed at wrongdoing is not so much its deterrent effect as its effect in constituting consciences, in moral education. We have also contended that the law must be designed to incapacitate irrational actors as well as to deter rational ones; hence, other types of sanctions, designed with incapacitation rather than deterrence in mind, are needed.

In this section we take this suggestion of the need for a range of sanctions a radical step further. This step was taken in Braithwaite's *To Punish or Persuade* where the argument was first made that compliance is most likely when an agency displays an explicit enforcement pyramid. An example of an enforcement pyramid appears in Figure 2.1. Most regulatory action occurs at the base of the pyramid where attempts are initially made to coax compliance by persuasion. The next phase of enforcement

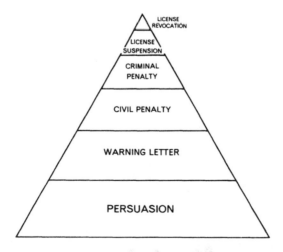

Figure 2.1. Example of an enforcement pyramid. The proportion of space at each layer represents the proportion of enforcement activity at that level.

escalation is a warning letter; if this fails to secure compliance, imposition of civil monetary penalties; if this fails, criminal prosecution; if this fails, plant shutdown or temporary suspension of a license to operate; if this fails, permanent revocation of license. This particular enforcement pyramid might be applicable to occupational health and safety, environment or nursing home regulation, but inapplicable to banking or affirmative action regulation. It is not the content of the enforcement pyramid on which we wish to focus during this discussion, but its form. Different kinds of sanctioning are appropriate to different regulatory arenas.

Defection from cooperation is likely to be a less attractive proposition for business when it faces a regulator with an enforcement pyramid than when confronted with a regulator having only one deterrence option. This is true even where the deterrence option available to the regulator is maximally potent. Actually, it is especially true where the single deterrence option is cataclysmic. It is not uncommon for regulatory agencies to have the power to withdraw or suspend licenses as the only effective power at their disposal. The problem is that the sanction is such a drastic one (e.g., putting a television station off the air) that it is politically impossible and morally unacceptable to use it with any but the most extraordinary offenses. Hence, such agencies often find themselves in the situation where their implied plea to "cooperate or else" has little credibility. This is one case of how we can get the paradox of extremely stringent regulatory laws causing underregulation (Mendeloff, 1979; Sunstein, 1990: 91–92). Regulatory agencies have maximum capacity to lever cooperation when they can escalate deterrence in a way that is responsive to the degree of uncooperativeness of the firm, and to the moral and political acceptability of the response. It is the same point as in strategic deterrence in international affairs; a country with a nuclear deterrent but no conventional forces may be more vulnerable than one that can bargain with a limited range of conventional escalations.[9] And it is the same point that has been demonstrated empirically in the domain of criminal justice: if death is the sentence for rape, juries that think this excessive will not convict rapists; if mandatory imprisonment is provided for drunk drivers, many police officers will decline to arrest them (see generally Feeley, 1983: 126–138).

A regulatory agency with only a sanction that cannot politically or legally be used in a particular situation is unable to deliver a punishment payoff. When a regulatory agency has a number of weapons in its armory, for any particular offense the rational offending firm will calculate that the regulatory agency will in practical terms be unable to use some of the weapons theoretically at its disposal. For those sanctions that can practically be used, it will calculate that the regulator can choose sanctions ranging in severity from s_1 to s_n with probabilities that these sanctions can actually be delivered ranging from p_1 to p_n. But the information costs of calculating these probabilities will be high even for a large company with the best legal advice. These information costs imply that the regulator with an enforcement pyramid may have superior resources with which it can bargain and bluff, a subject we return to later.[10]

Figure 2.2 lays out the dilemma more explicitly. It depicts a regulatory arena where five offenses of increasing seriousness are possible—A,B,C,D, and E—and where the law provides for only two possible punishments for these offenses—X and Y. X and Y are punishments that community sentiment judges to be suitable to offenses C and D. However, they are unacceptably severe sanctions for the less

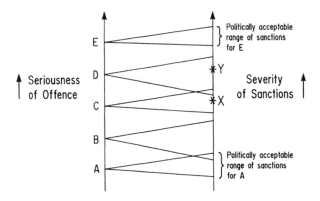

Figure 2.2. A regulatory arena with five offenses of seriousness (A–E), but sanctions with only two severities (X and Y).

serious offenses A and B. There is, therefore, no politically acceptable way of punishing these offenses. There is another type of problem with E. E can be punished (by X or Y) but only at a level that the community judges to be unacceptably lenient. A further implication of this problem may be that if the firm is bold and irresponsible enough to push noncompliance beyond certain limits, it will find a zone where the benefits of noncompliance will exceed the costs of all possible sanctions.

The solution to the dilemma depicted in Figure 2.2 is an appropriately designed enforcement pyramid that makes available to the regulatory agency at least three extra sanctions that fall within the bounds of political acceptability for offense types A, B, and E. Then every escalation of noncompliance by the firm can be matched with a corresponding escalation in punitiveness by the state. Again the strategic analogy is appropriate. If there is any level of escalation in either conventional or nuclear mobilization that is available to the Soviet Union but unavailable to the United States, then the United States is at a significant tactical disadvantage (Schelling, 1966). The disadvantage arises from the fact that the United States must either overreact, with the risk or escalating the conflict beyond bounds where it can be contained, or underreact, risking defeat.

> The idea of "graduated deterrence" and much of the argument for a conventional warfare capability in Europe are based on the notion that if passive deterrence initially fails, the more active kind may yet work . . . if the aggressive move takes time, if the adversary did not believe he would meet resistance or did not appreciate how costly it would be, one can still hope to demonstrate that the threat is in force, after he begins. If he expected no opposition, encountering some may cause him to change his mind. (Schelling, 1966:78)

The enforcement pyramid solves a serious problem with the negotiation of win-win solutions through simple TFT, a problem demonstrated by Langbein and Kerwin (1985). Langbein and Kerwin show that, contrary to the conclusions from static economic modeling of environmental and safety regulation, it is often irrational for firms to comply with laws when the costs of compliance are less than the benefits. If enforcement is the outcome of a process of negotiation, as it generally is, rational firms will avoid immediate compliance when it will be cheaper to negotiate a compliance deal with the agency. At the least, negotiation delays the firm's compliance costs; at the best, the firm extracts concessions that reduce compliance costs. This is only true, however, if holding back on compliance does not cause an escalation of penalties. The appeal of the enforcement pyramid is that it solves the problem with simple TFT bargaining raised by Langbein and Kerwin's model. Firms that resist initial compliance will be pushed up the enforcement pyramid. Not only escalating penalties, but also escalating frequency of inspection and tripartite monitoring by trade unions (see Chapter 3) can then negate the returns to delayed compliance.

The Pyramid of Regulatory Strategies

The pyramid of sanctions in Figure 2.1 is pitched at the target of the single regulated firm. But there is a more fundamental enforcement pyramid pitched at the entire industry. This is a pyramid of regulatory strategies.

To Punish or Persuade argued that governments are most likely to achieve their goals by communicating to industry that in any regulatory arena the preferred strategy is industry self-regulation. When self-regulation works well, it is the least burdensome approach from the point of view of both taxpayers and the regulated industry. When the state negotiates the substantive regulatory goal with industry, leaving the industry discretion and responsibility of how to achieve this goal, then there is the best chance of an optimal strategy that trades off maximum goal attainment at least cost to productive efficiency. But given that an industry will be tempted to exploit the privilege of self-regulation by socially suboptimal compliance with regulatory goals, the state must also communicate its willingness to escalate its regulatory strategy up another pyramid of interventionism. The pyramid suggested was from self-regulation to enforced self-regulation (see Chapter 4) to command regulation with discretionary punishment to command regulation with nondiscretionary punishment (Fig. 2.3). Command regulation with nondiscretionary punishment has its military analogue in the burning of bridges. If the bridges that are an army's only route of retreat are burned, the enemy knows that it must fight a bloody battle if it advances beyond a certain point. Burning bridges and enacting a policy of nondiscretionary punishment both have the effect of demonstrating commitment—of communicating to an adversary an intention never to give in.[11]

Again, this is just one example of the particular strategies that might be installed at different layers of the strategy pyramid. One could conceive of another pyramid that might escalate from self-regulation to negative licensing (see Grabosky and Braithwaite, 1986: 188), to positive licensing, to taxes on harm (Anderson et al., 1977). Another kind of pyramid from a totally free market to various forms of partial-industry regulation to industry-wide regulation will be considered in Chapter 5.

Escalation up this pyramid gives the state greater capacity to enforce compliance but at the cost of increasingly inflexible and adversarial regulation. Clear communication in advance of willingness by the state to escalate up the pyramid gives incentives

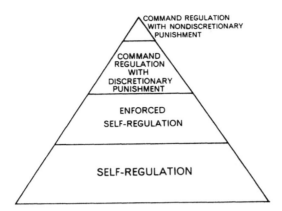

Figure 2.3. Example of a pyramid of enforcement strategies.

to both the industry and regulatory agents to make regulation work at lower levels of interventionism. The key contention of this regulatory theory is that the existence of the gradients and peaks of the two enforcement pyramids channels most of the regulatory action to the base of the pyramid—in the realms of persuasion and self-regulation. The irony proposed was that the existence and signaling of the capacity to get as tough as needed can usher in a regulatory climate that is more voluntaristic and nonlitigious than is possible when the state rules out adversariness and punitiveness as an option. Lop the tops off the enforcement pyramids and there is less prospect of self-regulation, less prospect of persuasion as an alternative to punishment.

Modeling of regulatory deterrence tends to fall into the trap of considering only the option of passive deterrence—deterrent credibility shaped by the potency of the sanctions waiting to be used. The modeling of deterrence in warfare, however, has long involved recognition of the importance of active escalation—a more dynamic modeling of deterrence as an unfolding process. The finesse with which escalation is executed can be as crucial to the efficacy of deterrence as the potency of passive sanctions.

The idea of the pyramid of regulatory strategies underlines the importance of transcending models of regulation as games played with single firms (e.g., Scholz, 1984a, b). The importance of business subcultures of resistance to regulation means that we must understand the significance of industry-wide forces beyond the agency of the single firm. In some respects industry associations can be more important regulatory players than single firms. For example, individual firms will often follow the advice of the industry association to cooperate on a particular regulatory requirement because if the industry does not make this requirement work, it will confront a political backlash that may lead to a more interventionist regulatory regime. Hence, the importance of the pyramid of regulatory strategies (Fig. 2.3) as well as the pyramid of sanctions (Fig. 2.1). Regulatory cultures can be transformed by clever signaling by regulatory agencies, public interest groups, and political leaders that an escalation of the interventionism of regulatory strategy may be in the offing. As even bigger costs and more unfathomable probabilities are involved in such threats, the potential for bluff is even greater. So much so that industry associations can often be coopted into disciplining and bluffing individual firms that free ride on the regulatory future of the industry.

The Benign Big Gun

The possibility that the range and the nature of the sanctions and strategies at the disposal of regulators may matter is suggested from the application of a variety of multivariate techniques to taxonomize ninety-six Australian regulatory agencies according to patterns of enforcement behavior (Grabosky and Braithwaite, 1986; Braithwaite et al., 1987). A "benign big gun" cluster of agencies emerged from this research. The benign big guns were agencies that spoke softly while carrying very big sticks. The agencies in the benign big gun cluster were distinguished by having enormous powers: the power of the Reserve Bank to take over banks, seize gold, increase reserve deposit ratios; the power of the Australian Broadcasting Tribunal or the Life Insurance Commissioner to shut down business completely by revoking licenses; the power of oil and gas regulators to stop production on rigs at extraordinary cost; the power of drug and motor vehicle safety regulators to refuse to allow a product on the market that has cost a fortune in development. The core members of this cluster of agencies had such enormous powers but never, or hardly ever, used them. They also never or hardly ever used the lesser power of criminal prosecution. Commentators in the past have described the Australian Broadcasting Tribunal's strategy as "regulation by raised eyebrows," and the Reserve Bank strategy as "regulation by vice-regal suasion."

   The data from this study are not adequate to measure the relative effectiveness of these ninety-six agencies in achieving their regulatory goals. Nevertheless, the very empirical association of speaking softly and carrying big sticks is an interesting basis for theoretical speculation. The pyramid of enforcement idea suggests that the greater the heights of punitiveness to which an agency can escalate, the greater its capacity to push regulation down to the cooperative base of the pyramid. Graduated response up to draconian final solutions can make passive deterrence formidable (even if the final solution has never been used, as in nuclear deterrence) and can give active (escalated) deterrence room to maneuver. Thus, the theory would be that the successful pursuit of cooperative regulation is predicted by:

1. Use of a tit-for-tat strategy;
2. Access to a hierarchical range of sanctions and a hierarchy of interventionism in regulatory style (the enforcement pyramids); and
3. Height of the pyramid (the punitiveness of the most severe sanction).

Figure 2.4 represents the predicted change in the shape of the enforcement pyramid as the most powerful sanction in the regulatory agency's armory increases in potency. As the capacity for regulatory escalation increases to greater heights as we move from left to right in Figure 2.4, we move to agencies that speak ever more softly (pushing more of the enforcement activity down to the cooperative base of the pyramid) while carrying ever bigger sticks. The bigger the sticks, the less they use

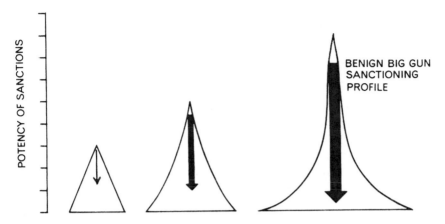

Figure 2.4. Model of the effect of increasing potency of maximum sanctions on the tendency of an enforcement pyramid to push enforcement down to the cooperative base of the pyramid.

them. Indeed, we could conceive of the pyramids in Figure 2.4 as regulatory "density functions" depleting the proportion of regulated firms governed by a particular form of regulation (with the area of the entire pyramid summing to 1 or 100 percent). Our argument is then that higher peaked pyramids will be skinnier at the top (a lower percentage of severe intervention) and fat at the bottom (a larger percentage of gentle intervention).

The empirical claim is not an implausible one. Again it is the same as that commonly made in international strategic debate. It is often said that the period between World War II and World War III is proving to be much longer than that between World Wars I and II because the superpowers have such big sticks.[12] Since the Cuban missile crisis, the superpowers have behaved like benign big guns toward each other. We might take comfort from this accomplishment were it not for the fact that the sticks are so big that one swipe could end us all.[13]

The Theory of Super-Punishments

Goodin (1984) has suggested that social life is not plausibly modeled either as a single-round prisoner's dilemma game where the players interact and then walk away for good, or by a repeatedly iterated game. Social life is, instead, a series of iterated but self-contained games. So conceived, how is it best to play the games? Goodin suggests that the best way is to follow two well-known political precepts, "Don't get mad, get even" and "Forgive but never forget." These precepts need not be contradictory when political life is viewed as a series of iterated but self-contained episodes.

> Politicians should indeed try to 'get even' within a single episode, 'forgive' each other between episodes, but 'never forget' the useful information they acquired in previous episodes about the others' styles of play. Consider the case of one

perennially large subset of American politicians, Democrats with presidential ambitions. Candidates would be mad not to try to get even with their opponents during the course of a primary election campaign or nominating convention. They would be equally mad to continue grinding that axe once their party's nomination is settled. Yet they would also be mad to forget all they had learned in the course of that campaign about who was trustworthy and who was not. (Goodin, 1984: 130)

An interesting implication Goodin draws is that vindictive tit-for-tat (VTFT), a strategy that proves ineffective in an endlessly iterated game, might be effective under the episodic model. VTFT is an unforgiving strategy that matches every one of the other player's defections from cooperation with multiple punitive defections of its own.[14] VTFT has been found not to be a successful strategy in iterated games: when VTFT plays TFT, a downward spiral occurs into more and more punitive defections (Taylor, 1976; Axelrod, 1984). This need not happen, however, when there is a "partial restart" after each discrete episode of iterations. Certainly the first episode should fall into the mutually destructive cycle of defections. But with the restart, grudges are canceled.

> [In the new episdoe] the TFT player will have marked his opponent as a 'don't tread on me' player, inclined toward vindictiveness and overreaction. He knows that unless he treats his VTFT opponent right he will fly off the handle. And knowing that, he *does* treat him right, even if—indeed, precisely because—they got into a fight last time. The consequence is that TFT will *never* thereafter defect when playing against VTFT [Goodin goes on the qualify this claim]. There should, therefore, be an endless run of mutually profitable co-operation throughout all subsequent episodes. Compare this with the ordinary outcome of a series of games between TFT and TFT players. They regularly revert to defection every thirty rounds or so, just to make sure their opponent is still playing TFT. Their opponent inevitably retaliates with costly defections, and both take some moderately heavy losses while the co-operative equilibrium re-establishes itself. (Goodin, 1984: 131)

Much could be said about the conditions under which this analysis is right or wrong. We will not delve into this except to say that the empirical evidence of business subcultures of resistance to regulation (Bardach and Kagan, 1982) suggests that in some contexts business executives who are dealt with vindictively may be more reluctant to set aside their grudges against government regulators than are Democratic presidential candidates.

Nevertheless, it does seem useful to model much regulation as a series of episodes. For example, the Australian nursing home inspection team experiences a sequence of regulatory encounters as it seeks to extract information and cooperation with changes needed to comply with nursing home standards. The episode of iterated opportunities to cooperate or defect continues as a draft report on the compliance rating of the home is negotiated and then as "Agreed Action Plans" are negotiated. It may continue over the next month or two through follow-up visits to check that these plans are being implemented. The episode then ends; the inspection team will not return for a year or two, when the next episode begins.

Similarly with dealings at the level of the industry association. This year the consumer protection agency deals with the bankers' association over consumer protection concerning aspects of Electronic Funds Transfer Systems. Will the industry control the abuses in this area through self-regulation or will escalation of regulatory intervention occur in the course of this extended episode? A year or two later a fresh start will be made between these two players in a new episode concerning misleading advertising of interest rates by banks. And so on.

If VTFT runs too great a risk of engendering a business subculture of resistance, other strategies for demonstrating that the regulator is a "don't tread on me" player may not. Making an example of a cheat in a single episode by iterated escalation of punishment up to the point of firing the big gun may be the better way to get the "don't tread on me" message out than VTFT. Strategic publicizing of the escalation to super-punishment against one player in one episode will get this message out to all players for all episodes. The industry grapevine readily assures this even in a loosely knit industry. Moreover, if the regulatory agency is patient and fair in its escalation, giving plenty of warning of the inevitablility of escalation and sufficient time to comply before moving up a rung in the enforcement pyramid, then it will enhance its reputation for justice as well as its reputation for ruthless retaliation against recalcitrance.

VTFT is not a desirable strategy where a government regulator is concerned because vindictive repeated punishment of citizens who are now complying with the law will undermine the legitimacy of the state and thereby threaten voluntary compliance (cf. Levi, 1987). However, we can accept Goodin's episodic analysis as applicable to much regulation and accept the advantages that Goodin demonstrates as flowing from a "don't tread on me" demonstration effect. Given the need for the state to be just, the better way for it to achieve this effect is by patient but inexorable escalation up an enforcement pyramid that ultimately crushes firms that persist in flouting the law.

The plausibility of VTFT regulatory strategies is broadly consonant with the recent literature on super-punishments. Dilip Abreu (1986), for example, has shown that oligopolists may be able to sustain greater compliance with cartel regimes by instituting threats of "extremal equilibria" or super-punishments. Such super-punishments are often characterized by:

1. The punishment consisting of a short "stick" period of discomfort followed by a longer "carrot" period of reintegration; and
2. The punished party itself being induced to cooperate with its punishers during the "stick" period.

The "stick and carrot" nature of super-punishment encourages cooperation of the punished firm and even self-punishment because by cooperating, the punished firm can more quickly move from the more painful "stick" to the less painful "carrot."

Super-punishments may be of use to agencies seeking regulatory compliance. By engendering a firm's cooperation in its own punishment, agencies can radically reduce the costs of punishing. This increases the fiscal feasibility of costly super-punishments in the most extreme cases. This is illustrated by the use of plea bargaining. By cooperating with punishment on one charge, the defendant may get the carrot of immunity from further prosecution on other, more serious, charges. If defendants "take their medicine," they can more quickly move to the carrot period of reintegration. If they do not, instead of stick–carrot, they get stick and more stick—an escalation up the pyramid. A functional equivalent in the business regulation domain has been the U.S. Securities and Exchange Commission stewardship of its scarce punitive resources by persuading firms such as E. F. Hutton (Orland and Tyler, 1987: 887–907) and Gulf Oil (McCloy, 1976) to pay for independent counsel to produce public reports on corporate malfeasance and on the need to dismiss or demote responsible senior managers.

Super-punishments thus broaden the notion of a responsive regulatory pyramid. First, super-punishments increase the height of the regulatory pyramid. Furthermore, the threat of the super "stick and stick" punishment preserves scarce regulatory resources by channeling violators to "stick and carrot" punishments (where violators cooperate in implementing self-sanctions). Also, by increasing the credibility of regulatory responsiveness it more effectively channels industry behavior to more cooperative paths to regulatory compliance. With effective super-punishments, agencies can more credibly deter noncompliance because they can more convincingly say "if you violate it is going to be cheap for us to hurt you (because you are going to help us hurt you)." The notion of escalating super-punishments even further broadens the notion that pyramids can engender cooperation—because super-punishment theory shows that, even within the most punitive portions of the enforcement pyramid, eliciting firm cooperation can enhance the channeling effects of responsive regulation.

The Image of Invincibility

There surely are good reasons to be pessimistic about the capacity of regulatory agencies to stand up to powerful industries. Yet the pathologically pessimistic might consider the regulatory power of a creature more socially accomplished than ourselves—the dog. How is it that a single Australian sheep-dog or cattle-dog can exercise unchallenged command over a large flock of sheep or herd of cattle every member of which is bigger than herself?[15] How is it that a dog can force the retreat of a man, even a man with a knife—when the man is bigger, more intelligent, and more lethally armed?

The first point to make about the regulatory accomplishments of the dog is that dogs are delightfully friendly to other creatures who cooperate with them. Second, dogs are convincing at escalating deterrent threats while rarely allowing themselves to play their last card. They bark so convincingly that a bite seems more inevitable and more terrifying than it is. And they know how to escalate interactively—in a way that is strategically responsive to the advance or the retreat of the intruder. Friendliness can turn to a warning bark, then a more menacing growl, posture and raising of fur transforms her—she is bigger and seems ready to pounce, teeth are bared, slightly at first, the dog advances slowly but with a deliberateness that engenders irrational fears that a sudden rush will occur at any moment. The dog's remarkable regulatory accomplishments are based on a TFT strategy (the intruder will be extended friendliness when reintroduced as a friend; the sheep will be protected, led to food and drink when they cooperate). The success is also based on finesse at dynamic interactive deterrent escalation, and at projecting an image of invincibility.

In this section we must now begin to ponder the possibilities for regulators to project an image of invincibility to industries that may be more powerful than themselves. Before erecting any more than our three propositions around the TFT, enforcement pyramid and benign big gun ideas, we require more empirical work to better ground theory construction. The starting place is to ponder Hawkins' (1984) seminal study of British water pollution inspectors. Hawkins found that much of the activity of the inspectors was interpreted by them as maneuvering to preserve their authority and in particular to sustain the myth that compliance with their requirements was inevitable. Now these water boards were anything but benign big guns. Their field officers played a game of regulatory bluff because the fines that actually flowed from the supposedly awesome prospect of prosecution were derisory. Puny penalties were dealt with by a degree of misrepresentation of the terrible consequences of prosecution and by inspectors alluding to the humiliation of a court appearance and adverse publicity rather than emphasizing the fine. All in all, ''Negotiating tactics are organized to display the enforcement process as inexorable, as an unremitting progress, in the absence of compliance, towards an unpleasant end'' (Hawkins, 1984: 153).

We can read Hawkins as instructing us that even though British water boards are not benign big guns, in a sense they struggle to give the appearance of being just so. There are costs of managing such an appearance, in backsliding and cross-negotiation to extricate the agency from the risk of an appeal or an unsuccessful prosecution. In a more litigious business regulatory culture such as in the United States, one wonders whether a regulatory agency could sustain for long such a fragile image of invincibility.

Notwithstanding this, the Hawkins study does sensitize us to the possibility that there may be a weak relationship between the reality and the image of the enforcement powers of regulatory agencies. What may predict cooperative, compliant outcomes is whether regulatory agencies are perceived by industry as benign big guns. That is, if the agency is perceived as cooperative even though it may be quite adversarial; if it is perceived as willing and able to repay uncooperativeness with awesome sanctioning even though it is not, then firms will cooperate and comply.

A number of possibilities follow. A regulatory agency that is legally able but politically unwilling to fire its big guns might get enormous mileage in management of the appearance of invincibility from a single famous case where it had political support to fire its big guns and where it brought a powerful corporation to its knees. Conversely, an agency that skates on thin ice in the management of these appearances (such as the British water boards) is vulnerable to a litigious firm determined to shatter its myth of invincibility. Equally, a benign big gun with awesome powers it is rarely willing to use is vulnerable to a legal defeat or to being forced into political capitulation on the first occasion it seeks to fire its big gun. In international relations we know that the image of superpowers as invincible is vulnerable to Vietnams and Afghanistans when political and moral exigencies mean that the level of escalation required for victory is impossible or imprudent.

An understanding of political power requires a grounding of how actors come to be granted the credibility of being benign big guns. Firing big guns causes a lot of fallout in resentment among those who are bullied by brute force. It can be a delegitimating business for the state, especially when the firing mechanism on the gun is untested or rusty. The superpower does better to coax and caress compliance from weaker nations whose very insignificance adds to the damage they will do if they successfully challenge the superpower's image of invincibility. When great powers do bully smaller countries, they must be sure to win. And so with political leaders. They must seek never to lose at the hands of a less significant adversary within the party. While being routinely benign, they must choose their moment to show that they hold the big guns by ruthlessly crushing an opponent. It must be believed that they are both good to those who are loyal, but invincible when they decide to bully the disloyal.

So there might be a more general benign big gun theory of power. If there is, it must stem from an understanding of how actors build appearances of invincibility by displaying their firepower in strategic contests. Certainly Hawkins' work suggests that this might be so in the arena of regulation.

To develop a benign big gun theory of regulation, we must build upon Hawkins' work on the day-to-day interaction of field officers with firms. We must move beyond this to study how agencies handle the crucial tests of their strength that occur at watersheds in their history—how they handle their Cuban missile crisis, their Vietnam. In addition we must study how regulatory agencies go about the business of preemptive efforts to construct an image of invincibility. This might include the study of how agencies pick the "right case" to show that an amendment to an act has "teeth." It might include research on how industry reacts to publicity campaigns calculated to create the impression that agencies with relatively weak powers are benign big guns.

Finally, we need empirical work on what happens when agencies that do have big guns say and do things that threaten their appearance of regulatory clout. For example, in 1987, the Chairman of the Australian Broadcasting Tribunal declared that certain legislative deficiencies made the agency "a toothless tiger." While the agency continued to have very big legal teeth with respect to other matters, one wonders whether across the board the agency came to be perceived as one that could only gum the industry as a result of headlines like "ABT is Toothless Tiger— O'Connor [the Chairman]" (*Australian Financial Review,* 9 November, 1987) and editorials like "Farce at the Broadcasting Tribunal" (*Australian Financial Review,* 10 November, 1987). Do senior executives of regulatory agencies in some ways foster a demeanor of confidence among their own staff, keeping doubts about the fragility of their powers to themselves and nurturing a culture of invincibility within the organization? Or are they frank with their staff on these matters, training them in how to bluff while skating on thin legal ice, how to bargain by making the law appear to cast a bigger shadow than it does?

We also need more empirical work on how actors in business socially construct what it is they fear from regulators (see, for example, the start in Fisse and Braithwaite, 1983). Then we can begin to ground a theory of compliance in the ways of thinking about compliance, the various forms of bounded rationality about regulatory threats and legal obligations, that regulated actors actually manifest. Here, we must explore how compliance constituencies *within* business exploit an exaggerated spectre of an all-powerful regulator to increase the authority or resources of their own safety, auditing, environmental or legal department (for evidence of this exaggeration of the regulator's power by corporate safety departments, see Rees, 1988: 56–59). This is the kind of program of research needed to ground a theory that might take up the ideas of TFT, the enforcement pyramid and the benign big gun approach to secure cooperative compliance.

Keeping Punishment in the Background

A case will be put in the next chapter for republican institutions that are oriented to persuading actors to deliberate in a socially responsible way (see also Braithwaite and Pettit, 1990). Under such institutions, the public interest is fostered as a result of such public-regarding modes of deliberation. These republican institutions are contrasted with market institutions that seek to foster the public interest by aggregating the endeavors of actors who all pursue their private interests.

We have illustrated in this chapter some of the variety in the modalities of what the republican considers socially responsible deliberation—directors of nursing who deliberate in terms of the well-being of patients instead of self-interest, mine managers pondering how to secure maximum safety for their employees, factory managers weighing how to minimize the pollution caused by their operation.

An interesting way of reframing our hypothesis is that without the spectre of sanctions in the background, such social responsibility concerns would not occupy the foreground of our deliberation. In contrast, where punishment is thrust into the foreground, it is difficult to also sustain public-regarding modes of deliberation in the foreground. Hence the attraction of TFT as a strategy that keeps punishment in the background until there is no choice but to move it to the foreground.[16]

To put some flesh on these bones, let us return to Smith filling out his tax return. As he sits surrounded by receipts, a method of cheating to reduce his tax enters his head. Almost simultaneously, the idea of getting into trouble with the tax authorities crosses his mind. This is enough to stop the cheating idea in its tracks. He does not go on to calculate rationally the chances of the spectre of "trouble with the Tax Office" eventuating or what the actual penalties might be. Rather, within an instant of this spectre crossing his mind, another thought has occupied the foreground of his deliberation. This is that it is morally wrong to violate the tax laws; he remembers his self-concept as an honest taxpayer; turning his mind to careful calculation of the risks and benefits of cheating would be a distasteful mode of deliberation for him. This rapid sequence of ideas in the foreground of Smith's consciousness—cheating, trouble and honesty—is perhaps more likely with a law where the enforcement agency enjoys both an image of invincibility and an image of fairness (Levi, 1987; Stalans et al., 1990; Tyler, 1990). Remember that Smith in this thought sequence never gets to the point of rational calculation. It is just the spectre of awesome and authoritative power that matters, not any realistic assessment of the possibility that such powers would actually be used and with what effect. This is what we mean by keeping awesome powers in the background to motivate socially responsible deliberation in the foreground.

A month later, Smith is audited. He had misunderstood the requirements of the tax law in one respect and claimed a larger deduction than was his entitlement. Smith is taken aback when the government auditor treats him as a cheat; he threatens Smith with punishment. This causes him to dig in his heels and fight. His motivation is now to beat the tax man, to retaliate against the person who threatens him. The socially responsible motivation to understand the law and comply with it (normally in the foreground of Smith's deliberation) has been driven off his deliberative agenda by accusation, innuendo of dishonest intent and threat of punishment. His preoccupation is simply to fight and to win.

Imagine, in contrast, that the auditor had attributed a different vocabulary of motive to Smith: "Here is a responsible citizen who has just misunderstood the law; I do not need to threaten punishment." A more likely response from Smith then is apology, remorse, offer of immediate repayment. By keeping punishment in the background instead of the foreground of the encounter, the auditor is more likely to keep Smith's law-abiding self to the fore. And given the economic and moral costs of consistently enforcing punitive law in such cases, sustaining a willingness of taxpayers to settle voluntarily is critical.

Is responsibility in the shadow of the axe really responsibility? Interestingly, we believe that it is usually so construed by human actors. When my boss trusts me with $50 to buy some flowers for a sick colleague, it may be trust against a background of a variety of forms of retribution should my boss detect its breach. Yet I may not view the trust any differently than I would if the $50 were entrusted to me by a person who had no power over me. If my boss reminds me of power ("If you don't spend every penny of that $50 on flowers, you're fired"), then I will not feel trusted. So whether actors feel trusted is a matter of subtle social construction about whether the principal is invoking threat.

It may be that trustworthiness is best secured when the obligations of trust are owed to principals with great power over the agent, where that power is threatening but never threatened. Because retaliation is not threatened, trustworthy agents can be motivated by the positive regard of being trusted. Because the power of the principal is nevertheless threatening, untrustworthy agents may calculate that it is best not to breach trust. The trick of domination is the presentation of a social reality wherein threat will be disguised for those who wish to be trusted, and threat becomes apparent to those who deliberate untrustworthiness. When domination works, compliance is seen as natural and right rather than compelled. My boss does not need to threaten retaliation if the obligations of the trust she confers are violated; her power to so retaliate is clear from her authority. In contrast, the stranger in the street may have to threaten to "come after me" if I do not spend his $50 on flowers. But as soon as he does that, he shatters any illusion that I am trusted.

We should not underestimate the capacity of human actors (like Smith as he completes his tax return) to opt for a prosocial interpretation of their own action—trustworthiness—in preference to interpreting their action as submission to compulsion, even in the face of evidence of compulsion. So there is nothing baffling about the capacity of trust in the shadow of the axe to persuade actors that they are trusted, while also persuading them at other moments that they had better watch out if they are untrustworthy.

Considered together, therefore, these accounts suggest that regulators should not do without an image of invincibility in the background, and should be reluctant to push punishment to the foreground of day-to-day regulatory encounters. They do best when they are benign big guns.

Poorly conceived regulatory strategies, like that of the U.S. Occupational Health and Safety Administration (OSHA), do just the opposite of this. They constantly nip at firms with flea-bite fines. In most encounters with OSHA inspectors, petty punitiveness is in the foreground and no big guns are in the background (see Bardach and Kagan, 1982; Rees, 1988). The result of routine flea-biting is that cooperation is destroyed without any of the benefits that can flow from tough enforcement being secured. When scholars point to an agency like OSHA to conclude that punishment and persuasion are incompatible, they have not understood the foregrounding of cooperation and backgrounding of punishment that benign big guns can accomplish.

The Minimal Sufficiency Principle

Unfortunately, when people think about social control, they tend not to grasp the importance of subtlety and salience in how we underwrite persuasion with punishment. Instead, in most respects, lay psychology involves a crudely economistic model of social control. A series of experiments by Boggiano et al. (1987) showed that parents and college students adopt a "maximal-operant" theory of how to motivate students to work at academic tasks. The subjects believed that long-term commitment to academic tasks varies positively with the size of short-term extrinsic rewards. This belief is wrong.

What the maximal-operant principle forgets is that what may be best for short-term compliance might also be counterproductive for long-term internalization of a desire to comply. And this long-term internalization is the more important matter in almost any domain of social control because it is usually impossible for society to organize its resources so that rewards and punishments await every act of compliance or noncompliance.

As opposed to the maximal-operant principle, a great deal of empirical evidence supports a minimal-sufficiency principle: the less salient and powerful the control technique used to secure compliance, the more likely that internalization will result (Lepper, 1973, 1981, 1983; Lepper and Greene, 1978). Experimental research on children and college students demonstrates the counterproductive effect salient rewards and punishments can have: long-term internalization of values like altruism and resistance to temptation is inhibited when they view their action as caused by a reward or punishment (Lepper, 1973, 1983; Lepper and Greene, 1978; Dix and Grusec, 1983; Hoffman, 1983).

> Over 50 studies examining the effect of extrinsic incentives on later intrinsic motivation indicate that inducements that are often perceived as controlling (e.g. tangible rewards, surveillance, deadlines), depending on the manner in which they are administered, reduce feelings of self-determination and undermine subsequent motivation in a wide variety of achievement-related activities after the reward is removed. (Boggiano et al., 1987: 867)

The minimal-sufficiency principle seems to be of fairly general import, being supported in a variety of domains including moral behavior, altruism, personal interaction, aggressive behaviors, and resistance to temptation (Lepper, 1973; Dienstbier et al., 1975; Dix and Grusec, 1983; Boggiano et al., 1986). Just as strong external incentives retard internalization, using reasoning in preference to power-assertion tends to promote it (Cheyne and Walters, 1969; Parke, 1969; Hoffman, 1970; Baumrind, 1973; Zahn-Waxler et al., 1979).

There is one important sense, however, in which Boggiano et al. (1987) found that citizens were not narrowly economistic in their views on social control. They did understand the positive effects of attributing positive intrinsic motivations to encourage desired behavior. Therefore, adults rated the strategy of telling children that they (children) really seemed to "get a lot of pleasure" out of being helpful, or that they (children) were "the kind of person" who enjoys helping others, as a better strategy than reward, punishment or noninterference for increasing helping behavior. Recall that Braithwaite's nursing home inspectors also frequently use positive attribution as a compliance strategy. And the experimental evidence is encouraging that positive attribution works (Pittman et al., 1977; Grusec et al., 1978; Grusec and Redler, 1980; Rushton, 1980).

Together, the minimal-sufficiency principle and the positive attribution principle ground in tested psychological theory why it is best to have a TFT strategy wherein: (1) escalating to punishment is a last resort, and (2) the resort will be only to a point up the enforcement pyramid that is minimally sufficient to secure compliance. At the same time it can be argued that the big gun idea shakes these theoretical foundations. However, in the previous section we attempted to solve this problem by showing how the benignness of the big gun can mean that the gun has low salience for actors who are intrinsically motivated to comply (being kept in the background of deliberation). At the same time the big gun can be made salient for actors who have no intrinsic motivation to be resonsible that is worth nurturing, and who can only be moved by bringing forward the extrinsic incentive.

Effective regulation is about finesse in manipulating the salience of sanctions and the attribution of responsibility so that regulatory goals are maximally internalized, and so that deterrence and incapacitation works when internalization fails.

Rational choice theorists like to urge the design of institutions that economize on virtue (Brennan and Buchanan, 1985). They believe that institutions are less likely to fail if they minimally depend on citizens being virtuous. The benign big gun institution economizes on motivation, not just virtuous motivation. It does not depend on citizens being virtuous. If they are not virtuous, guns are ready to be fired. But because guns are not fired at the virtuous, and because the threat of the gun is kept so far in the background that people are not forced to think just in terms of it, virtue is saved from being undermined; indeed virtue is nurtured. The benign big gun institution does not depend on citizens being economically rational. If the threat of the gun—say a monetary penalty—does not motivate them, a variety of forms of persuasion are available—appeals to social responsibility or law abidingness, positive attribution, praise, holding up other organizations as models of how to solve a problem successfully.

If both money and a sense of responsibility fail to motivate, the benign big gun institution can mobilize an incapacitative sanction such as temporary license suspension or permanent corporate capital punishment. If noncompliance is a result of neither greed nor irresponsibility, but of incompetence, the benign big gun institution can seek to persuade management to accept consultancy advice. As an institution economizing on motivation, it has a solution to the problem of noncompliance regardless of what motivates the noncompliance. And it avoids the profound danger of institutions that economize only on virtue—the danger that they will not only fail to nurture virtue but will actively crush it.

Conclusion

We have shown that analyses of what makes compliance rational and what builds business cultures of social responsibility can converge on the conclusion that compliance is optimized by regulation that is contingently cooperative, tough and forgiving. In Scholz's (1984a, b) work, forgiveness for firms planning to cooperate in the future is part of maximizing the difference between the cooperation and confrontation payoffs. In Braithwaite's (1985) work, forgiveness is advocated more for its importance in building commitment to comply in the future. In Scholz's formulation, punishment is all about deterrence. Braithwaite places greater importance on the moral educative effects of punishment (Braithwaite, 1989a; see also the next chapter), and on the role of punishment in constituting an image of invincibility within a regulatory culture. When analyses grounded in very different accounts of human motivation can converge on the virtue of the same policy idea, then there is some hope that this may be a robust idea.

If there is a theme beyond transcending the debate between regulation and deregulation that permeates this book, it is the pursuit of such convergence. Much of contemporary social science is a stalemate between theories assuming economic rationality on the part of actors and theories counterposing action as variously motivated by a desire to comply with norms, to maintain a sense of identity, to do good or simply to act out a habituated behavioral sequence. We think robust policy ideas are most likely to be discovered when we pursue areas of convergence between analyses based on *Homo economicus* and those based on *Homo sociologicus*. Unfortunately, however, our disciplinary predilections are to seek battlegrounds for new clashes between them. Perhaps such convergence will be rare, but where we do find it we might be in the domain of policies that have intended effects instead of the more common unintended effects. The pursuit of such convergence is taken up in a different way in the next chapter.

In this chapter we have seen how an economic and a social defense of TFT move away from the notion of an optimum static strategy, and instead move toward the idea of an optimum way to play a dynamic enforcement game. This too contributes to robustness because the enforcement game is of course dynamic rather than static.

For Scholz, it is the fallback deterrence payoff that determines the level at which firms will voluntarily comply. We have made a number of points about this fallback deterrence payoff here. First, the setting of the deterrent payoff is also a dynamic rather than a static matter. What deterrent can be imposed will depend on interactions between the regulatory agency and other actors in its environment—prosecutors, courts, political leaders—a fact that sophisticated firms understand. When regulatory agencies have maximum deterrents that are beyond their political capacity to deliver, firms are not likely to take note of the maximum in calculating a deterrence payoff. What they may take greater note of is whether the agency has at its disposal such a range of sanctions (including sanctions that can be imposed without going to court) that it is always likely to be able to respond to evasion with a punitive reply. Furthermore, if firms note that the agency has in place a hierarchy of enforcement response, they may calculate that even though they can tolerate the politically feasible deterrent response from a given level of evasion, escalation to the next round of the enforcement pyramid in a subsequent evasive encounter may be less bearable.

So we might think of the literature as winding toward a more sophisticated account of the possibilities of regulatory enforcement being used to steer corporate behavior away from socially harmful forms of conduct. First, there was the assumption that the more stringent the enforcement of tougher laws to protect say, the environment, the better the environment would be protected. Then there was the caveat that tougher laws would reduce environmental degradation up to the point where the costs of compliance exceeded expected punishment costs. But once an optimum level of stringency is passed, as the law becomes even tougher, compliance falls (see Viscusi and Zeckhauser, 1979). When the compliance standard is set so high as to threaten the survival of firms, many will decide that it is better to be hung for a sheep than for a lamb. Ultimately, the environmental gain from higher standards is outweighed by the environmental loss from lower compliance with those standards. So the economist's advice to the environmental activist is to do best by the environment by lobbying for optimum stringency rather than maximum stringency.

But then Scholz (1984a, b) takes the economists to task for thinking statically in terms of an optimum compliance level in the standard. Rather, it is the fallback deterrence payoff put in the context of a dynamic enforcement strategy that predicts compliance. Now we are taking Scholz to task for adopting a static view of that fallback payoff. Different fallback payoffs will have differential credibility depending on the social context in which an attempt is made to apply them. There is no simple linear relationship between the potency of "a" fallback deterrence payoff and compliance under a TFT strategy. Rather compliance is most likely when regulators (1) have access to an armory of deterrent and incapacitative weapons, and (2) when they avoid both the mistake of selecting a sledge hammer to swat a fly and selecting a flyswatter to stop a charging bull. Compliance is predicted by both the existence of an awesome armory and by the avoidance of clumsy deployment of it.

In summary, the possibility has been advanced that compliance is responsive to the existence of TFT strategy, the existence of an enforcement pyramid appropriate to the particular regulatory domain, and the potency of the upper limits of sanctioning within that pyramid. Empirical work is needed to build an understanding of how regulatory agencies succeed or fail in maintaining the appearance that noncompliance is a slippery slope that will eventually lead to these ultimate sanctions unless the firm reforms.

A worry about a policy that delivers to regulatory agencies discretion to shift the degree of regulatory intervention or nonintervention up and down two pyramids, such as shown in Figures 2.1 and 2.2, is that there will be abuse of discretion—perhaps capture by the malevolent or victimization of the innocent. The next chapter explores republican tripartism as a strategy for addressing this worry.

In emphasizing this participatory solution for assuring the accountability of discretion, we do not mean to pretend that it is enough. In any shift from autonomous to responsive law, as Nonet and Selznick (1978) point out, there is a risk of jettisoning the major advances that autonomous law involved as a movement away from coercive law (where the law is no more than an extension of the administrative power of the state). Therefore, it is essential to preserve rights of appeal against regulatory decisions to courts that enjoy substantial autonomy from the state. Although we have seen the virtues of giving regulatory agencies big guns, it is crucial that the state set limits on the maximum sanctions that can be imposed and on the offenses for which they can be applied. Obviously, the rule of law is needed as protection against the excesses that we have seen from regulators with the backing of the ruling party in countries such as China, excesses that have included execution and arrest without trial. The rule of law is not only essential to a republican regulatory order, it is definitional of it (Braithwaite and Pettit, 1990: 54–136). And in a republican state, however participatory and open is the context in which regulatory discretion is exercised, the process must be monitored by representatives elected by the entire citizenry who can legislate to forbid or constrain a particular kind of discretion.

Should our regulatory institutions, therefore, be designed for knaves or should they be designed to foster civic virtue? Our answer has been that they should be designed to protect us against knaves while leaving space for the nurturing of civic virtue. This requires the design of dynamic rather than static institutions. First, we should seek to solve our regulatory problems by appeals to the social responsibility of the firm. If that fails, the dynamism of a responsive strategy enables us to shift our motivational appeal to rational self-interest by escalating through deterrent threats. If that fails, if we confront a firm that irrationally resists deterrent threats or that commits an offence so lucrative as to be beyond deterrence, the control strategy shifts from deterrence to incapacitation. Ultimately, this means corporate capital punishment when we withdraw the licence or charter of the company. This is how we can design institutions that avoid the mistake of assuming that actors will be rational or that they will be virtuous.

3

Tripartism

In this chapter we argue that features of regulatory encounters that foster the evolution of cooperation also encourage the evolution of capture and corruption. Solutions to the problems of capture and corruption—limiting discretion, multiple-industry rather than single-industry agency jurisdiction, and rotating personnel—inhibit the evolution of cooperation. Tripartism—empowering public interest groups—is advanced as a way to solve this policy dilemma. A game-theoretic analysis of capture and tripartism is juxtaposed against an empowerment theory of republican tripartism. Surprisingly, both formulations lead to the conclusion that some forms of capture are desirable. The strengths from converging the weaknesses of these two formulations show how certain forms of tripartism might prevent harmful capture, identify and encourage efficient capture, enhance the attainment of regulatory goals, and strengthen democracy. Although the case we make for tripartism is purely theoretical and general in its application to all domains of business regulation, our conclusion is a call for praxis to flesh out the contexts in which the theory is true and false.

The Problem

Business regulation is often modeled as a game between two players—the regulatory agency and the firm. Naturally the world is more complicated than this. On the state side there are other players like prosecutors and oversight committees of legislators, whereas on the business side there are other players like industry associations. On both sides, individual actors wear many hats. Therefore, it is a rash simplification to interpret individual actions as those of the faithful fiduciary of the profitability interests of the firm on the one hand, and the fiduciary of agency interests in securing compliance with its statute, on the other.

This chapter seeks to problematize somewhat this simplification by modeling the idea of capture. Capture is a notion that has enjoyed political appeal among critics of regulation from both the right and the left. Among economists, models of regulatory capture have gained wide acceptance (Stigler, 1971; Peltzman, 1980). Yet capture has not seemed to be theoretically or empirically fertile to many sociologists and political scientists working in the regulation literature (Quirk, 1981). Here we will consider whether capture has proved analytically barren for these social scientists because of a failure to disaggregate different forms of capture. Ironically, it is an economic analysis that clarifies the disaggregation needed to enable a more fertile social analysis of capture.

The Evolution of Cooperation, Corruption, and Capture

Although the simplifications involved in modeling regulation as a game between two players with unproblematic interests are transparent, such simple models, with their elegance and clarity, can be the foundations on which we build more subtle and complex accounts. Moreover, simple prisoner's dilemma models of regulation do have some capacity to explain regularities in regulatory outcomes. These are models that construe regulation as a game between two players, each of which can choose between cooperating or defecting from cooperation with the other player. For the firm, defection means law evasion; for the regulator, defection means punitive enforcement. Whatever the other player does, defection results in a higher payoff than cooperation. The dilemma is that if both defect, both do worse than their joint cooperation payoff.

Let us illustrate this explanatory capability and in doing so go to the nub of the theoretical concern of this chapter. Grabosky and Braithwaite's (1986) study of ninety-six Australian business regulatory agencies found that agencies were more likely to have a cooperative (nonprosecutorial) regulatory practice when they regulated: (1) smaller numbers of client companies; (2) a single industry rather than diverse industries; (3) where the same inspectors were in regular contact with the same client companies; and (4) where the proportion of inspectors with a background in the regulated industry was high.

Grabosky and Braithwaite interpreted these findings as support for Black's (1976) notion of formal law increasing as relational distance between regulator and regulatee increases, and more ambiguously as support for capture theory. But equally these findings are just what would be predicted from the theory of Axelrod (1984) and Scholz (1984a) on the evolution of cooperation. This theory shows that the evolution of cooperation should occur only when regulator and firm are in a *multiperiod* prisoner's dilemma game. Repeated encounters are required for cooperation to evolve because the discount parameter that crucially determines the evolution of cooperation is a product of "the perceived probability in any given round that there will be another round" (Scholz, 1984a: 189). Thus, cooperation should be more likely when the same inspector is repeatedly dealing with the same firm. Similarly, when an agency regulates a small number of firms in a single industry the chances of repeated regular encounters are greater than with an agency that regulates all firms in the economy. And indeed inspectorates recruited from the industry may be in a better position to secure an evolution of cooperation because they are enmeshed in professional networks that give more of an ongoing quality to their relationship.

Yet the fact that such findings can be interpreted in either capture or evolution of cooperation terms goes to the heart of our dilemma. The very conditions that foster the evolution of cooperation are also the conditions that promote the evolution of capture and indeed corruption. A revolving door simultaneously improves the prospects of productive cooperation and counterproductive capture. Where relationships are ongoing, where encounters are regularly repeated with the same regulator, corruption is more rewarding for both parties: the regulator can collect recurring bribe payments and the firm can benefit from repeated purchases of lower standards. Moreover, ongoing relationships permit the slow sounding out of the corruptibility and trustworthiness of the other to stand by corrupt bargains (and at minimum risk because an identical small number of players are involved each time).

This is why if you are looking for corruption in a police force, you look at those areas where there is regular contact between police in a particular squad and long-term repeat lawbreakers—prostitution, illegal gambling, other vice squad targets, and organized drug trafficking (Simpson, 1977: 88–108). You are less likely to find it in police dealings with robbers, burglars, and murderers. The ninety-six-agency Australian regulation study found (via highly speculative data) that corruption was more likely in agencies that had two qualities: they maintained close cooperative relationships with the industry, and engaged in regular sanctioning of the industry (Braithwaite et al., 1986). Cooperation corrupts; cooperation qualified by the possibility of defection corrupts absolutely!

Classically, enforcement agencies deal with the risks of corruption and capture by regular rotation of personnel (Kaufman, 1960; Grabosky and Braithwaite, 1986: 198). Contrary to the policy prescription required for the evolution of co-operation, the anticorruption policy is to ensure that the suspect confronts different law enforcers on each contact. Officers are rotated between regions and among sites within regions.

Another variant of the same policy dilemma arises with discretion. Wide discretion ''presents a real danger of corruption and capture'' (Davis, 1969; Lowi, 1969; Handler, 1988: 1027). But narrow discretion results in rulebook-oriented regulation that thwarts the search for the most efficient solutions to problems like pollution control (Ackerman and Hassler, 1981; Bardach and Kagan, 1982; Scholz, 1984b). When the reward payoff for cooperation is low as a result of such confining discretion, then the evolution of cooperation is unlikely. Might it be possible, however, to allow discretion to be wide, but to replace narrow rule-writing to control capture with control by innovative accountability for the exercise of wide discretion?

This then is the policy nut we seek to crack. How do we secure the advantages of the evolution of cooperation while averting the evolution of capture and corruption? Our answer lies in a republican form of tripartism. Tripartism is a process in which relevant public interest groups (PIGs) become the fully fledged third player in the game.[1] As a third player in the game, the PIG can directly punish the firm. PIGs can also do much to prevent capture and corruption by enforcing what Axelrod (1986) calls a metanorm—a norm of punishing regulators who fail to punish noncompliance. Here the effect of the PIG on the firm is mediated by the PIG's effect on the regulator—instead of directly punishing firms, it punishes regulators who fail to punish firms. Axelrod's (1986) simulations show how the introduction of metanorms can dramatically increase the prospects of stable compliance. The fully fledged tripartism we consider, where PIG's are empowered to punish firms directly, is a more radical option that has been conspicuously unanalyzed, in spite of incipient instances of its implementation in many countries (e.g., Carson and Henenberg, 1988).

Who Guards the Guardians?

In another sense this chapter is about who guards the guardians (M. Shapiro, 1988). The problem of guardianship, as eloquently formulated by Susan Shapiro (1987), is that we tend to deal with failures of trust by accumulating more and more layers of guardianship. The untrustworthiness of nth order guardians is monitored by $n+1$th order guardians, and so on in infinite regress. In the present case, who will guard the PIGs? PIGs can be captured and corrupted; history is littered with cases of PIGs caught with their snouts in the trough.

We hope to show that this way of setting up the problem entails a rather too mechanistic conception of guardianship. What we put in its place is a notion of contestable guardianship. The idea of contestable markets arises where there is such a small number of producers in a market as to provide little direct guarantee that they will vigorously compete to hold each other's prices down. According to the theory, firms will nevertheless hold prices down because, as long as there are not formidable barriers to entry, they will fear that high prices will cause the entry of a new competitor who will seize their market share with lower prices (Baumol et al., 1988).

The trick of institutional design to deal with the problem of regulatory capture, we suggest, is to make guardianship contestable. This is no easy matter, just as it is no easy matter to render economic markets contestable.[2] Of course, the fact that economic markets rarely fit the theory of contestability says nothing about the possibilities for rendering political influence contestable in a democracy. To secure contestability, what is required is a regulatory culture where information on regulatory deals is freely available to all individual members of a multitude of PIGs. Also required is a vital democracy where PIG politicians are always vulnerable to accusations of capture by competing PIG political aspirants who stand ready to replace them. If talk of competition for PIG influence seems unreal, it is only because we are thinking of arenas where PIGs are powerless; where PIGs are empowered, aspirants emerge to contest the incumbency of PIG politicians.

Contestability can mean more than simply competition within the PIG sector for seats at the bargaining table. It can also mean, in a manner more directly analogous to contestable markets, pro-consumer discipline exercised by the potential of PIG entry into a regulatory domain that PIGs have decided not to enter. In a regulatory culture characterized by consumer groups becoming politically active whenever major consumer interests are threatened, the mainstream players of the regulatory game may guard against such consumerist assault by being mindful of consumer interests.[3]

What Is Tripartism?

Tripartism is defined as a regulatory policy that fosters the participation of PIGs in the regulatory process in three ways. First, it grants the PIG and all its members access to all the information that is available to the regulator. Second, it gives the PIG a seat at the negotiating table with the firm and the agency when deals are done. Third, the policy grants the PIG the same standing to sue or prosecute under the regulatory statute as the regulator.[4] Tripartism means both unlocking to PIGs the smoke-filled rooms where the real business of regulation is transacted and allowing the PIG to operate as a private attorney general.

Generally in this book we refer to the simplest model of tripartism where a single PIG is selected by the state (or by a peak council of PIGs) as the most appropriate PIG to counterbalance the regulated actors. That PIG then elects its representative to participate in that regulatory negotiation. Contestability in this simple model is, therefore, accomplished by (1) different PIGs competing for the privilege of acting as the third player in the regulatory negotiation;[5] and (2) different PIG politicians within each PIG competing for election to the negotiating role. The simplest model will not always be the most appropriate—the appropriate model of tripartism will be an historically and institutionally contingent matter. However, the simplest model has definite attractions: it should delay minimally decision making in arenas where no decision is the worst possible decision. And it should maximize the prospects of genuine dialogue around the table leading to a discovery of win–win solutions, instead of a babble of many conflicting voices talking past each other. In this book, tripartism is considered as a strategy for implementing laws and regulations that have already been settled. If one wanted to extend its application to the rule-making process itself, an extension that may have merit, then clearly the simple tripartism model would provide too narrow a basis for PIG participation.[6]

But who are the PIGs? Here it is best to resist pleas for a clear definition of the public interest and who represents it. One reason is that what we ultimately favor is a contested, democratic theory of the public interest rather than an account that can be neatly packaged in advance of the operation of democratic process (Keane, 1988). Second, what we urge democratic polities to do is identify, on an arena-by-arena basis, the group best able to contest (rather than "represent") the public interest embodied in a particular regulatory statute. These groups are thrust into the breach to fight for the public interest the legislature intended to be protected by a regulatory statute; but, in fact, they will more often than not be private interest groups.

An environmental group empowered as the third party in environmental regulation may be a PIG largely devoid of private interest. But we include as PIGs trade unions empowered to defend the interests of their members in occupational health and safety regulation. Indeed, it could even be that a suitable group to contest the public interest in a consumer protection statute to guarantee the quality of automobiles could be the industry association of car rental firms.[7] The most knowledgeable group to intervene in a cozy regulatory arrangement that maintains oligopolistic prices for wheat may be the industry association of flour millers.[8]

As Meidinger (1987) cogently argues, there is no touchstone, no objective standard, by which we can separate the public interest from private interests. Social life seems "almost always to involve a combination of pecuniary interest-pursuit and citizenship" (Meidinger, 1987: 30). In practical terms, citizen concerns about themselves motivate their identification of public concerns: "reason is most likely to be applied by passion—in the form of interests" (Meidinger, 1987: 31). This is not to support the crude "deals thesis" that one sometimes sees in law-and-economics writing (Stewart, 1983). Regulation is largely contested in a public-regarding discourse; it is a shallow analysis to view interest groups as unashamedly using the state regulatory apparatus as no more than a vehicle for advancing their private interests. Certainly, our conclusion will be that this latter form of discourse should be discouraged by our regulatory institutions. Public-regarding discourse, which is already encouraged in many ways by regulatory agencies and the courts, should be further encouraged (Macey, 1986). As Baar (1989) points out, achieving regulatory effectiveness through a balance of control is not about simply striking a compromise of interests. It is about understanding each other's needs and then sharing ideas in the pursuit of risk management strategies that deliver acceptable protection at acceptable cost. As the negotiation experts have instructed us, we will all do better if we focus less on positions and more on designing new solutions that are responsive to mutually understood needs, new solutions that may bear no relation to initial bargaining positions (Fisher and Ury, 1981).

An assumption implicit in our analysis is that for most business regulatory statutes in a democracy, there will be an appropriate PIG. We assume this because we think it unlikely that statutes that threaten the interests of business would ever have been enacted in the absence of an interest group pushing for them. This assumption will not always be true, however, even after empowerment has increased incentives for PIG formation (see Walker, 1983). The question that immediately comes to mind is which PIGs could play the corporate tax enforcement game, say with the IRS in the United States? Perhaps groups like the Citizens for Tax Justice who have been concerned with the issue of fair corporate tax contributions. But this difficult case may be unusual because tax laws are peculiar in the way they are brought into existence by the state to serve the needs of the state rather than in response to clamorings from external interests.

The simplest arena to understand how tripartite regulation would work is with occupational health and safety. In a unionized workplace, elected union health and safety representatives would have the same rights to accompany the inspector in the workplace as the company safety officer. They would have the right to sit in on and ask questions at any exit conference at the end of the inspection and at any subsequent conference. They would receive copies of the inspection report and of any subsequent correspondence between the parties. If they perceived an unwarranted failure to prosecute, to shut down a machine or to take any other enforcement action, they would have the same standing as the government inspector to pursue that enforcement action. With minor variations, this has been the thrust of recent occupational health and safety reform in most Australian states.

Of course, one could usefully grant the same rights to a nonunion safety representative elected at a nonunionized workplace. But that raises issues of where this individual would turn for technical assistance and for legal assistance in going to trial. These problems are remediable in principle by public funding of legal aid, hazardous chemical information bureaus, and the like. Where there is no power base and no information base for the weaker party, tripartism will not work. The tripartism idea is fundamentally about transcending the shallow liberal notion that all you need to do to solve the problems of weaker parties is to give them legal rights (Handler, 1986, 1989; Unger, 1987). Beyond rights, the state can cede real decision making power to weaker parties and can resource them so that they can hire technically competent consultants to help them use that power effectively.

Tripartism may also allow us to move to a regulation model from a prohibition model for some areas of the black economy. Corruption has always been the fear in allowing cooperation to evolve in de facto police regulation of prostitution. But if conditions are imposed on brothel licenses by a tripartite committee, we might secure an evolution of cooperation in the battles against AIDS, declining amenity for neighborhoods, assault of prostitutes, and ensnarement of teenage girls, while forestalling the evolution of police corruption. A variety of third players might perform this role—the women's movement, the church, a prostitutes' union.

In the next part of the chapter, we build on the work of Scholz to develop a game-theoretic notion of capture and then model, game theoretically, the effects of tripartism. After that, we consider the limits of this kind of economic analysis of tripartism. Then we consider an alternative (empowerment) analysis of tripartism, and in turn consider its limits. Finally, we explore the possibility that a synthesis of the two traditions can leave us with an analysis of tripartism where the weaknesses of one approach are covered by the strengths of the other. Readers who are intimidated by mathematical notation can skim over the second section (pp. 63–68). After reading the first section (pp. 60–63), they can extract the most important conclusions from the second section by reading the summary in the third section (pp. 68–71).

The Economic Analysis

The Game-Theoretic Model of Regulation

In two important articles, John Scholz (1984a, b) proposed that agencies might be able to engender "egoistic cooperation" from the firms they regulate if they undertake a regulatory enforcement strategy that is "at once vengeful and forgiving." Building on the seminal work of Robert Axelrod (1980, 1984), Scholz reconceived the interactions between an agency and the regulated firm as a repeated prisoner's dilemma game in which the agency and the regulated firm must each choose whether to cooperate in enforcement of regulations. Scholz began with a simple game of pollution regulation set out in Figure 3.1.

The regulated firm must choose whether to "comply with" or to "evade" the regulations; the agency must choose whether to adopt a "cooperative" or "deterrence" enforcement strategy. The social optimum is reached if both the agency and the regulated firm cooperate. For Scholz, a cooperative enforcement strategy from the agency entails less regulatory supervision and monitoring; consequently, the agency will tolerate literal violations of regulations. Joint cooperation is Pareto optimal because the agency does not have to expend as much resources in monitoring and the regulated firm can more efficiently spend its resources on meeting the underlying goals of the regulation instead of meeting the literal rules of the regulation. This is an equilibrium where the agency enjoys the savings of flexible enforcement by overlooking minor or technical violations in return for the firm's extra-legal efforts to reduce harm in ways not directly addressed in the regulation. In Figure 3.1, this outcome is depicted with both the agency and the firm receiving their reward outcomes: the agency achieves 100 tons of sulfur being removed from the air, and the firm only has

AGENCY'S ENFORCEMENT OPTIONS

		COOPERATIVE (goal-oriented)	DETERRENCE (rule-oriented)
	COMPLY	R = 100 TONS VOLUNTARY COMPLIANCE r = –$2 million	T = 125 TONS HARASSMENT s = –$4 million
FIRM'S INITIAL COMPLIANCE OPTIONS	EVADE	S = 50 TONS OPPORTUNISM t = –$1 million	P = 75 TONS LEGALISTIC BATTLES p = –$3 million

Agency payoffs (capital letters) represent expected amount of pollution reduced annually.

Firm payoffs (small letters) represent total expected annualized costs of compliance and sanctions.

Cell labels reflect the situation as seen from the firm's perspective.

The dilemma defined: $T>R>P>S$ and $t>r>p>s$
$2R>S+T$ and $2r>s+t$

Figure 3.1. The enforcement dilemma: payoffs for joint compliance and enforcement decisions (reprinted from Scholz, 1984a: 186, with permission of author).

to pay $2 million by implementing an innovative pollution-saving production technique ($R = 100$; $r = -\$2$ million).

Scholz suggested that under certain assumptions about the compliance and monitoring technology, there may be short-run incentives for both the firm and the agency to defect from joint cooperation. If the agency adopts a cooperative strategy, the regulated firm has, under Scholz's assumptions, a short-run incentive to act opportunistically and "evade" both the letter and the spirit of the regulation. Firm defection is represented in the lower left box of Figure 3.1 with the firm receiving the temptation payoff of only paying $1 million in pollution prevention and with the agency having only fifty tons of sulfur removed from the effluent.

Similarly, if the agency knows that the firm is going to cooperate with the underlying goals of removing sulfur pollution, the agency may have a myopic incentive to defect from its cooperative strategy and require subsequent *rule compliance* in addition to the cooperatively achieved goal compliance.[9] Scholz thus describes agency defection: "the firm may cooperate by developing and implementing innovative pollution-saving production techniques only to have the agency insist later that the legally required scrubber be installed as well" (Scholz, 1984a: 187). In Figure 3.1, agency defection gives the agency the temptation payoff of 125 tons of removed sulfur and the hoodwinked firm the sucker payoff of $4 million dollars compliance costs.[10]

The temptations to defect from cooperative behavior can lead to the standard prisoner's dilemma result of Pareto inefficiency, represented in Figure 3.1 by the lower right-hand box. The agency undertakes an inefficiently high amount of monitoring and the regulated firm responds by inefficiently fulfilling the letter of the regulation while bypassing its spirit and foregoing innovative cleaning techniques that, while not meeting the letter of the regulations, are more effective at removing the sulfur. At this inefficient short-sighted equilibrium, the agency succeeds in only removing seventy-five tons of sulfur, while the firm is forced to spend $3 million on regulatory compliance.

In formal game-theoretic terms, this regulatory game can be represented by defining the strategies that each player can make and the resulting payoffs for each strategy. For the one-period game:

f_t = the firm's strategy in the tth period;
a_t = the agency's strategy in the tth period;
    where 1_t = cooperate and 2_t = defect;
$V_{ft}(t,a_t)$ = the firm's payoff for the tth period; and
$V_{at}(f_t,a_t)$ = the agency's payoff for the tth period.

For example, the agency's payoffs in Figure 3.1 would be represented:

$V_{at}(1_t,1_t)$ = 100 tons (reward payoff);
$V_{at}(1_t,2_t)$ = 125 tons (temptation payoff);
$V_{at}(2_t,1_t)$ = 50 tons (sucker payoff); and
$V_{at}(2_t,2_t)$ = 75 tons (punishment payoff).

For a multiperiod game of uncertain duration, the present discounted value of the single-period payoffs would equal:

$$V_f(f,a) = V_{ft}(f_t,a_t) + \delta V_{ft+1}(f_{t+1},a_{t+1}) + \delta^2 V_{ft+2}(f_{t+2},a_{t+2}) + \ldots \quad (1)$$

where δ is the discount parameter;[11] and f and a are the firm's and the agency's respective multiperiod strategies. The discount parameter, δ, is inversely related to the discount (or interest) rate, r: $\delta = 1/(1 + r)$ (Rasmusen, 1989). Therefore, as the discount rate (r) rises, the discount parameter (δ) falls.

Multiperiod strategies determine what choice a player will make in every period of the game: "Strategies may be simple rules such as 'always defect' and 'alternately defect and cooperate' or complex rules which use the history of play" (Scholz, 1984a: 188). A central insight of Axelrod's research is that for large enough δ a TFT strategy can be an equilibrium strategy for both players in a repeated period prisoner's dilemma that engenders the Pareto optimal jointly cooperative payoffs.[12] In the TFT strategy, a prisoner's dilemma player cooperates until the opponent defects and responds by defecting until the opponent cooperates. Because cheating against a TFT strategy necessarily entails future punishments, if the discount rate is low enough today's temptation is outweighed by tomorrow's punishment (Ayres, 1987).[13]

Scholz, by extending Axelrod's "evolution of cooperation," is able to demonstrate the possibility of efficient agency cooperation. A provokable, but forgiving, strategy such as TFT in which the agency adopts more discretionary monitoring during episodes of cooperation, can thus avoid the prisoner's dilemma inefficiency. However, the very discretion that promotes cooperation may also allow agencies to abdicate their public-regarding responsibilities to the interests of the very firms they are regulating. In the next section, Scholz's model is formally extended to explore how capture can destabilize the evolution of cooperation.

A Game-Theoretic Model of Capture

In a capture model, through lobbying the regulated firm is able to win the hearts and minds of the regulators. In a sense capture is achieved as the lobbying causes the regulators to care about different things. At the captured extreme the regulators think that "what is good for GM is good for America."

The possibility of capture can be formally included in the enforcement game described earlier if we define the agency's "captured" single-period payoff as:

$$V'_{at}(f_{t'}a_t) = \alpha \; V_{ft}(f_{t'}a_t) + (1 - \alpha) \; V_{at}(f_{t'}a_t)$$
$$\text{where } 1 \leq \alpha \leq 0. \tag{2}$$

The variable α is a measurement of capture. When $\alpha = 0$, the agency's payoff is simply the same as in the original enforcement game (in which implicitly the agency was trying to maximize social welfare). When $\alpha = 1$, however, capture is complete in that the agency payoff is identical to the regulated firm's payoff. For intermediate values of α, the agency's payoff is a weighted average of the public and private concerns.

To simplify the analysis, let us (1) monetize both the firm's and agency's payoffs (so that the captured weighted average payoff of equation [2] can be more readily calculated); and (2) transform the uncaptured payoffs so that the payoff matrix is symmetric.[14] The uncaptured matrix of payoffs can be generally represented as in Figure 3.2. In this symmetric game, efforts to capture cause the agency's temptation payoff to fall ($T' < T$) and the agency's sucker payoff to increase ($S' > S$).

Capture can take three different forms that can have strikingly different impacts on firm behavior. In uncaptured multiperiod games, the only plausible equilibria are joint cooperation and joint defection.[15] Hence, we need to consider only the effect of capture in moving payoffs and outcomes away from either a joint cooperation equilibrium or a joint defection equilibrium.

An important thrust of the works of Axelrod and Scholz has been to suggest that in a wide range of regulatory contexts, the parameters of the game support the evolution of cooperation. Accordingly, we first analyze situations where the agency's discount rate is sufficiently low that joint cooperation has evolved. If capture increases the sucker payoff for the regulatory agency above its punishment payoff ($S' > P$), then an agency will not retaliate if the firm defects. Capture has changed the payoff matrix from $T > R > P > S$ to $T > R > S' > P$.[16] Because the captured sucker payoff for the agency is higher than its punishment payoff, firm defection will not lead to the joint defection equilibrium, but to the firm defect:agency cooperate equilibrium. This is an inefficient shift away from the Pareto optimal joint cooperation equilibrium. This

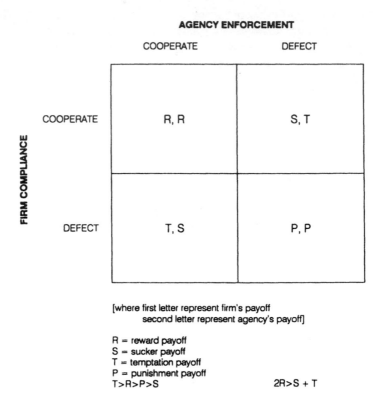

Figure 3.2. A regulatory game with symmetric agency and firm payoffs.

clearly undesirable form of capture, which we call inefficient capture, is the first of our three possible forms of capture.

The other two types of capture take as their starting point the situation in which the agency's discount rate is sufficiently high so that the joint TFT strategy is not stable; the equilibrium devolves to joint defection. Understanding how capture affects shifts away from the joint defection equilibrium is not as simple as understanding how it affects the joint cooperation equilibrium. In situations in which multiperiod cooperation is unstable, capture can potentially move the enforcement game from the joint defection equilibrium to either the joint cooperation equilibrium or the firm defect: agency cooperate equilibrium (look ahead to Fig. 3.4). Now we consider each of these moves in turn.

The movement from joint defection to firm defection:agency cooperation is possible because capture increases the agency's sucker payoff. If the agency's captured sucker payoff increases above the punishment payoff of the joint defection equilibrium ($S' > P$), then the agency will choose to cooperate with even a noncooperating firm. Capture causes the agency's sucker payoff to increase because the captured payoff is a weighted average of the firm's temptation payoff and the agency's uncaptured sucker payoff:

$$S' = \alpha \, T + (1 - \alpha) \, S = \alpha \, V_{fi}(2,1) + (1 - \alpha) \, V_{at}(2,1). \tag{3}$$

The movement from the joint defection equilibrium to the firm defect:agency cooperate equilibrium has ambiguous welfare consequences: the firm does better, but the agency (and the rest of society) does worse. Because it is theoretically uncertain whether these gains outnumber the losses, we refer to this movement from joint defection to firm defection:agency cooperation as ''zero-sum'' capture. The net effect on welfare can be theoretically positive if:

$$T + S > 2P. [17]$$

It is likely, however, that $T + S < 2P$ in many regulatory situations. In the pollution context, for example, moving to the firm defect:agency cooperate outcome is likely to hurt the community more than it benefits the firm. In other words, the higher temptation payoff $(T - P)$ may not outweigh the detriment to the rest of society $(P - S)$ so that together $T - P < P - S$, which, adding P and S to both sides, would imply that $T + S < 2P$. The firm's gains from zero-sum capture will thus often represent an inefficient redistribution of assets. ''Zero-sum'' capture redistributes from society to the regulated firm, but the process of redistribution is likely to consume resources. [18] Beyond these welfare effects, the movement of zero-sum capture seems clearly inequitable. First, cheating firms get an advantage that law-abiding firms miss. Second, the gain to cheating firms is at the expense of innocent (noncheating) pollution victims.

Now for the third form of capture. A movement from the joint defection equilibrium to the joint cooperation equilibrium is possible because capture reduces the agency's temptation payoff below the reward payoff:

$$T' = \alpha S + (1 - \alpha)T = \alpha V_{fi}(1,2) + (1 - \alpha)V_{at}(1,2). \tag{4}$$

If the captured temptation payoff falls below the reward payoff of the joint cooperation equilibrium $(T' < R)$, then even in a single-period game, the agency would not have an incentive to defect if the regulated firm is cooperating. [19] If there is no agency defection to be reciprocated by firm defection, then a source of devolution to joint defection in the multiperiod game will have been averted. [20]

Moving from joint defection to joint cooperation is clearly Pareto efficient. Strikingly, this form of capture will unambiguously increase welfare. How can this be? Remember capture works by getting the agency to care more about the regulated firm's welfare. Although we spoke of the agency's uncaptured payoff as being public regarding, the agency's original, uncaptured payoffs did not reflect complete social welfare because they excluded the effects on one member of society, the regulated firm. This efficient capture has the potential of increasing welfare, because it causes the agency to consider the real harm it can inflict on the regulated firm.

In equation (4), the agency's captured temptation payoff is reduced because, cum capture, the agency begins to consider how its defection will hurt part of society (by the sucker payoff imposed on the cooperating firm). Once the agency's temptation to defect is removed, the firm may be able to move to the joint cooperation equilibrium with impunity.

To understand whether zero-sum or efficient capture is more likely to be manifested, let us return to our earlier discussion. Equations (3) and (4) can be rearranged to solve for critical values of α. From equation (3) zero-sum capture will only be possible if:

$$S' = \alpha T + (1 - \alpha) S \geq P.$$

By algebraic manipulation this inequality yields a critical lower bound of zero-sum capture, α^{zs}, that would stabilize a firm defect:agency cooperate equilibrium:

$$\alpha^{zs} = (P - S)/(T - S). \tag{5}$$

Similarly, from equation (4), efficient capture can only occur if:

$$T' = \alpha S + (1 - \alpha)T \leq R,$$

which implies a critical lower bound of capture, α^P, below which Pareto-efficient capture would not be stable:

$$\alpha^P = (T - R)/(T - S). \tag{6}$$

An agency maximizing total welfare will maximize the sum of payoffs V_f and V_a. Maximizing the sum is the same as maximizing the simple average (the sum divided by two). This means that if the degree of capture rises to $\alpha = 1/2$, joint cooperation should be stable because the agency will then be maximizing the total payoffs to society. There will be no longer a temptation payoff for the agency when $\alpha = 1/2$. Indeed, we can prove that α^P will always be less than $1/2$. Our initial assumption that $2R > S + T$ implies:

$$-S > T - 2R,$$
$$T - S > 2T - 2R,$$
$$1/2 > (T-R)/(T-S).$$

To determine which type of capture will take place, we need to say more about how firms capture. We assume that capture is "purchased" by lobbying expenditures, L, such as preparing submissions, the time involved in building friendships with regulators, and the cost of bribes. Under this conception, corruption is just one kind of lobbying technology for securing capture. It is reasonable to assume that the degree of capture, α, is a positive function of lobbying expenditures:

$$d\alpha/dL > 0.$$

Unfortunately, there is no necessary order between α^{zs} and α^P. Comparing equations (5) and (6), we find α^{zs} will be greater than α^P if and only if:

$$P - S > T - R.$$

Since our prior assumptions about these firm payoffs do not necessarily conform with this inequality, either lower bound can be greater, as illustrated in Figure 3.3

Because the firm clearly prefers zero-sum capture to the reward payoff of efficient capture, if the agency is sufficiently captured to support both forms the firm will always choose zero-sum capture by simply choosing to defect (knowing that the agency will continue to cooperate). Thus, if $\alpha^{zs} < \alpha^P$, as depicted in Figure 3.3A, zero-sum capture will be the only capture.

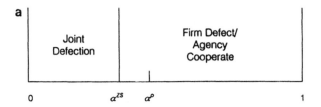

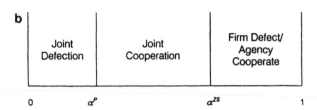

Figure 3.3. Two possible orderings for lower bounds of zero-sum capture and pareto-efficient capture.

Conversely, when $\alpha^{zs} > \alpha^{p}$, either type of capture is possible. The firm may only be willing to lobby enough to establish α^{p} with its reward payoff or the firm may incur the greater lobbying costs of making α^{zs}, which yields the larger temptation profits.

The lobbying technology is critical to this choice. Because the $\alpha(L)$ is monotonically increasing, an inverse function exists and the lower bounds α^{p} and α^{zs} have corresponding critical values of L^{p} and L^{zs}. In other words, minimum lobbying expenditures will be needed to produce these minimum amounts of capture.

A firm in deciding whether to invest lobbying expenditures will compare the costs of Pareto-efficient and zero-sum capture, L^{zs} and L^{p}, respectively, with the increased profits of capture.

In moving from joint defection to joint cooperation the firm receives the reward instead of the punishment payoff. Accordingly, the firm will only "purchase" efficient capture if:

$$R - P > L^{p}.$$

The firm's greater return from zero-sum capture stems from its getting the temptation payoff. This form of capture will only occur if:

$$T - P > L^{zs}.$$

Most generally, lobbying may be so costly [as represented by a steep $\alpha(L)$ function] that neither form of capture is cost-effective, therefore, in choosing how much to lobby, the firm will maximize:

$$\max [0, T - P - L^{zs}, R - P - L^{p}].$$

That is, the firm will choose the level of lobbying ($L = O$, L^p, or L^{zs}) that generates the highest net payoff, and the highest may be zero. In that case, no lobbying will be preferable to spending money on L^p, or more money on L^{zs}.

It is important to note that the foregoing has modeled capture and lobbying to change simultaneously and symmetrically both the agency's temptation and the sucker payoffs. However, some forms of lobbying may disparately impact these off-diagonal agency payoffs. For example, lobbying the agency not to defect from the joint cooperation equilibrium may be compelling because, as described earlier, agency defection from joint cooperation reduces total welfare. Lobbying the agency to "be reasonable" and "fair" by rejecting the temptation payoff is likely to be cheaper than lobbying the agency to "sell out" by sitting on its hands when a firm cheats.

There is an interesting policy question here that neatly brings together the economic and cultural analyses in this book. Is it possible to promote a kind of socialization of regulators that renders them more open to lobbying that promotes efficient capture, more resistant to lobbying that promotes zero-sum capture and inefficient capture? It is clearly possible; indeed, what we may be formalizing here is Bardach and Kagan's (1982) notion of "regulatory reasonableness." It is possible to inculcate through training and precept a regulatory ethic that construes it as wrong to go for the temptation payoff when the firm is cooperating. Such a posture is socially constructed in the regulatory culture not as capture but as regulatory reasonableness. At the same time, a failure to reciprocate cheating by the firm with agency defection from cooperation is socially constructed as capture or corruption, as selling out.

To preserve the advantages of efficient capture while averting inefficient and zero-sum capture, what we must do is overlay our economic analysis of the incentives of agencies to be captured with a social analysis of how to transform those incentives. Capture that reduces the agency's temptation payoff is welfare enhancing; capture that increases the agency's sucker payoff undermines cooperation and can reduce welfare. What is needed is a regulatory culture that allows the agency's T' to fall by attaching negative social approval sanctions to the temptation payoff (the regulator is disapproved as "unreasonable and uncooperative"). But the regulatory culture also protects S^1 from rising in response to capture by adding social disapproval sanctions when this happens. Looking back to Figure 3.3B, social disapproval sanctions that allow the agency's T^1 to fall while protecting S^1 from rising will push α^p down and α^{zs} up, leaving a wider range of situations where joint cooperation will prevail. It will push α^{zs} up to a cost that will more likely be prohibitive.

Social disapproval, through changes to T and S, can also encourage joint cooperation in multiperiod games: by extending the range of discount rates where TFT joint cooperation will remain stable.[21] Hence, for example, joint cooperation can emerge for rather lower perceived probabilities that there will be another round, or that firm and agency will continue to influence each other's payoffs into the future.

Summary: The Game-Theoretic Analysis of Capture

Using simple algebra, we have attempted to model the effects of lobbying to capture or bribing to corrupt a regulatory agency. We have shown that when capture causes agencies to start caring about the welfare (payoffs) of regulated firms that the evolution of cooperation can be either enhanced or undermined. Specifically, the game-theoretic analysis has disaggregated capture into three distinguishable forms (Fig. 3.4):

1. *Inefficient capture:* where joint cooperation shifts to a firm defect:agency cooperate equilibrium.
2. *Zero-sum capture:* where joint defection shifts to a firm defect:agency cooperate equilibrium.
3. *Efficient capture:* where joint defection shifts to a joint cooperation equilibrium.

The first is the most sinister form of capture: the welfare effects of moving away from Pareto-optimal, joint cooperation are unambiguously negative. The third has unambiguously positive welfare effects in moving from joint defection to joint cooperation. The second, zero-sum capture, has ambiguous welfare effects, but clearly unfair distributive effects in advantaging cheaters over noncheaters.

Attempts to capture agencies operate crucially through changes in the agency's temptation and sucker payoffs. In both the single and multiperiod contexts, capture

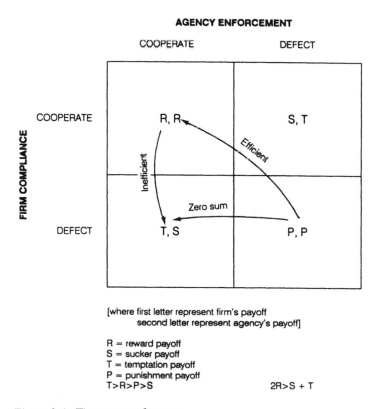

Figure 3.4. Three types of capture.

that tends to reduce the agency's temptation payoff is welfare enhancing; capture that tends to increase the agency's sucker payoff undermines cooperation and can reduce welfare. This result matches the simple intuition of the prisoner's dilemma: reducing the agency's myopic temptation to defect increases cooperation; and increasing the sucker payoff makes the agency less provokable. As Axelrod has eloquently explained, the threat of TFT retaliation is credible only if defection provokes your opponent's ire.[22]

Empirically there can be no doubt that regulatory agencies cooperate much more than they defect.[23] This evidence, by itself, indicates that something is working to overcome the prisoner's dilemma and move the regulatory equilibrium away from joint defection. Our analysis, however, goes beyond Scholz and Axelrod to suggest that some ''solutions'' to the prisoner's dilemma may actually make society worse off. Although we suggest that one form of capture (i.e., efficient) reinforces the evolution of cooperation, we have shown that two other forms of regulatory capture (i.e., inefficient and zero-sum) may reduce social welfare.

Empirically, it is natural then to ask where (in which box) are current regulatory equilibria and why. Joint cooperation can be caused by either the pure multiperiod effects of the evolution of cooperation or the temptation-reducing effects of efficient capture. A firm defect:agency cooperate equilibrium can be caused by either zero-sum or inefficient capture. These are areas for further research. Although we believe that a majority of regulated firms join the agency in cooperation, we are agnostic as to whether joint cooperation is caused by efficient capture or the evolution of cooperation.[24] For those instances in which the agency fails to retaliate against firm defection, there are good reasons for believing that inefficient capture of one type or another is responsible.[25] For most agencies, firm defection must be of extraordinary proportions to overcome the attitudinal resistance of regulators to punishment. Failure of regulators to defect from cooperation to retaliate against cheating firms is likely to be the predominant regulatory problem[26] and the focus of our proposed tripartism reform.

Finally, we have argued that to solve the policy problems the economic analysis has uncovered, we must complement an understanding of economic institutions with an understanding of socializing institutions. It is possible to promote a socialization of regulators that renders them more open to lobbying that promotes efficient capture, more resistant to lobbying that promotes zero-sum and inefficient capture. A regulatory ethic can be engendered that construes it as wrong to go for the temptation payoff when the firm is cooperating and wrong to acquiesce in cheating. When we add to the economic model the social and self-disapproval sanctions from a regulatory culture that is reasonable but firm in this way, efficient joint cooperation can be accomplished in a wider range of situations.

In the next section, we seek to show that tripartism dramatically increases the costs of capture in the economic analysis. This is all to the good when tripartism deters inefficient and zero-sum capture. As with regulators, however, so with PIGs we do not want to deter efficient capture. Because we seek a social rather than an economic solution to preserving the benefits of efficient capture, we must design institutions to involve PIGs as well as regulators in a tripartite culture of regulatory reasonableness. As we move into a republican analysis of regulation in the following sections, we show how it is both desirable and plausible that republican tripartism will discourage PIGs from seeking the temptation payoff.

Deterring Capture With Tripartism

Empowering Public Interest Groups with standing to enforce agency regulations can serve as a powerful deterrent to the various forms of capture discussed. To extend the capture model to include the possibility of PIGs, consider a model with N PIGs, each receiving the same payoffs as the uncaptured agency, V_f. The PIGs, as their name indicates, have payoffs that are public regarding. But as stressed earlier these payoffs exclude the firm's profitability. The strategy set of each PIG consists of whether to enforce the law or not. In terms of the original model, the decision to enforce is equivalent to strict rule enforcement or noncooperative defection. Any individual PIG by litigation can effectively substitute for the agency defecting from cooperation. Indeed, cooperative enforcement will pertain only if neither the agency nor any of the individual PIGs choose to defect. Any individual PIG can cause defection.

PIGs crucially affect the regulated firm's ability to capture, because in the presence of empowered PIGs the firm must capture PIGs as well as the agency to be effective. But as the foregoing analysis has indicated, the different forms of capture have different equitable and efficiency effects. Public policy should seek to deter agency defection from the joint cooperative equilibrium but should enhance the ability of agency and PIGs to defect from the firm defect:agency cooperate equilibrium.

Consequently, as shown in Figure 3.5, policy should be set to discourage PIGs from defecting from the joint cooperative equilibrium while simultaneously facilitating their capacity to defect when the firm has done so. To accomplish this, we want to render PIGs susceptible to the same social and self-disapproval sanctions discussed earlier in relation to agencies. We want PIGs to be full participants in a culture of regulatory reasonableness—a culture that rewards those who are "fair but firm." We have more to say on this later in our discussion of republican tripartism wherein all players are given an interest in working together to discover options for mutual gain— to empathize with the needs of the other.

By focusing on agency defection from the firm defect:agency cooperate quadrant, public policy can deter the inequity and questionable efficiency of zero-sum capture and the clear inefficiency of inefficient capture without undermining the welfare enhancement of Pareto capture.

If the N PIGs are given standing to enforce the law, a firm will only be able to achieve zero-sum or inefficient capture if it captures the PIG's individual payoffs as well as the agency's. We can thus consider that each PIG could be lobbied and captured independent of agency lobbying. In formal terms, let the payoff for the ith PIG be $V_f = \alpha_i V_f + (1 - \alpha_i) V_a$ where α_i, the level of PIG capture, is a positive function of the lobbying expenses, L_i, devoted to the ith PIG.

To accomplish zero-sum capture, the regulated firm must not only raise the agency's degree of capture (now termed α_a to distinguish it from the PIGs') above α^{zs}, but also ensure that the degree of capture for each PIG is above this magnitude.

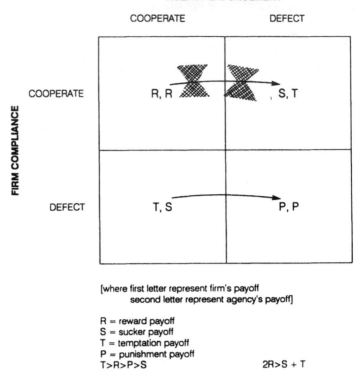

AGENCY ENFORCEMENT

COOPERATE   DEFECT

FIRM COMPLIANCE

COOPERATE   R, R   , S, T

DEFECT   T, S   P, P

[where first letter represent firm's payoff
          second letter represent agency's payoff]

R = reward payoff
S = sucker payoff
T = temptation payoff
P = punishment payoff
T>R>P>S   2R>S + T

FIRM COMPLIANCE

Figure 3.5. Public policy responses to two forms of agency defection.

The firm's degree of effective capture α_e, will accordingly be as low as that which it has achieved with the least captured PIG:

$$\alpha_e = \min (\alpha_a, \alpha_i) \qquad\qquad (7)$$
for $i = 1, N$.

To accomplish zero-sum capture, the level of effective capture must exceed α^{zs}:

$$\alpha_e \geq \alpha^{zs}.$$

which implies:

$$\alpha_i \geq \alpha^{zs}$$
for $i = 1, N$.

As in the bilateral model, there will be a L_i^{zs} associated with each α. Furthermore, to minimize costs, a firm interested in establishing a certain level of capture will lobby to establish that same amount with each PIG, as lobbying to capture one PIG more than another cannot, from equation (7), affect the capture equilibrium and thus would entail needless lobby expense. If each PIG has the same lobbying technology function as the agency:

$$\alpha_i(L) = \alpha_a(L)$$
for all L,

then to establish zero-sum capture for any individual PIG will entail lobbying expenses of:

$$L_i^{zs} = L_a^{zs}$$
for $i = 1, N$.

To effectuate zero-sum capture under these assumptions would require:

$$L_e^{zs} = (N + 1) L_a^{zs}$$

as a firm would need to invest L_a^{zs} lobbying expenses in the agency and each (of the N) PIGs.

Tripartism (and beyond) can thus dramatically increase the costs of capture as can be seen in the increased slope of the effective lobbying technology:

$$d\alpha_e/dL_a = (N + 1) \, d\alpha_a/dL_a.$$

The firm's benefits from inefficient or zero-sum capture are fixed at $T' - R$ and $T - P$, respectively. Introducing multiple PIGs raises the cost of capture without increasing its benefits. Because a rational firm will not spend more on lobbying agencies and PIGs than it can potentially gain, tripartism offers the hope of retarding deleterious forms of capture.

In fact, the simple assumptions of our model understate the potential impact of tripartism in two ways. First, if the idea of contestable guardianship is right, then it is not enough to capture only all relevant PIGs presently on the scene. Assume PIG capture is achieved by paying a bribe to all relevant PIG politicians. Under conditions of contestability, this capture will give reason for other PIG members to replace their unfaithful fiduciaries. Or if they cannot succeed in this, it will give them reason to resign and form a new PIG. Indeed, conditions of across-the-board capture of PIGs will create opportunities and incentives for citizens presently uninvolved in PIGs to set up new PIGs with a reform agenda. Thus, perfect contestability means that the number of bribes to be paid is not N but ∞.

Second, the assumption that each PIG has the same lobbying technology function will usually be wrong, and wrong in an interesting way. There exist individuals who for all practical purposes are incorruptible and immune to all available forms of capture. Individuals of this sort are particularly likely to be found among PIG activists. What company would be foolish enough to consider offering Ralph Nader a bribe? The point is that as N (the number of PIGs) rises, the risk increases that one of them will be immovable by any level of lobbying expenditure. Then the lobbying expenditure on all the others will have been wasted.

Types of PIGs

In this section we summarize what has been suggested so far about four ideal types of PIG behavior. This leads us to open up what is our major concern about tripartism: the zealous PIG.

The Rational PIG. We assume that it is possible to identify PIGs whose mission is the same as that embodied in a regulatory statute: environmental groups for environmental statutes, animal welfare groups for animal welfare statutes, civil liberties groups for privacy statutes, women's groups for affirmative action legislation, an so on. If this assumption is correct, the rational PIG will behave in the same way as a rational regulator. If TFT is the rational way to play the game, as Scholz (1984a) and Axelrod (1984) suggest it is so often, then the rational PIG will monitor that the regulator is playing the game that way. When the captured regulator cooperates in a temptation payoff for the firm, the PIG will know this (because tripartism has given it access to the same information as the regulator). The rational PIG would then seek in the courts the deterrence payoff the rational regulator should have sought. Sticking with the simplistic motivational account of the rational actor model, if we assume the judge to be a rational uncaptured upholder of the public interest embodied in the law, then the judge will enforce the law on accurate evidence of law evasion supplied by the PIG. The judge will replace the temptation payoff the firm has achieved through capture with the confrontation payoff. Thus, the firm can no longer escape the prisoner's dilemma by capturing the regulator.

The Captured PIG. However, the firm can capture all the PIGs as well, and then escape the prisoner's dilemma. The captured PIG will behave in the same way as the captured agency. But we have shown that it is unlikely to be profitable or even possible under conditions of tripartism for the firm to spend an amount on capture that will enable it to defect with impunity.

The Tempted PIG. We have shown that there is a form of capture, efficient capture, that increases welfare. For regulatory agencies, we showed that we can encourage efficient capture by reducing the agency's temptation payoff. Similarly, we can encourage efficient capture by reducing the PIG's temptation payoff. In the case of agencies, we saw that to achieve this result we must supplement the economic analysis with an analysis of incentives derived from regulatory socialization (regulators are disapproved of when they are ''unreasonable'' and ''uncooperative''). There is reason for optimism that regulatory socialization can and does steer agencies away from seeking the temptation payoff. Empirically, it has been shown that regulators are mostly ''of manners gentle'' (Grabosky and Braithwaite, 1986). There is no such empirical basis for optimism that PIGs will be of manners gentle. Firms have good reason to be nervous that PIGs will prove both uncapturable and so ill-mannered that they will readily succumb to the temptation payoff.

The Zealous PIG. The problem of the tempted PIG is so far unsolved. But the problem may be worse than one of simple rational temptation. Certain facts about PIG socialization might be just the opposite of those of regulator socialization; PIGs may be socially selected to be combative rather than cooperative and well-mannered. Hence, PIGs may zealously seek the temptation payoff even when this is irrational according to the parameters of our simple model.

The Problem of the Zealous PIG

One empirical study is consistent with this analysis of the problem of the zealous PIG (but contrast the discussion below of PIG spinelessness from the studies of Rees [1988] and Carson and Henenberg [1990]). Scholz (1991) himself sought to predict the effectiveness of the Occupational Safety and Health Administration in preventing worker injuries across thirty-four states. Consistent with his hypothesis that "vengeful and forgiving" TFT enforcement will maximize compliance, he found that states with what he called cooperative enforcement (firm enforcement concentrated on the "bad apples") had more effective enforcement. However, he also found that labor involvement in regulation reduced the effectiveness of enforcement.

We do not want to dwell on this study because it may be enforcement ineffectiveness that increases labor involvement, especially since the latter was measured by the number of complaints per worker filed with OSHA. Also needless to say, the right to file a lot of complaints with the regulator is such a pale form of PIG participation as to approximate PIG exclusion rather than tripartism, if that is the only participation involved. In fact, the rather interesting analysis in Scholz's (1991) paper is based in part on this very observation. Scholz points out that when PIGs are locked out of meaningful participation in a regulatory regime, opportunities to invoke enforcement have the qualities of a one-shot game (which recommend the temptation payoff). Locked out constituencies are best to lock in temptation payoffs whenever the law gives them an opportunity to do so. If they fail to mobilize legalistic enforcement to lock in their preferred outcome, that preferred outcome will be undone on future occasions when they are locked out. The implication, from our theoretical perspective, is that disempowered PIGs are likely to be supporters of regulatory inflexibility and opponents of the regulatory discretion needed to constitute win-win solutions precisely because they are disempowered.

There are good theoretical reasons for expecting that PIGs will not always act as rational maximizers of the public interest embodied in the law, the interest they purport to represent. PIG behavior, like any social action, can be understood in useful and limited ways as (1) a process of displaying and being faithful to an identity (Bowles and Gintis, 1986; Etzioni, 1988); and (2) a rational pursuit of goals. For PIG activists, sustaining the identity of a knight on a white charger may be quite important. A commonplace observation of Australian Labor Party politicians is that PIGs too often indulge the politics of the "warm inner glow" in preference to achieving results. Trade union leaders can sometimes win more votes from their constituency by glorious but unsuccessful confrontations with evil capitalists than by cooperatively negotiating satisfying resolutions to conflict. The environmental group that thrives on conflict may suffer a decline in financial contributions or membership if it becomes conciliatory (Harris and Milkis, 1989; see also Quirk, 1989).

This connects with Edelman's (1964) theory that diffuse publics get symbolic rewards while concentrated interests get tangible rewards. Consumers, for example, are usually diffuse interests. Concentrated interests have the power (particularly the staying power) to hold out for tangible rewards. Could it be that PIGs so often settle for symbolic rewards because that is all they have the capacity to hold out for? They derive satisfaction from the enactment of a new regulatory law (symbolic reward), when 10 years later it is found that the law has never been enforced (the elusive tangible reward).

What then is our theory of why PIGs are sometimes zealots, "irrationally" going for symbolic rewards associated with the temptation payoff? Drawing on Edelman (1964), the theory is that PIGs focus on deriving satisfaction from symbolic victories to the extent that they are excluded from tangible victories. When PIGs are empowered, they will be more focused on the more durable, and ultimately more persuasive, appeal of tangible long-term progress toward goals that are important to their members.[27] Powerful PIGs, like the contemporary Australian Council of Trade Unions (ACTU) or the Swedish Trade Union Confederation, rarely sacrifice tangible rewards to symbolic rewards; they systematically prefer cooperation with business and government to short-sighted seizure of a temptation payoff.[28] Tripartite empowerment removes the conditions for the irrational zealotry that, in advance of empowerment, seem the strongest argument against tripartism (see also Boyer and Meidinger, 1985: 962).

One dynamic that underlies this is that PIG politicians are driven to emphasize symbolic rewards because that is all they can deliver to the membership to justify their own reelection or their continued funding. The leadership has an interest in duping the membership into believing that symbolic victories are not Pyrrhic. It follows that communication to the membership of tangible outcomes from the regulatory process will undermine the appeal of symbolic politics. The open-information aspect of tripartism, therefore, undermines the political foundations of PIG zealotry. The more the regulatory system succeeds in widely communicating knowledge about the benefits secured from cooperation, the more likely that PIG constituents will support rational TFT policies; the more likely they will remove zealots from office.

A common source of PIG zealotry is that PIG leaders, rather than being faithful fiduciaries for their members, are captured by fourth interests. PIG activists are sometimes captured by political affiliations; their motivation can be less to be a rational fiduciary of the PIG and more to use PIG activism as a stepping stone into politics. It is possible, for example, for a trade unionist to be captured by a left political party, and for this capture to explain "consciousness raising struggles" that leave members worse off than they would have been through a more cooperative strategy. To the extent that PIG zealotry is explained as capture by fourth interests, again the solution is maximum engendering of awareness among PIG members of the payoffs their agents are delivering on their behalf.

We now develop a further, more formal, argument concluding that tripartism may be a cure rather than a fillip to seemingly irrational PIG advocacy of the temptation payoff. When the PIG is excluded from information,[29] it is more rational for it to harass the regulated firm, to opt more often for deterrence when the firm is cooperating. Uncertainty makes it more difficult for a PIG to determine whether a firm is cooperating or defecting. Consequently, uncertainty makes it more difficult for the PIG to join the agency in a TFT strategy against the firm. If the PIG is excluded from information, it will only be able to play TFT with error and these errors will tend to destabilize the evolution of cooperation. Because uninformed PIGs will sometimes mistakenly believe that a cooperating firm is defecting, the firm's payoff from cooperating is reduced. Analogously, because uninformed PIGs will sometimes mistakenly believe that a defecting firm is cooperating, the firm's payoff from defecting is increased. Both types of error work to increase the firms' incentives to defect. At the extreme, a PIG would have no idea whether the firm was defecting or cooperating, therefore, from the PIG's perspective the 2×2 matrix would collapse to a 1×2 matrix depicted in Figure 3.6. In Figure 3.6 β is the PIG's estimate of the probability that firm is cooperating. Because $T > R$ and $P > S$, the completely uninformed PIG will prefer defection for any value β $(1 \geq \beta \geq 0)$.

It follows from our theory that the admitted attraction of PIGs to the adversarial temptation payoff is not a problem that is unleashed by tripartism, but a problem reigned in by our conception of tripartism. In addition to this, one must not lose sight of the fact that under tripartism the combative zealot will end up having to persuade a judge to zealotry against the weight of evidence submitted by the two other players.

Under conditions of full tripartism, PIGs would tend to view going to court in the same way that agencies currently tend to view it—as a last desperate measure to force compliance, as an "admission of failure."[30] As we see later, empowered agents have an interest in not handing over that power to courts. Here, it is important to distinguish our tripartism proposal from the trends that have led to the emerging malaise of American administrative law over the last 20 years (ably described by Shapiro [1988] and Melnick [1983]). That malaise can be described first as paralysis in dealing with the tough rule-making issues, and second as a shift in power within regulatory agencies "from those who are really concerned about making policies that work to those concerned with defending them in court" (Shapiro, 1988: 152).

The malaise was largely caused by the American fear of capture; PIGs addressed this fear by fighting legal battles for rules to narrow agency discretion. Judges who had "read and accepted the literature on agency 'capture'" (Melnick, 1983: 362) agreed, and undercut regulatory flexibility. The tripartism proposal involves accepting wide discretion, allowing flexible regulation, but safeguarding against its abuse by PIG participation at the front end of the regulatory process. Front-end participation

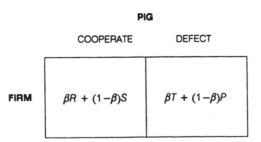

Figure 3.6. Expected payoffs for asymmetrically informed PIG.

in actually negotiating outcomes is more empowering than back-end participation in attempting to reverse these deals in the courts.[31] Nevertheless, back-end standing is a prerequisite for front-end submissions to be taken seriously. It requires an extremely pessimistic view of PIG irrationality to believe that PIGs would systematically prefer back-end to front-end participation. Back-end participation is not only less empowering, it is also more expensive to go to court.

The relevant feature of regulatory problems here is that they tend to be polycentric (Fuller, 1978), such that a solution to any side of the problem will affect how the other sides of it can be solved. Polycentrism means, first, that formal rule adjudication cannot unravel this complex fabric, and second that the many sides of the problem can be mutually adjusted to constitute non–zero-sum solutions. Thus, at the same time that polycentrism undermines the rationality of legalistic adjudication, it also creates the conditions where mutuality can constitute high reward payoffs in the prisoner's dilemma game.

The central message of this section has been that seemingly irrational PIG zealotry is not an inevitable fact of life; it is a product of structural conditions that make zealotry the PIG's best shot. Tripartism might transform those structural conditions.

Limits of the Economic Model

We started with a simple economic model that enabled us to see with clarity the different forms of capture and the possible effects of tripartism on them. But we quickly came to see that it is a model that only gets us started toward understanding how we can secure the advantages of the evolution of cooperation while averting the evolution of inefficient capture and corruption. It is now time to summarize the limits of the game-theoretic model revealed so far, and to add some more.

Notwithstanding its limits, the simple model makes two steps toward greater complexity compared with the Scholz (1984a) model in that (1) it problematizes the interests of the two original players—from simply pursuing structurally determined unitary interests to being captured by the interests of the other; and (2) it adds a third player to the game. However, we have already seen that whether tripartism will cost-effectively advance compliance with the law cannot be assessed without considering the relevance of the capture of regulatory players by fourth interests outside the model. Furthermore, as we saw in the previous chapter, regulation is better conceived as a simultaneous pursuit of multiple interrelated games. Hence, for example, the regulator plays cooperatively with an employee or subunit of the firm at the same time as it plays confrontationally with the firm itself in communications with its chief executive. As that chief executive plays confrontationally with the regulator, she plays another game cooperatively with the regulator's political masters to bring their influence to bear.

It is often assumed that the problem of the nonunitary nature of the corporation is a source of regulator impotence, but in fact it is not. One of the reviewers of our manuscript advanced this common assumption clearly: "[T]he large corporation suffers from a bifurcation of goals between top management which must play ball with regulators and activists and middle managers who are judged on short-term financial criteria. In fact, the real problem is that middle managers get mixed signals—be socially responsible and maximize business performance in the short run. Of course their career advancement is predicated on the latter.'' The problem of nonunitariness is in fact a strategic advantage for the regulator. When middle management is irresponsible and adversarial but top management is cooperative, the regulator can choose to switch the venue of regulatory negotiation to the offices of top management. If, as also often happens, middle management is more cooperative than top management would want them to be, regulatory negotiation can quietly proceed at this lower level of the organization without top management finding out about the nature of the deals that are done. Of course, this venue-shopping advantage often cuts the other way. If the inspector is not captured, the firm can go to their supervisor; if the supervisor is not captured, to the head of the agency and ultimately to the political masters. To the extent that tripartism deters corruption and capture, our hypothesis is that it will have an effect at all levels of the regulatory bureaucracy. To this extent, the effect of tripartism is to curtail the venue-shopping advantage of the firm while leaving the venue-shopping advantage of the regulator untouched.

Having disaggregated capture into its welfare-damaging and welfare-enhancing forms, we have glimpsed the insight that the key to a policy for preserving efficient capture while preventing inefficient capture will lie with a *social* analysis of regulatory cultures.

We have seen the error of assuming that the lobbying technology function is the same for all PIGs, and the importance of this error for underestimating the effects of tripartism in deterring capture. Beneath this error lies a deeper error inherent in economic modeling. This is the assumption that actors are maximizers, or at least satisficers (Simon, 1982), of some value. We pointed out that for many PIG fiduciaries the lobbying technology function will have a slope of zero. On some matters some PIGs and some regulators will not be maximizers or satisficers of some utility, least of all one that can be monetized; they will be deontologists. They will seek to secure some approved state irrespective of the cost, without regard even to the possibility that doing so will worsen attainment of that same value in the long run.

Hence, the union will insist that millions of dollars be spent in attempts to dig out miners trapped miles underground even if that will mean there will be no money for subsequent improvements in the safety of the mine that are likely to save more lives. The environmental group will adopt the position that no economic benefit can justify the extinction of a species. Even corporate actors frequently enough reason deontologically: "This company is committed to complying with the law. Price-fixing is against the law. We will refrain from price-fixing whatever the cost.''[32] It is the case that actors sometimes think this way; and good moral arguments can be advanced as to why actors ought to think this way (Yeager, 1990). We fail to capture this sort of is and ought with economic models that monetize values that actors are assumed to want to maximize.

A further limitation is in assuming that when capture does occur, it occurs as a result of lobbying expenditure by the firm. Capture may be hegemonic (Gramsci, 1971; Bocock, 1986), a product of tendencies for capitalism to inculcate an identification among all citizens of the interests of capital with their own interests. Capture may be the result of a judgment that in a capitalist economy people who believe that "what is good for General Motors is good for America" are the people who win (Cohen and Rogers, 1983: 51–58). In neither case does the firm benefiting from capture have to spend money to gain the benefit.

One of the most plausible noneconomic theories of capture is the most mundane: regulators like to cooperate with firms because they seek a conflict-free worklife.[33] Most of us regularly conciliate in circumstances where we could achieve a better result by fighting; we do this because fighting is nasty and unpleasant, especially when fighting means a gladiatorial battle in a court of law. Regulators confront incidents where ugly conflict can flare much more regularly than actors confront in almost any walk of life; little wonder they seek to minimize their exposure to conflict, even when conflict is in the public interest.

Our economic model assumes that noncompliance with the law occurs as a result of calculations to break the law. Often noncompliance will occur as a result of ignorance; if the firm had known what the law was, it would have complied; the costs and benefits of compliance had nothing to do with it. Or they might know what the law is, but fail to grasp the fact that it applies in particular circumstances, or lose sight of this fact.

Noncompliance sometimes occurs because the firms believe the law is a bad thing; they will resist the law even when they know it is economically irrational for them to do so because they are against the law in principle. Obversely, if the regulator can persuade them that it is a good law, they may comply even when it is economically irrational for them to do so. Business executives regularly comply with laws that have such low deterrence payoffs and probabilities associated with them that compliance is almost always economically irrational (see, for example, Kagan, 1978). Kagan and Scholz (1984) define three models of the firm that are relevant here: the *amoral calculator* as assumed in our economic model; the *political citizen* that fails to comply because of principled disagreement with a command; and the *organizationally incompetent* firm that fails to comply because of poor management systems.

For some laws, there is no temptation payoff for the firm. There is no temptation payoff for a trucking firm that defies the law against driving on the left hand side of the road. When laws of this kind are broken, which they often are, the explanation is usually incompetence. The prisoner's dilemma model does not incorporate incompetence as an explanation. Social control policies designed to deal only with rational action, to the exclusion of extrarational action, will fail. Theories that preclude alternative modes of reasoning in favor of one narrow version of rationality will mislead.

The key question in all of this is the following. If firms behave other than as profit-maximizing monoliths, if regulators have other motivations besides the impartial enforcement of the law, does taking into consideration these alternative motivations make tripartism a better idea or a weaker idea? We conclude that a consideration of motivational dissensus makes tripartism even more appealing as a policy solution to the contradictions of cooperation and capture.

The economic model assumes a knowledge of compliance outcomes, and implicitly a level of resources, that regulators rarely have. How often does the environmental agency realize how many tons of pollution result from its enforcement decisions? This is not simply a question of information costs naturally being high because of the complexity of the facts. Firms can actively contrive complexity, conceal evidence, and engage in downright deception (Braithwaite, 1984).

A related error with the simple two-person model is that it implicitly assumes an equality of power between the agency and the firm. A hidden assumption is that the agency will have the same capacity to deliver the deterrence payoff that the firm has, that there are no phenomena, such as political interference, to prevent the agency delivering deterrence.

These are not all of the limitations of the game-theoretic modeling of regulation; they are only the most consequential ones in attempting to understand how to secure the advantages of the evolution of cooperation while averting the evolution of corruption and capture.

An Empowerment Theory

What we attempt now is a complementary theory of tripartism, an empowerment theory, that addresses these deficiencies of the economic model. The empowerment theory of tripartism combines both explanatory and normative propositions grounded in the application of a republican theoretical tradition to regulation (Pettit, 1989; Braithwaite and Pettit, 1990).

First, we distinguish the empowerment analysis of tripartism as one that assumes inequality of power and seeks to remedy it. Second, we show that empowerment gives regulatory players an interest in building trust, cooperation and dialogue within regulatory communities. A communitarian tripartism of this sort, we show, can solve the problems left unsolved by the pure economic interests model of tripartism. It can address problems that are not best understood as an outcome of the rational pursuit of interests; it can advance compliance by engendering a commitment to the rightness of the law and to the unthinkableness of breaking the law; and it can engage in dialogue with the firm for whom the question is not "should we do the right thing," but "what is the right thing to do?" (Schelling, 1974).

The Case for Countervailing Power

We have seen that the Scholz game-theoretic approach implicitly assumes equality of power. The empowerment theory starts from an explicit assumption of inequality of power. This assumption is that regulatory institutions are structured to institutionalize the power of some stakeholders (in particular those who bear the costs) over regulatory outcomes, and to exclude the influence of others (those who derive the benefits). The reason, drawing again on Edelman (1964), is that beneficiaries are systematically more likely to be diffuse interests, whereas those who bear the costs are more likely to be concentrated interests. The process frequently goes so far that an industry regulatory system that is theoretically a benefit to consumers and a cost to industry becomes the reverse (Bernstein, 1955; Kolko, 1965).

Idealizing, let us assume that we are dealing with a good regulatory law that properly reflects the will of a democracy. Limiting of the regulatory game to two effective players profoundly undermines this democratic will. If we assume the regulatory agency is an uncaptured fiduciary of the democratic will embodied in the law, then it will bargain for the level of intervention required by the law. The firm that acts in the profitability interests of shareholders will bargain for a level of intervention lower than required by the law. It will play games with the political masters of regulators to mobilize pressure for such lower intervention. The result of any plausible outcome to bargaining from these starting positions will be a level of intervention higher than the company wants and lower than the law requires.

Now if a PIG becomes a third player in the bargaining game, we assume it will advocate a level of intervention higher than that required by the law. The result of this exercise of countervailing power in the bargaining game will be that the final result will be closer to the democratic will embodied in the law. What are the circumstances where this would not occur? If the starting position of the PIG were more than twice as much above the legal standard as the starting position of the firm were below it, and if the PIG had equal countervailing power to the firm, then the outcome, post-PIG, would be further from the legal standard than the outcome pre-PIG. This is a highly implausible set of circumstances. It is not only implausible because of the extremeness of PIG demands required and the improbability that PIGs will match industry in power, but also because liberal legal systems properly make it easier to appeal state interventions beyond that provided by the law than state interventions below that provided by the law.

A complaint of industry against the idea of PIG empowerment, related although not the same as the complaint against PIG zealotry, is that PIGs will improperly demand a higher standard than that required in the law. It may be that such demands are improper. But the empowerment theory suggests that to the extent that PIGs make them, they will only partially counterbalance the demands made by industry for a lower standard than that provided by the law. The outcome under tripartism should be closer to the legal standard settled upon through the democratic process.[34]

The defense of tripartism under the empowerment theory is not only in terms of outcome but also in terms of process. An opportunity for participation by stakeholders in decisions over matters that affect their lives is a democratic good independent of any improved outcomes that follow from it. With the regulation of risk, risk-takers and risk-bearers should both be involved in decision making about the distribution of risk (Frank, 1990). Normatively we require a theory of policy that directs our attention to the equitable distribution of burdens as well as to the maximizing of benefits.

The power of all citizens to vote for those who make their laws is an equalizing institution that gives Western democracies a profound participatory superiority over other existing political systems. But the fact is that this democratic superiority is systematically undermined by unequal power relationships at the implementation stage (Handler, 1988). Laws that have popular support, that reflect the capacity of ordinary citizens to prevail over powerful corporate interests in the legislative arena, are thwarted by the superior capacity of corporate interests, and the inferior capacity of individual citizen interests, to be mobilized at the implementation stage. When it is powerful interests being regulated, the law in the books will usually be closer to democratic preferences than the law in action, because the law in the books is more directly influenced by the power of ordinary citizens to vote.

It follows that a state with a democratic vision limited to the vote will be a democracy undermined by the powerful. Genuine democratic influence over regulatory institutions requires that we supplement the power to vote for the platitudes of party platforms with innovative participatory mechanisms that follow legislative will through to executive implementation (Boyer and Meidinger, 1985; Meidinger, 1987). Empowerment means creating a more vital, active democracy—a democracy less under the thumb of the corporate sector.

Citizens have limited capacities and motivation for participation. For some citizens, environmental protection will be such a vital concern that an empowered environmental movement will give them an opportunity to follow through on their special concern; for others it will be broadcasting regulation; for others, motor vehicle safety, and so on. Tripartism may be a route to a more participatory democracy, a more genuine democracy, but a practical democracy that does not make unrealistic demands of mass participation in all institutional arenas.

The trick here is to steer a course between the practical impossibility of mass participation and the danger of participation only by PIGs that have become oligarchies (Michels, 1915). That middle course is to be found in the idea of contestable PIG guardianship. It requires the open communication to PIG constituents that is a defining requirement of our tripartism. The policy of the democratic state should be to deny empowerment to PIGs that are not democratically constituted, to stand ready to disempower PIGs with a declining base of popular support in favor of PIGs with rising popular support. Doing favors for the PIG with the strongest base of support in this way is generally good politics for political leaders in any case. In this sense, contestable tripartism has the strength of some practical political appeal. Judicious PIG empowerment can be good for political survival.

We reject the utopianism of a democracy where all citizens actively participate in decisions regarding the running of their workplace, the administration of their children's schools, the planning of the neighborhoods where they live, the policy planning of the police force that serves them, the framing of the environmental policies to protect the wilderness areas of their nation. None of us could bear the information overload from such participatory demands. However, opportunities should be available for citizens to participate actively in these and all other important spheres. For our theory to work, all that is then required is for *enough* people to absorb the information made available and take up the opportunities for participation to supply countervailing regulatory power and to render that power contestable.

These demands, we hypothesize, are minimal enough to be realistic, particularly when the state motivates political engagement by empowerment and the provision of tangible resources for PIGs. Consider the case of the elected worker health and safety representative who participates in regulatory negotiations, the results of which are reported on workplace notice boards. Will many workers be interested in taking a turn as the health and safety representative? No. Will many workers read the inspection report pinned on the notice board? No. However, will someone be interested in being the health and safety representative? Generally yes, at least in high-risk workplaces.

Will some workers read the posted inspection reports and make a fuss if they don't like what they see? Will some workers notice if their representative fails to follow through on their complaints? Again we suspect that the answers to these less demanding questions will often be yes, even if the answer to whether most representatives will initiate enforcement action against their employer is no (Carson and Henenberg, 1990). For the latter to be realistic, activism by salaried PIG lawyers is probably needed.

In the case of the Australian Federation of Consumer Organizations that puts consumer representatives onto many significant and not-so-significant government committees, how many consumers read the reports their representatives are required to produce from those meetings, or the minutes of the meetings? Not many. But during the period when one of the authors headed that Federation, some staff and most members of the executive read them in case a debate ensued when they were tabled at an executive meeting. And other constituents, if only constituents who were interested by virtue of being former representatives on the committee, read reports frequently enough to provoke occasional oustings of representatives.

We do not envision a tripartism where most beneficiaries of regulation participate in PIGs, where most who do participate in PIGs will be interested enough to process the information made available to them, where the incumbency of PIG representatives is frequently contested. We only assume that incumbency will be contestable, and spasmodically contested, because a sufficient number of citizens will absorb the information required to stir opposition to perceived infidelity to the interests of constituents. The vision of democracy is of extended periods of peaceful apathy punctuated by infrequent ringing of alarm bells occasioning gushes of grassroots participation, and even more infrequent purges.

Democratic organization of diffuse publics that are then empowered achieves two key outcomes. First, the very organization, the defeat of disorganization, is a remedy for the malady of diffuseness that allows concentrated interests to implement capture with impunity. Second, the democratic-participatory potentialities structured into the organization are a remedy to the second-order capture problem of the PIG representative being captured.

Empowerment and Trust

The next move in developing the empowerment theory is the proposition that empowerment builds trust and trust builds power. Power and trust are mutually constituting. How does this work in the tripartism case? There is no reason for us to trust those who have no influence over our lives; but once an actor is empowered in relation to us, we are well advised to build a relationship of trust with that actor. The boss may have little reason to build a relationship of trust with a particular worker; but once that worker is elected as health and safety representative with the power to stop production until safe conditions are restored, the prudent employer will seek to build rapport and ultimately establish a relationship of trust. Power constitutes trust. If it does not constitute trust, at least it constitutes responsiveness.[35]

Trust certainly makes us more vulnerable. Yet this is a two-way street: we can either gain power by exploiting the vulnerability of those who trust us, or we can lose power by being exploited. How then does trust constitute power? We consider three ways. First, players who build trust will gain more resources from win–win solutions in non–zero-sum games. Second, when players trust each other, their intentions (as opposed to uncontrolled external contingencies) will better explain outcomes. Third, the complexities and uncertainties of modern societies must be controlled by those who want to be powerful; making trust work for you is the most cost-effective, perhaps the indispensable, route to such mastery.

The union representative and the boss who trust each other are both able to get more power. Trust creates an environment of communication and mutual understanding of positions; distrust means misperception of the preferences and agendas of the other. Given that most regulatory games are not zero-sum games,[36] trust therefore opens the way for win–win solutions and reduces the prospects of lose–lose solutions. And if the solutions must be win–lose, trusting negotiators can take it in turn to lose on the occasions when it is least damaging for them.

Furthermore, if distrust breaks out, the players will lose the power to decide outcomes to other institutions (like courts of law) and to environmental contingencies that determine who will win out in a test of strength (like fluctuating market conditions that might decide how long the firm or the union can hold out during a strike). To put it another way, under conditions of trust, intentions of the players determine more of the variance in outcomes; under conditions of distrust, outcomes are more in the hands of uncontrolled external contingencies.

Macaulay's (1963) classic text on noncontractual relations in business can be read in these terms (see also Clegg, 1975). Consider two comments by businessmen from the Macaulay study:

> You can settle any dispute if you keep the lawyers and accountants out of it. They just do not understand the give-and-take needed in business.(p. 61)

> If something comes up, you get the other man on the telephone and deal with the problem. You don't read legalistic contract clauses at each other if you ever want to do business again. One doesn't run to lawyers if he wants to stay in business because one must behave decently. (p. 61)

We can read these as assertions that if you want to be powerful in business, don't hand your power over to the law and lawyers, instead, build trusting relationships with other powerful players that enable the direct negotiation of mutual accommodation.

Finally, trust engenders power simply because it is the most cost-effective strategy in dealing with many of the complexities and uncertainties of the modern world (cf. Luhmann, 1979; Reichmann, 1988). If Reiss (1984: 33) is right that "modern societies and their organizations are increasingly built on trust relationships," then power in modern societies depends on making trust relationships work for you. A stockbroker will become powerful only if he or she becomes trusted by others with power. Modern transnational corporations are empires built on trust. Japanese megacorporations may have a comparative advantage in the modern world because intracorporate trust has deeper cultural roots than in the West. Equally, many Third World businesses may be hindered in the acquisition of power because although trust works well in their cultures among kin or tribal affiliates, it does not work well when those affiliations are lacking (Gambetta, 1988: 229; Hart, 1988). [37] So Arrow

(1972) contends, "It can be plausibly argued that much of the economic backwardness in the world can be explained by the lack of mutual confidence."

An important economic property of trust to note in connection with its constitution of power is that trust is not a resource depleted through use[38]; trust is depleted through not being used (Gambetta, 1988: 234; Hirschman, 1984). It must be granted that at the time of empowerment, the PIG wins the increased power and the firm loses. But once empowerment is in place, conditions of trust further empower both the firm and the PIG: both become winners.

Trust, as it is conceived here, means a relationship where the other player can be taken at his or her word, where there is a commitment to honest communication, to understand the needs of the other, to agreed rules of fair play and a preference for cooperation. As a social matter, the fact that cooperation is part of what makes for trust means that trust is threatened whenever regulatory agencies should impose a deterrence payoff. The firm will usually try to invoke the symbolic capital of cooperation and trust in these circumstances: "Okay we made a mistake. We regret it. Let's work together to ensure it doesn't happen again."

An important advantage of tripartism is that it makes it easier for regulators to sustain cooperation and trust while imposing the required deterrence payoff. Regulators are given a strategic advantage in sustaining cooperative social relationships by occupying a middle ground between countervailing constituencies (Braithwaite, 1989b). They appeal to the firm that it surely understands that unless they invoke the deterrence payoff, the PIG will step in and do so, leaving them open to criticism from their superiors and embroiling all the players in a protracted confrontation. Indeed, the nature of the situation should make it clear to the firm that the agency has no choice but to impose the deterrence payoff, without any need for the agency to verbalize its appeal to this fact. Empirically, even in the absence of tripartism, regulators who want to get tough while maintaining cooperation often leak strategic information to PIGs whom they know will put the agency under outside pressure to act.

Finally, we saw earlier that when the PIG is excluded from information and participation, consistent pursuit of the deterrence payoff is more likely to be its best strategy. Tripartism, we say, transforms these incentives toward more cooperative preferences. Lock PIGs outside the gates and their best strategy is to hurl missiles across the fence (mostly by scattergun media assaults); invite them inside to sit at the table, and they are more likely to find that they do best through cooperative negotiation. In all these ways, therefore, PIG empowerment constitutes trust, cooperation, and communication among the three types of players.

Synthesis

Plugging the Gaps in the Economic Analysis

Once we have transcended the game-theoretic notion of cooperation as a simple manifestation of self-interest—when tripartite trust, cooperation, and communication are in place as social phenomena with momentum of their own—we can solve some of the problems we listed with the pure economic model. When the agency enjoys a relationship of trust with the firm, the agency can deal with noncompliance caused by incompetence by playing the role of regulator-as-consultant instead of the role of regulator-as-punisher (Kagan and Scholz, 1984). Trust is necessary to this enterprise because honest communication of managerial and technological break-downs is a prerequisite.

When the agency deals with an industry that breaks a law because it thinks the law is silly, or because it does not understand its requirements, the agency can use its good channels of communication with the industry to attempt to convince it that there is in fact a good reason for the law, or to bring the industry to an understanding of what the law requires. Similarly, union safety representatives can exploit a communicative relationship with bosses to explain from a shop-floor perspective why compliance with a particular law is necessary. Because they bring a different perspective and knowledge base to the problem compared with the other two regulatory players, often they will be able to suggest a more cost-effective way of securing compliance than has crossed the minds of resistant bosses.

More generally, cooperative open communication may produce more efficient regulatory outcomes because bad arguments and bad solutions are less likely to go unchallenged. And genuine communication means that when challenges are ad-vanced, they are listened to. Furthermore, three heads are better than two in ensuring that all the arguments are properly considered (Vroom, 1969: 227–240). The PIG will bring different experiences and perspectives to enrich regulatory deliberation. As the bedridden president of the Residents' Council of an American nursing home put it: "A lot of things you have to live it in order to see it." The informational advantages of the PIG at the follow-through stage of regulation may be particularly profound. The erroneous assumption of solid agency knowledge of compliance outcomes was identified earlier as an important defect of the economic model. Let us imagine that the nursing home inspector, the proprietor, and the Residents' Council agree on a new system to ensure that food from the kitchen is not cold by the time it gets to the residents. Because it is the residents who eat the food, and because the inspector only gets back to the nursing home once a year (while they are there every day of the year), the Residents' Council is the player best able to monitor whether the agreed solution is implemented and works. It is also in the best position to detect whether routine compliance is combined with intermittent deceit.

The neocorporatists of European political science (e.g., Streeck and Schmitter, 1985: 22–23) have identified another advantage that tripartite deliberation can have at the follow-through stage. This has to do with legitimation to secure the governability of capitalist societies. When the state acts as an umpire between interest groups under a liberal–pluralist model, it is hard put to find a general justification that appeals to the plurality of interests, and it generally fails to do so. When the rules are indexical, everyone hates the umpire. Tripartism can solve this problem by differentiating legitimation. In the classic case of the industrial agreement, the trade union uses one set of arguments to explain to the workers why they should stick with the deal; the industry association uses a radically different set of arguments and appeals to different values to secure the consent of its members. When agreements are differentially legitimated in this way, the players are more likely to make the agreement work than when the state is stuck with finding a legitimating message that is generalizable.

Conditions of trust and cooperation increase the prospects that the parties will end up with a commitment to making the agreed solution work (Vroom, 1969: 233–237). As a company safety officer said in the Rees (1988: 135) study of worker empowerment in an occupational health and safety self-regulation scheme: "Prior to voluntary self-inspection . . . the employees generally perceived the responsibility for safety as belonging to the company. . . . Now we have employee involvement." The economic model is silent on this matter of commitment, as it is on the more general matter of legitimation. The naive implied assumption is that once the payoff is settled, the agency can walk away from the firm and assume that the payoff will happen. If and when it can do this, it is because of trust.

The original Scholz (1984a) model assumes that the joint cooperation equilibrium will be the best equilibrium for both players. However, a social process of honest communication is required to constitute this reward payoff. The reward payoff is no less than a win–win payoff that can only be arrived at by communication. The better, the more honest that communication, the wider the range of creative win–win options that can be explored to further enhance the joint cooperation payoff (Zartman and Berman, 1982). In this regard, de Bono (1985: 124) sees special merit in having a third party at the negotiation table during a conflict. For de Bono, the advantage of having the third party is not about assisting compromise or consensus. It is about the contribution to the design of solutions. De Bono believes that the three-dimensional exploration of problems leads to better designed solutions than two-dimensional exploration; his advocacy is of "triangular thinking."

The landmark study by Rees (1988) of OSHA's Cooperative Compliance Program again casts some empirical light on how superior payoffs can be constituted under cooperative tripartite regulation compared with OSHA command and control regulation. When the latter model applies, OSHA enforces the regulations and the firm contests the legality of this enforcement at every opportunity. Yet, according to the designers of the Cooperative Compliance Program, the proportion of lost-time injuries that can be prevented by enforcement of the regulations ranges from 40 to 60 percent (Rees, 1988: 138). The tripartite safety committees at the workplaces studied by Rees solved this problem by refusing to be rule bound on "easy cases," and the overwhelming majority of problems that arose were easy cases:

> [An] indication is the tenor of weekly safety committee meetings. Because the task environment readily lends itself to consensual problem solving, "[i]t's very seldom that there's a divergence of opinion at the meetings," says a safety engineer. "Everybody pretty much agrees on what has to be done." "There's not too much discussion on the issues," says a labor representative on another job site. "Usually, we come to a meeting of the minds right away. A guy will bring up a problem, somebody will immediately come up with a solution, everybody looks around and nods, usually nobody says anything against it, and we buy it." Indeed, the safety committee's task environment is so congenial to a strong problem-solving ethos, says another labor representative, that on most issues "it isn't even a matter of agreement so much as somebody brings up a problem and we resolve it." Under these congenial conditions there is little if any need to appeal to "outside" authorities for guidance, such as OSHA rules; practical sense is authority enough. (Rees, 1988: 155)

While this is the routine reality, disagreements occasionally arise that are beyond the pale of labor–management consensus. When these serious conflicts arose, Rees found that the players became rule bound. Management adopted the position that they would not agree to any change that the workers could not show to be required under the regulations. The workers had no choice but to accept these terms. If they could not agree on whether the desired improvement was required under the regulation, an OSHA umpire could be called in.

The implication of cooperative tripartism here seems to be this. Most of the time, a consensus was reached on a practical solution to secure safety with minimum transaction costs, regardless of whether this solution was required by the law. This constitution of reward payoffs contrasts with traditional bipartite OSHA inspection where: (1) the regulations can only be mobilized to solve about half these problems; (2) often it will not even solve that 50 percent because the evidence acceptable to a cooperative safety committee will not always be acceptable to an adversarial court of law; (3) when the regulations can be mobilized, frequently they will not mandate the most cost-effective of all possible solutions; and (4) whenever mobilization of the regulations are attempted, transaction costs are high. These are the reasons why cooperative tripartism could constitute higher reward payoffs. Even when conflict erupted and the players became rule bound, they were able to constitute reward payoffs less depleted by transaction costs because it was rare for them to fail to agree among themselves on how the rule applied to the case.

This rosy analysis of the Rees data must be qualified by a concern that when conflict did break out and decisions were made "by the book," management was sometimes domineering and workers deferential to the power of management to decide what the rules required without giving reasons. A labor representative manifests this failure of the republican ideal in the following quote:

> . . . the reason he [the management rep on the safety committee] is a superinten-dent is that he's not bashful about making decisions. In his role as a superintendent he doesn't feel the need to explain his decisions. If he had to explain his actions it would weaken his position. So what he would do is just say, 'This is the way it is boys.' In his dealings with the safety committee the same tone prevailed. (Rees, 1988: 157–158)

We must be realistic about the difficulties in enabling regulatory empowerment policies to swim against the current of class domination or patriarchy or ageism in the power relations of the encompassing social structure. Both the Rees study and the work of Carson and Henenberg (1990) and Cheit (1990: 177) suggest that it is not PIG zealotry that is the major problem with making tripartism work, but weakness, disorganization or apathy (see also Noble, 1986).

Tripartism is relevant to constituting reward payoffs in another sense. Imagine there are two coherent policy packages to solve an environmental problem: ABCD and WXYZ. The PIG clamors in the media for the first package because it likes A and B. The industry lobbies for the second because it likes Y and Z. The two are bitter adversaries who do not communicate. Then, a likely political compromise is the incoherent policy package ABYZ. Our best hope of dealing with this problem is tripartite communication and understanding. Under such conditions, the PIG and industry might quickly agree that ABYZ is so incoherent as to be one of the worst possible solutions.[39] Tripartite communication is a means of constituting high reward payoffs in the prisoner's dilemma game.

Another endemic kind of undercutting of reward payoffs that occurs in the absence of tripartism is as follows. The firm and the agency agree on a pollution control plan; the firm invests in the technology to put it in place. An environmental group, not privy to the plan at the time, fires up a political protest when it later finds out about the plan. The media and political fallout force the agency to saddle the firm with a sucker payoff—in addition to the investment it made under the agreed plan, it will have to implement the solutions favored by the PIG. While PIG participation in the design of the original plan cannot guarantee the elimination of this kind of undermining of the reward payoff, it certainly makes it less likely.

A further limitation of our economic model was that it assumed capture to be a result of lobbying expenditure by the firm. We paid particular attention to the plausibility of capture being explained by a distaste for confrontation: people like to be loved, they prefer a smoothly running work life to a conflict ridden one, and they do not like the extra work associated with fighting battles. Qualitative data from Braithwaite's current study on nursing home regulation suggest that one of the very reasons that inspectors leave the industry to take up government service is the pursuit of a job with fewer worries. Now if the reason for capture is a retreat from conflict, this reason evaporates in a tripartite regulatory system where capture means conflict with a PIG.

But the more general point is about the possibility for the communicative attributes of tripartism raised by the empowerment theory to cover for the weaknesses of a narrowly economic model of tripartism. The most general proposition is: To the extent that players identify with different modes of rationality (sometimes deontological, sometimes value maximizing), different conceptions of their interests and their identity, indeed different ways of thinking that bear little resemblance to conceiving of interests and behaving rationally, then the best way to uphold the value embodied in a democratically supported regulatory statute is through cooperative communication (Handler, 1990). Tripartism opens up prospects for regulatory players to comprehend each other's ways of thinking and to accommodate them so as to avoid mutually harmful outcomes.

This returns us to the insight of the economic analysis that some forms of capture are good. Implicitly we are also recognizing this in the empowerment analysis. We are saying that better outcomes will be achieved if PIGs and agencies are open to internalizing the interests of firms, and firms are open to internalizing the interests protected by the law. This reduces to an advocacy of mutual capture, of each player having an α of 0.5 to multiply by the welfare of the other. Regulatory statutes also implicitly recognize this when they regularly specify that compliance only be required "so far as is reasonably practicable" (Gunningham, 1984: 100). In the simple terms of the economic model we could operationalize the "reasonably practicable" standard as an α of 0.5. At the very least, this kind of provision is normally read to mean that firms are not required to comply whatever the cost.[40] It follows from our analysis that there can be virtue in such provisions (but see Gunningham, 1984: 318–319); the virtue could be that of structuring the deliberations of courts so that they strike down PIG enforcement when it frustrates efficient capture. It is appropriate for agencies, PIGs, and courts to weigh the economic costs of compliance to the firm. In the extreme case, in deciding whether to approve a merger between Ford and General Motors, who could argue it to be an inappropriate form of capture to weigh the economic consequences for General Motors?

The communicative form of internalization of the interests of the other is a more variegated phenomenon, however, than just α. We may want to foster in business executives the deontological view (that so many of them already have [Footnote 32; Victor and Cullen, 1988: 114]) that once something is a serious criminal offense, we must comply whatever the cost. We can struggle to change the law, but while it is the law of our democracy, we have an obligation to comply. That is, there may be virtue in a republican version of tripartism that leaves business vulnerable to persuasion by PIGs and regulators that in some areas their deliberative habits should not be calculative, but rather constrained to honor what is right (cf. Braithwaite and Pettit, 1990).

Dialogue and Accommodation

The relevant feature of tripartism here is that it involves dialogue. Empirically, there can be no doubt that dialogue transforms the nature of regulatory encounters. In bipartite regulation at the agency that administered the U.S. wage-price freeze of 1971, Kagan (1978) found that negotiators were twice as likely to get accommodative responses from the agency when they made their submissions in person than when they did so in writing, and that this was true whether the supplicants were small businesses, giant corporations, or unions. Kagan interprets his finding in the discourse of efficient capture:

> Whenever an inquirer arranged to present his case in person, he almost automat-
> ically broke through any propensity toward blatantly legalistic or retreatist case
> processing. The agency official who met the inquirer face to face almost unavoid-
> ably became cognizant of the inquirer's problems and was forced to attend to the
> fairness and economic impact of decision. (Kagan, 1978: 152)

In such bipartite arrangements, however, there is no protection against regulators seeking interpersonal rewards by succumbing to inefficient as well as efficient capture. We should not be distracted by this debate here. Our point for the moment is that face-to-face negotiation will often transform confrontational disputes into accommodative encounters where the concerns of the other are internalized.[41] Because face-to-face negotiation among PIG, agency, and firm is by definition a feature of tripartism, it follows that tripartism will result in each player internalizing the interests of the other more than in nondialogic regulation where the players keep their distance.

The sociological literature richly informs us of another crucial difference between the way we go about the business of the social control of deviance when we do it at a distance from the way we do it when we must communicate with the deviant in our daily lives. Wilkins (1964) has pointed out that people who live in village cultures have much more complex experiences of each other as total personalities. Or as Christie (1981: 81) has argued:

> All other things being equal, though obviously they are not, it seems to be a
> plausible hypothesis that the greater the amount of information on the totality of the

life of the relevant system members, the less useful (and needed) are generalized
concepts such as 'sickness,' 'madness,'—and 'crime.' The system members come
to know so much about each other, that the broad concepts in a way become too
simple. They do not add information, they do not explain.

Thus, in an anonymous urban community it is easier to label a neighbor as
"mentally subnormal" and therefore "dangerous" than Jack, "who is so kind, so
complex, who has problems enough, whose total biography many know" (Christie,
1981: 90): "[m]aybe he drools, but he is also known to be harmless, and his father
was a good workman" (Wilkins, 1964: 68).

This is important. It means that under conditions of communitarianism, social
control can work better. Under conditions of communitarianism, shaming becomes
part of the ongoing dialogue with others with whom one maintains bonds of respect.
Braithwaite (1989a) calls this reintegrative shaming—shaming without outcasting,
shaming while sustaining bonds of respect. Impersonal shaming—shaming at a
distance—tends to stigmatization; instead of dealing with an essentially good person
who has done an evil deed, we see ourselves as dealing with an evil person.
According to Braithwaite (1989a), reintegrative shaming rather than punishment or
stigma is the key to effective social control. This is why families are mostly better at
social control than police. Reintegrative shaming is our best shot at inducing guilt and
responsiveness in the wrongdoer; stigmatization is most likely to induce anger and
resistance. The denial of respect involved in stigma motivates the accused to preserve
her self-respect by rejecting her rejectors.

When PIGs and agencies seek to change business executives and their corporations by stigmatizing them, they too are more likely to induce anger and resistance. If
PIGs and agencies reproach wrongdoing across a negotiating table as they struggle to
sustain ongoing relationships of respect, they have a better chance of eliciting guilt
and responsiveness. In the next section we have more to say on the possibility that the
key to effective regulation is dialogue and reintegrative shaming in communities that
sustain mutual respect.

Regulatory Communitarianism

Earlier the point was made that the way to allow efficient capture and to prevent
inefficient capture is to build a regulatory culture wherein regulators are socialized to
be tough on cheaters (armed against inefficient capture) and cooperative with firms
who are cooperating. This means reducing the agency's temptation payoff by
directing social disapproval within the regulatory culture against regulators who are
"unreasonable."

Now we are saying that it is possible (plausible interest configurations make it
possible) for PIGs to be susceptible to the same forms of disapproval within the
regulatory culture. Even in the United States, hardly the seedbed of tripartism in the
modern world, interesting recent regulatory scholarship is exploring the existence of
regulatory communities that incorporate PIGs as well as agency and industry.
Meidinger's (1986: 25) work on federal air and water pollution regulation character-
izes these arenas as regulatory communities wherein the key players have long-term

relationships with each other and seek to retain each other's respect and trust. Meidinger (1986: 20) quotes a PIG lawyer:

> I've been in this [air pollution regulation] for a long time, and I plan to be in it for a long time. I'm a firm believer in personal reputations. And I think people need to know who they're dealing with, and when somebody says something to them that they can expect that what they tell you will come true.

The notion of regulatory culture here is not a monolithic one, but the kind of conception advanced by Van Maanen and Barley (1985: 33): "culture can be understood as a set of solutions devised by a group of people to meet specific problems posed by the situations they face in common." Hence, we might fruitfully talk of an executive of General Motors participating in the culture of General Motors, in a motor vehicle safety regulatory culture and in the culture of his or her church. Norms may be largely specific to the context of the community that constitutes each culture; but equally they may have influence beyond their normal institutional terrain.

It is the notion of regulatory communitarianism that brings the empowerment theory within the republican tradition of normative theory. Liberal theory finds special attraction in market institutions that assume that individuals will behave in a self-interested way; institutions are designed so that such self-interested actions will aggregate to produce the public benefit. Our game-theoretic analysis of tripartism was an exercise in the design of market institutions. While market institutions purport to leave the psychology of individuals untouched, socializing institutions are designed to affect citizens in such a way that they behave as if they were primarily concerned with the public benefit (Braithwaite and Pettit, 1990). Although liberal theory finds special appeal in market institutions, republican theory finds special appeal in socializing institutions. Socializing institutions seek civic virtue by changing the deliberative habits of citizens. Our analysis of a republican tripartite regulatory culture is an example of institutional design focused on a socializing institution. The regulatory culture advocated seeks to modify the deliberative habits and behavioral dispositions of actors, not just to tinker with payoffs of actors whose psychology is untouched. Through mobilizing social disapproval against those who sell out to cheaters and those who are unreasonable with cooperators, the regulatory culture seeks to foster an internalization of a concern for the other player that is in the public interest.

Note now a special case of why it is important to reform deliberative habits and not just the payoff matrices of unreformed individuals. This is the case of the regulator who takes a bribe to succumb to efficient capture. The normative implication of the pure economic analysis is that this is good because it is welfare enhancing. Yet, such a judgment is clearly contrary to our moral intuitions. The normative focus of the republican interpretation of the tripartite institution (on deliberative habits) allows us to make a clear distinction not only between efficient and inefficient capture, but also between capture and corruption, regardless of whether the corruption has good or bad consequences. The republican is able to say that taking a bribe manifests an unacceptable form of deliberation. In this sense the republican construction of tripartism allows us to reflect a proper moral concern with means as well as ends.

So we need regulatory institutions designed to allow questioning of the commodity values that are inescapably central in market economies—inescapable but not immutable. As Stewart (1983: 1563) argues, we must seek a society that enhances "the capacities and opportunities of citizens to expand and enrich the available conceptions of the good. This objective requires the nurture of non-commodity values of aspiration, mutuality, civic virtue and diversity . . ."

The republican version of tripartism as a normative theory is built on a different explanatory theory of why actors comply with the law than the deterrence theory at the foundation of the economic model. The republican explanatory theory is that most citizens comply with the law most of the time because it seems wrong to them to break the law. They refrain from crime not because they calculate that the costs of crime exceed its benefits; crime is simply off their deliberative agenda; murder is never thought of as a solution for dealing with an obstinate competitor. It is not that the expected utilities turn out badly; they do not know the sentence and the probability of detection to be able to calculate them. More often, it is just that the offense is unthinkable. The sense of the wrongness of law breaking, and its unthinkability, are constituted by shaming.

Shaming is important as a simple deterrent. When tripartism succeeds in building bonds of trust and respect among business executives, regulators, and PIGs, then they will be able to deter each other by communicating disapproval for breaking the law, for being unreasonable, for selling out. Social disapproval for being captured is more potent when extended by someone whose opinion we respect. But the more important effect of shaming is in constituting consciences, in fostering the internalization of norms (Braithwaite, 1989a). Hence the most important effect of the mobilization of tripartite disapproval against a company that breaks the law is not the specific deterrent effect on that particular company, nor even the general deterrent effect on other companies who may fear "there but for the grace of God go I." The most important effect is the internalization of a sense of right and wrong among those who observe and participate in the shaming; such internalization is required to constitute a republican regulatory culture. In the same way, republican tripartism can be constituted by the pride when an actor is praised for reasonableness, provokability, or for obeying the law even when it is costly to do so.

Shaming can also help solve the dilemma of who guards the guardians. The most important point about contestable markets for guardianship is not that corrupt guardians will be ousted and thereby deterred. The important point is that the social process of shaming corrupt guardians constitutes the unthinkableness (for most guardians) of taking a bribe.

Strength in the Convergence of Weaknesses

Earlier we catalogued some weaknesses of the pure economic model of capture and tripartism. But the empowerment analysis has its own flaws. Republican ideals of active democracy, of building cooperative regulatory cultures, of trust, honest communication, respect for others and their concerns may be fine ideals, but can they withstand profound economic incentives to free ride, to cheat? Even where the players have strong rational incentives to cooperate, will they do it? Could business executives and PIG activists with a long history of distrust come to cooperate, especially given the tragic possibility that a prisoner's dilemma player who trusts the other may still defect because of fear that the other will not trust her (Gambetta, 1988: 216)? Is not trust a psychological disposition conducive to capture? Won't the presence of a third party sometimes chill communication between the other two parties rather than enhance communication?[42] Isn't all this communication expensive? Won't it slow down decision making?

Some of these problems are clearly the obverse of problems identified with the economic model. Communication slows decision making; yet dialogue is a solution to the problem of a decision being made and then reversed by PIG lobbying. Slower progress forward is better than spurting in one direction, stopping, then heading off in another. Building trust is costly, but as Lorenz (1988: 209) argues, "lack of trust is more costly still." As Luhmann (1979) shows, without heavy reliance on trust we cannot begin to cope efficiently with the complexity and uncertainties of modern social and economic life. When PIGs have in place a working policy of "trust and (selectively) verify," they will selectively turn down opportunities for participation in circumstances where they believe their trust in the other two players is well placed, or where the outcomes are not especially critical. Then costs will fall.

Trust may be a psychological disposition conducive to capture. Yet, the economic analysis, converging with the empowerment analysis, shows that capture up to levels of $\alpha = 0.5$ is desirable. And it shows that at any level of α, tripartism increases the punishment of firms who benefit from capture, and of regulators who dispense it. Tripartism may, therefore, foster counterbalancing effects here—increasing a psychological disposition conducive to capture (trust in the empowerment analysis), and increasing the economic disincentives for capture (the provokability effect in the economic analysis).

Our theoretical enterprise is to bring together economic and empowerment theories of tripartism, theories comprised of very different kinds of explanatory and normative claims, yet that converge on tripartism as a route to securing efficient, cooperative regulation that also avoids inefficient capture and corruption. Standing alone, each is a weak theory. But we hope to have shown how the weaker points of one theory are covered by the stronger points of the other.

Our empowerment theory of republican tripartism is a naive idealist theory about actors cooperating to sort out win–win solutions. Our prisoner's dilemma analysis is a crude materialist account that reduces all human motivation to economic rationality. What we have argued, nevertheless, is that the interplay of economic interests in the game-theoretic account can underwrite the idealism of the empowerment theory. Tripartism will increase rational incentives of regulatory actors to cooperate—incentives that the game-theoretic work shows to be already quite profound in many contexts. In the context of regulation, actors have incentives to build trust, not only because it solves problems of complexity and uncertainty, but also because it helps to increase their power. Cooperation and trust pay. Even disapproving of cheaters pays, because we all enjoy gossiping about the terrible deeds of others; we all enjoy affirming our own sense of moral uprightness by disapproving the moral inferiority of others. Most crucially, we have shown that cooperation and trust will produce higher payoffs for PIGs under conditions of tripartism than under conditions of regulatory exclusion, and that agencies get lower returns for inefficient capture and corruption under tripartism.

The economic analysis, therefore, shows how the interplay of interests constitutes the social conditions that make it possible for the idealism of the empowerment theory to work. Obversely, the workings of the ideals involved in the empowerment theory allow the economic theory to work. Honest communication, we showed, is needed to constitute reward payoffs in the regulatory game; the more trusting that communication, the higher the possible cooperative payoffs. The TFT strategy is "inconceivable in relation to humans without at least a predisposition to trust: when the game has no history a cooperative first move is necessary to set it on the right track, and unconditional distrust could never be conceived as conducive to this" (Gambetta, 1988: 227).

Trust has to work if the agency is to be assured that an agreed joint cooperation solution will be maintained; the agency cannot afford to return every day to check that it is still in place. More fundamentally, the whole system of exchange that delivers the economic payoffs could not be constituted without trust.[43] There are thus some quite crucial ways that the elements of one theory constitute the possibility of the other theory; the empowerment and economic theories are, at least in part, mutually constituting theories, not just complementary theories.

Yet it is their complementaries that make for the robustness of tripartism as a policy idea. These complementaries are too numerous to repeat. We will just repeat two fundamental ones. The internalization of a commitment to cooperation and reasonableness will build good faith among some of its beneficiaries and be exploited by others. For actors who are shameless cheaters, tough sanctions with economic bite are needed to sustain the commitment of fair players to the justice of the game and as we saw in the last chapter, tough incapacitative sanctions (e.g., licence revocation) are needed for actors who are beyond deterrence. Regulatory agencies will rarely have the resources to detect, prove, and punish cheating with sufficient consistency for it to be economically rational not to cheat (Moore, 1987). Hence, it is necessary to build a regulatory culture in which players generally do not want to cheat. Tripartism can increase the punishment of cheaters (the game-theoretic analysis); tripartism can supply the community denunciation of cheating that makes some forms of law-breaking unthinkable to most business executives most of the time (the republican analysis).

This is not to deny that there are also contradictions between the economic and the empowerment analyses of tripartism. The economic analysis is grounded in a classical positivist view of interests and rationality as pre-given and structurally determined (Hindess, 1988). Under the empowerment analysis, interests become contingent; their structural sources are problematized as we conceive of capitalists as internalizing the interests in the law, PIGs as internalizing the interests of firms and regulators, and both as having their interests shaped by third and fourth structural linkages. Indeed a virtue of tripartite institutions is that they further foster something that already happens: Interests are discovered by democratic struggle; far from being pre-given, interests are constructed and reconstructed through participation in social action (see Meidinger, 1986).

Conceived as grist for the democratic struggle over alternative visions of the good and the rational, the oppositions between the two models can have virtue. In the domain of consumer product safety, our game-theoretic analysis must monetize human lives lost from unsafe products. Under tripartism one would expect and hope that consumer groups would argue that it is morally wrong to put a dollar value on human life, that economic rationality should not be the mode of reasoning that drives our deliberation on such matters, and perhaps that we should be deontological rather than utilitarian in our approach. Equally, we would expect and hope that business groups more impelled by the economic mode of analysis would argue that it is not in anyone's interests to spend infinitely on reducing consumer product safety risks to zero; that if we do not commodify risk, human lives will not count in forms of deliberation where dollars are important; that courts must put a value on human lives if they are to sanction firms responsible for loss of life.

The way a democratic dialogue will and should resolve such a contradiction is an open question: republican theory raises some interesting ways of reconciling constraint-based and value-maximizing visions of the right (Pettit, 1988; and Braithwaite and Pettit, 1990). The point is the virtue of struggling for principles of institutional design that do not seek to paper over these contradictions. Rather we should flush them into the open to reconstruct them through democratic dialogue. As Bernstein (1983) has argued, however contradictory the visions of Gadamer, Habermas, Rorty, and Arendt, their common central theme is dialogue, communal judgment, reciprocal wooing, and persuasion, which is minimally coerced by power relations. For Gadamer (1975), for example, there is no objective knowledge that we can apply to resolve contradictions; but through dialogue citizens can acquire hermeneutical understanding, and the greatest threat to hermeneutical understanding is abdication to experts. As Handler (1990) has argued, there is no need to despair in postmodern confusion over the contradictions we perceive: dialogism "can orient our practical and political lives" (Bernstein, 1983: 163).[44]

Conclusion

The idea of tripartism can be applied to enforcement at any level of the enforcement pyramids discussed in the previous chapter. PIGs can be involved in self-regulatory enforcement, enforced self-regulation and so on up the pyramid. Indeed PIG involvement can strengthen the acceptability of deregulatory shifts by injecting public accountability and resistance to supine enforcement under the softer options. PIG involvement can also provide the data on noncompliance that justifies escalation of state regulatory intervention. In these senses, the ideas of tripartism and the enforcement pyramids are complementary ways of transcending the regulation versus deregulation debate.

Whether tripartism will work is culturally, institutionally, and historically contingent. All we have done is shown that there are some plausible theoretical reasons of a general kind as to why tripartism might foster the evolution of cooperation while preventing the evolution of inefficient capture and corruption. It is not a practical proposal ready for implementation; for that, there is no escape from detailed empirical investigation of the relevant institutional arena, and of the implementation modalities it enables and forestalls. We have said nothing about the costs of tripartite versus bipartite regulation (cf. Cheit, 1987). Local empirical research is needed to assess the cost effectiveness of, for example, the 14,000 workplace health and safety representatives versus the 200 government inspectors in the state of Victoria, Australia.

Axelrod (1984: 126–141) concludes his book by giving five bits of advice to "participants and reformers" on "how to promote cooperation." Let us show how we have followed Axelrod's advice with the tripartism proposal:

1. *"Enlarge the shadow of the future."* Tripartism solves the problems of capture and corruption by means other than rotation of personnel. The proposal implies the creation of regulatory communities that remain stable until capture or corruption becomes a problem (as opposed to designing transience into regulatory encounters in advance of capture or corruption). Furthermore, we have shown how a tripartite regulatory culture that decreases the temptation and sucker payoffs for regulators will extend the range of discount rates where joint cooperation will remain stable in multiperiod games.

2. *"Change the payoffs."* Tripartism reduces the temptation payoff the firm can achieve by corruption or capture. When tripartism builds a republican regulatory culture, it also reduces the temptation payoffs of agencies that are "unreasonable," the sucker payoffs of agencies that "sell out," and the reward payoffs for cooperating players who benefit from superior win–win solutions.

3. *"Teach people to care about each other."* Tripartite empowerment engenders incentives for regulatory players to develop trust and to reap rewards by learning to be concerned about the interests of the other. The negotiation literature instructs us that to be effective in negotiation, we must learn to understand the needs of the other so that we can move on to invent options for mutual gain (Fisher and Ury, 1981). Republican socializing institutions are fundamentally about "teaching people to care about each other." The regulatory communities described in the work of Meidinger (1986, 1987) are both part of the existing reality of regulation (even in noncommunitarian modern America), and a form of communitarianism to be nurtured (Braithwaite, 1989a: 149–151).

4. *"Teach reciprocity."* The form of republican tripartism we applaud mobilizes both social disapproval and usurpation of those who fail to be provoked by cheaters. It also teaches reciprocation of cooperation by mobilizing social disapproval against those who are "unreasonable" in pursuit of the temptation payoff.

5. *"Improve recognition abilities."* Under tripartism, PIGs can add substantially to the capacity of agencies to monitor outcomes. The eyes and ears available for verification are multiplied. The attraction of the PIGs themselves to cooperative strategies is enhanced by their direct involvement in the game and by the new information they thereby gain. When tripartism succeeds in building trust and honest communication, all players will be better able to recognize when the others are cooperating.

Praxis

If, as we have suggested, the value of our joint theory of tripartism can only be assessed through praxis in concrete institutional arenas, then how should we do this? The normative thrust of the empowerment analysis supplies a clear answer. It is the same answer as Handler's (1988: 1093): "We must create Bernstein's [dialogic] regulative ideal at the bottom end of the structure of power."

Nursing home residents are arguably the least powerful individuals in modern societies. Most of them, have been rendered indigent by their extended illness. They are mostly unable to vote with their feet as consumers or to give political speeches; they are generally even afraid to complain (Ronalds, 1989). They enjoy less freedom of movement than slaves: in the United States, 38 percent of them are physically restrained,[45] mostly by tying them into chairs, and many more chemically restrained. As Handler (1989: 5) remarks, even prisoners can riot: "dependent clients, and especially the frail, elderly poor, either fail to pursue or even conceptualize grievances; they develop a 'culture of silence' [Friere, 1985]."

One of the authors is exploring the possibilities for tripartite praxis through an international study of nursing home regulation and a consultancy with the Australian government.[46] The rationale for this choice is methodological as well as normative. The methodological rationale is the virtue of selecting a crucial case study (Eckstein, 1975). Crucial case studies test theories against least likely cases—those that can be expected to disconfirm a theory if any case can. There is no group that it is more difficult to empower than nursing home residents; so in this sense nursing home resident empowerment becomes a crucial case study.

The issue then is whether we can make tripartism work at the bottom of the power structure by empowering nursing home residents through the election of Residents' Councils. What might tripartism mean in this context? When state inspectors come to the nursing home, the Residents' Council and individual residents would become their more important source of information than medical records under the control of the institution. A representative, or representatives, of the Residents' Council would attend the exit conference (with a legal advisor or other advocate if they choose) and participate in negotiation on what plans of action should be put in place to correct noncompliance with the regulations. It would be widely publicized that a report on the inspection and the agreed action plans were available to all residents requesting them. The Residents' Council would have the same standing to take enforcement action against the nursing home as the inspector. The state would fund advocacy groups to make lawyers available to do the bidding of Residents' Councils. This funding is important as it would seem a triumph of hope over experience to expect that participation rights will be exercised when they are most needed unless there is active resourcing and collegial support for such participation.

It may be that tripartism in nursing home regulation is politically unachievable, and if achieved, it would fail. Attempting to see if this is true will be the first small step of a research program to explore the possibilities for tripartism. We do not imagine that PIGs can secure the resources to put tripartism into effect across the board any more than we imagine that regulators have the resources to put bipartism into effect across the board. Our concern is more modestly with finding out whether tripartism can work, if and when it can be applied.

Future work to address whether tripartism can work must avoid hopelessly utopian aspirations. It would be a triumph of hope over experience to expect that adding a representative of the Australian Federation of Consumer Organizations to the Australian Automotive Industry Authority would change the historical reality of unions and the automobile industry joining forces to rob consumers by securing high tariff protection for an inefficient industry. What we might hope for, however, is that empowered consumers might occasionally form successful alliances (with anti-protection elements of the bureaucracy, with industries that are also major car purchasers) against car industry unions and employers. We might not hope for a world where such alliances regularly prevail against unions and employers, but for a world in which countervailing power against organized interests is more often deployed than at present. We might hope for a world where sometimes consumers and unions will unite to defeat employers, where sometimes employers and consumers will unite to defeat unions, without having any illusions that most of the time unions and employers will continue to unite against the interests of consumers.

There is little prospect of consumer representatives being as influential as industry technical experts on a committee that writes consumer product standards (Cheit, 1990). However, the mere presence of technically literate consumer group nominees might motivate those who do the technical drafting to be more mindful of consumer interests. If they fail to elicit this motivation, the consumer representative might raise an alarm that puts the captured technocrats under pressure from a wider political campaign. Perhaps then the realistic aspiration is not for PIGs to become equal partners with industry and government but for them to be enabled to be credible watchdogs.

We see no prospect of a praxis that reveals tripartism as a panacea to the problems of regulatory capture and corruption. Yet, we have shown that there are good theoretical grounds for experimentation to ascertain where and how tripartism might contribute to more decent, democratic, and efficient regulatory institutions. Praxis is needed to specify the contexts where tripartism will fail because of the opposing critiques of those who forebode citizen apathy and excessive PIG weakness and those who forebode zealotry and excessive PIG power.

4

Enforced Self-Regulation

In this book we have attempted to make the case that a requirement for breaking out of the sterile contest between deregulation and stronger regulation is innovation in regulatory design. Perhaps the greatest challenge facing regulatory design is not at the apex of the pyramid of regulatory strategies discussed in Chapter 2 (see Fig. 2.3), where a variety of well-tested punitive strategies exist.[1] Nor is it at the base of the pyramid, where there is experience of the successes and failures of the free market and of self-regulation in protecting consumers. The need for innovation is at the intermediate levels of the pyramid of regulatory strategies.

The enforced self-regulation model is one idea to fill this gap. We do not present it as the best idea or even as an innovation that is desirable in most circumstances. The contention of this book is that there is no such thing as an ahistorical optimal regulatory strategy. There are just different strategies that have a mix of strengths and weaknesses. The appropriateness of a particular strategy is contingent on the legal, constitutional, and cultural context and the history of its invocation. If dropping an atomic bomb was the optimum strategy for dealing with Japanese recalcitrance in 1945, it does not follow that it would be today. It may, however, be useful to talk of the state signaling a willingness to consider regulatory escalation through a range of options, where some are more useful to flag than others. It seems to us that intermediate strategies like enforced self-regulation may be particularly valuable in this sense. The enforced self-regulation model presented in this chapter is about negotiation occurring between the state and individual firms to establish regulations that are particularized to each firm. Each firm in an industry is required to propose its own regulatory standards if it is to avoid harsher (and less tailored) standards imposed by the state. This individual-firm, as opposed to industry-association, self-regulation is "enforced" in two senses. First, the firm is required by the state to do the self-regulation. Second, the privately written rules can be publicly enforced. Enforced self-regulation is, therefore, a more radically innovative proposal than coregulation (discussed in the following section), although the two are functionally equivalent in the pyramid analysis of Chapter 2 as intermediate strategies.

The plan of this chapter is as follows: first, distinguish enforced self-regulation from the concept of industry coregulation. Second, outline the concept of enforced self-regulation, sketch its theoretical underpinnings, and illustrate its application in the context of corporate accounting standards. Third, argue the merits of enforced self-regulation. Fourth, point to areas in which necessary empirical research could be conducted by discussing incipient manifestations of partial enforced self-regulation models in the aviation, mining, and pharmaceutical industries. Fifth, consider in some detail the weaknesses of the proposed model. Sixth, make the case for a mix of regulatory strategies wherein enforced self-regulation is a valuable option, and seventh, consider a slight variation to the model where enforced self-regulation is based more on corporate case law than rules.

Enforced Self-Regulation
Distinguished from Coregulation

Enforced self-regulation represents an extension and individualization of "coregulation" theory. Coregulation, as distinct from enforced self-regulation, is usually taken to mean industry-association self-regulation with some oversight and/or ratification by government (Grabosky and Braithwaite, 1986: 83). Ideally, in light of what we have discussed in Chapter 3, coregulation should also involve participation by public interest groups. An example of a coregulatory scheme is the Code of Conduct for Computerized Checkout Systems in supermarkets negotiated between the Australian Retailers Association, the Trade Practices Commission, and consumer groups. The scheme is coregulatory in that it was designed in a tripartite process. It provides for ongoing oversight by government and consumers, and provides for self-enforcing mechanisms in the hands of consumers—if consumers can find a product for which the wrong price is charged at the checkout, they get it for free. For the retailers, it was a deregulatory step away from legislation that had been introduced into one Australian parliament to mandate individual item pricing in supermarkets, and much more. The British system for regulating financial services (Clark, 1986; Michael Levi, 1987; Page, 1987) is also coregulatory. Rule making and enforcement are primarily in the hands of industry and professional associations such as the Securities Association and the Association of Future Brokers and Dealers. A degree of tripartism is secured with the Stock Exchange, for example, through a chairman's Liaison Committee of market users. And the state is involved, for example, by the power to rewrite the rules of the self-regulatory organizations.

Whereas coregulation schemes of these kinds establish industry-wide voluntary standards out of a process of negotiation with industry associations, the thrust of this chapter is to investigate negotiations between the state and *individual* firms that result in flexible, particularistic standards and enforcement.

The Enforced Self-Regulation Idea

The Theory of Self-Regulation

Ronald Coase (1937) in his seminal work "The Nature of the Firm" proposed that firms would be organized to produce goods and services when internal production was cheaper than external market transactions. There are costs to both internal "command" production and external production "by contract." Coase argued that firms would internally produce products that they could make cheaper than buy on the open market.

The public goods produced by government are in many ways distinct from the private goods produced by firms,[2] but at a basic level the same Coasian insights apply. Although it is unusual for us to think about government subcontracting of regulatory duties, at least at a conceptual level, it makes sense that government should only internally produce "public goods" when internal public production is cheaper than external contracting.

In this chapter, we analyze enforced self-regulation as a form of subcontracting regulatory functions to private actors.[3] In particular, enforced self-regulation envisions that in particular contexts it will be more efficacious for the regulated firms to take on some or all of the legislative, executive, and judicial regulatory functions. As self-regulating legislators, firms would devise their own regulatory rules; as self-regulating executives, firms would monitor themselves for noncompliance; and as self-regulating judges, firms would punish and correct episodes of noncompliance. We stress that which particular regulatory functions should be "subcontracted" to the regulated firms will be contingent on the industry's structure and historical performance. Delegation of legislative functions need not imply delegation of executive or adjudicative functions.

Indeed, an important part of making self-regulation effective is to embed self-regulation in schemes of escalating interventions (as argued in Chapter 3). In particular, we argue that retaining public enforcement (detection and punishment) of privately promulgated standards is likely to be an important component in constituting genuine private self-enforcement. Far from arguing that enforced self-regulation is always warranted, we seek to articulate the particular contexts in which delegation or subcontracting of regulatory functions to the regulated firms is likely to be cheaper and more effective than the more traditional "integrated" forms of public regulation.

Self-regulation, whether or not fortified with the refinements proposed in this chapter, is an attractive alternative to direct governmental regulation because the state simply cannot afford to do an adequate job on its own. Fiscal pressures invariably prevent governmental inspectors from regularly checking every workplace for occupational safety offenses, environmental quality lapses, crooked bookkeeping, or faulty product design. The uniformly abysmal inspection coverage in these areas and others can and should be improved, but they will never reach a satisfactory level. Even in a domain where the risks of disaster are so profound that citizens might expect detailed government inspection—for example, nuclear regulation—the facts of life are that the wealthiest state in the world monitors only 1 or 2 percent of "safety-related" activities at nuclear plants annually (Manning, 1989).

It is important, however, to distinguish efficiency from liquidity motivations for self-regulation. As argued earlier, self-regulation will be more efficient than public regulation when subcontracting regulatory functions to the regulated firms is cheaper. But in this age of government fiscal deficits, there will be independent pressures for self-regulation simply to alleviate fiscal pressure.

Publicly mandated self-regulation represents both a hidden tax and a hidden expenditure. For example, we could imagine that firms and regulators might have identical costs in performing certain product quality tests. Mandating that private firms perform the tests might foil the "tax and spend" criticisms of the political right. Indeed, liquidity constrained legislatures may be forced to pursue self-regulatory strategies even when they are more expensive than public regulatory enforcement.[4]

Industry association self-regulation can dramatically expand coverage. Under the terms of Section ISA of the Securities Exchange Act of 1934, for example, the National Association of Securities Dealers (NASD) inspects the offices, books, and records of its members for violations of SEC regulations. In 1968, 45 percent of NASD members were inspected under this program. By way of contrast, in 1969, SEC inspectors surveyed only 5.5 percent of the dealers who were not members of the NASD (Katz, 1976: 161, 167).

Self-regulation can also achieve greater inspectorial depth. In the international pharmaceutical industry, for example, a number of the more reputable companies have corporate compliance groups that send teams of scientists to audit subsidiaries' compliance with production quality codes. In one Australian subsidiary of an American firm where Braithwaite did fieldwork, inspections by the headquarters compliance group were conducted twice yearly and were normally undertaken by three inspectors who spent over a week in the plant. The government health department inspection, on the other hand, consisted of an annual 1-day visit by a single inspector. Although employees had advance warning of the government inspection, the corporate compliance group arrived unannounced.

Corporate inspectors also tend, at least in the pharmaceutical industry, to be better trained than their government counterparts. Many have doctorates. Corporate inspectors' specialized knowledge of their employer's product lines also make them more effective probers than government inspectors who are forced to be generalists. Their greater technical capacity to spot problems is enhanced by a greater social capacity to do so. Corporate compliance personnel are more likely than government inspectors to know where "the bodies were buried," and to be able to detect cover-ups. One American pharmaceutical executive explained in part why this is so:

> Our instructions to officers when dealing with FDA inspectors is to only answer the questions asked, not to provide any extra information, not to volunteer anything, and not to answer any questions outside your area of competence. On the other hand we [the corporate compliance staff] can ask anyone anything and expect an answer. They are told that we are part of the same family, and, unlike the government, we are working for the same final objectives. (See also Rees, 1988: 60–61)

Perhaps this statement exaggerates the good will between company employees and internal compliance inspectors. Braithwaite asked the production manager of the Guatemalan subsidiary of another company: "Do you think of the internal quality auditors from headquarters a part of the same team as you?" His answer probably grasped the reality: "I think of them as a pain in the ass."

While anyone telling us how to do our job is a pain in the ass, interventions from "outsiders" are harder to take. Rees (1988: 147) found how worker participation can improve occupational health and safety self-regulation in this respect:

> "When I'm sitting there and doing something stupid," a worker explains, "something that I know damn good and well is wrong, but I'm doing it anyway, and the safety man comes up to me and corrects me on it, well, it'll upset me. I may not say anything. Or I'll say, 'Okay, fine, you're right.' But I will lose my temper over it, it will aggravate me, *because he's just not one of us"* [My emphasis]. By contrast, a labour representative observes, "Usually, if I come up and jump on somebody, they listen to me more than a safety engineer because he's not a construction worker. The hands will look at him and think, 'What's he telling me for? I've been doing this for years and I'm still around.' The difference between me and the safety man, is that *I am* a construction worker. . . . Of course, I get that kind of bullshit too. The difference is that they know I've been there and know what the situation is."
> "There's a different reaction," another labour representative observes. He can be more blunt compared to the safety engineer, he explains, yet less offensive, because the safety engineer is an 'outsider.'

> "I've been working around this area some twenty odd years. I know most of the people in the crafts and they know me. So I can go up and tell them something, and really get hostile with them, and chew their butt out. But still, there won't be any lasting animosity to it. Whereas if the safety man himself were to confront them on the same thing it would be exactly the opposite." (Rees, 1988: 147)

The power of corporate inspectors to trap suspected wrongdoers is often greater than that possessed by government investigators. One quality assurance manager told Braithwaite of an instance where this power was used. His assay staff was routinely obtaining test results showing the product to be at full strength. When they found a result of 80 percent strength, the manager suspected that the laboratory staff would assume that the assay was erroneous, simply mark the strength at 100%, and not recalculate the test. The manager's solution was to "spike" periodically the samples with understrength product to see whether his staff would pick out the defects. If they did not, they could be dismissed or sanctioned in some way. Government inspectors however, do not have the legal authority to enter a plant and entrap employees with a spiked production run.[5] Another example of the greater effectiveness of internal inspectors concerns a medical director who suspected that one of his scientists was "graphiting" safety testing data. His hunch was that the scientist, whose job was to run 100 trials on a drug, instead ran 10 and fabricated the other 90 so they would be consistent with the first 10. The medical director possessed investigative abilities that would have been practically impossible for a governmental investigator. He could verify the number of animals taken from the animal store, the amount of drug substance that had been used, the number of samples that had been tested, as well as other facts. His familiarity with the laboratory made this easy. As an insider, he could probe quietly without raising the kind of alarm that might lead the criminal to pour an appropriate amount of drug substance down the sink.

We have seen that corporations may be more capable than the government of regulating their business activities. But if they are more capable, they are not necessarily more willing to regulate effectively. This is the fundamental weakness of voluntary self-regulation. A voluntary program will stop many violations that cost the company money and others that are cost neutral; it will even halt some violations that benefit the company financially in the short term, for the sake of the long-term benefit of fostering employee commitment to compliance.[6] Recommendations that involve consequences beyond the cost neutral or short term, however, commonly will be ignored.

Enforced self-regulation, on the other hand, can ensure that internal compliance groups will not be lightly overruled. Under the model proposed in this chapter, a compliance director would be required to report to the relevant regulatory agency any management overruling of compliance group directives. A director who neglected this duty would be criminally liable. Such a provision would be the strongest method[7] of ensuring that compliance unit recommendations would be followed by management. Companies that regularly ignored such directives would fall under the regulatory agency's special scrutiny. The agency could concentrate its limited prosecutorial resources on companies that continually and irresponsibly disregarded compliance group recommendations. Thus, enforced self-regulation combines the versatility and flexibility of voluntary self-regulation, but avoids many of the inherent weaknesses of voluntarism.

The Model

The concept of enforced self-regulation is a response to the delay (Weidenbaum, 1979), red tape (Neustadt, 1980), costs (Moran, 1986), and stultification of innovation (Schwartzman, 1976; Wardell, 1979; Stewart, 1981) that can result from imposing detailed government regulations on business, and to the naiveté of trusting companies to regulate themselves (Cranston, 1978: 61–64). Under enforced self-regulation, the government would compel each company to write a set of rules tailored to the unique set of contingencies facing that firm. A regulatory agency would either approve these rules or send them back for revision if they were insufficiently stringent. At this stage in the process, PIGs would be encouraged to comment on the proposed rules. Rather than having governmental inspectors enforce the rules, most enforcement duties and costs would be internalized by the company, which would be required to establish its own independent inspectorial group. Where feasible, PIGs would be represented on this inspection group (e.g., the union on the workplace occupational health and safety group). The primary function of governmental inspectors would be to ensure the independence of this internal compliance group and to audit its efficiency and toughness. Naturally, old-style direct government monitoring would still be necessary for firms too small to afford their own compliance group.

State involvement would not stop at monitoring. Violations of the privately written and publicly ratified rules would be punishable by law.[8] This aspect of the enforced self-regulation model, perhaps sounding radical, is actually not as extreme as it first might seem. Regulatory agencies would not ratify private rules unless the regulations were consonant with legislatively enacted minimum standards.

To say that rules would be rejected if they failed to meet a minimum standard is not to say that the goal of the approval process ought to be standards as uniform as possible. It can be argued that striving for uniformity of standards under enforced self-regulation would not be desirable. Viscusi and Zeckhauser (1979) have developed the following rationale for nonuniformity. People normally assume that the higher the standards set by government for pollution, safety, and the like, the better will be industry's performance in meeting these criteria. Viscusi and Zeckhauser show formally that this is not the case. It is not so because whenever a standard is set, some firms will decide that the costs of compliance are greater than the costs of noncompliance (the probability of detection multiplied by the costs if detected). As standards are made more stringent, the costs of compliance increase steeply while the costs of noncompliance remain more or less constant. Hence, as standards become more stringent, the performance of firms that comply improves, but additional firms choose to risk penalties for noncompliance. Viscusi and Zeckhauser thus demonstrate that at some point further tightening of a standard may lower overall performance. But this point will be different for different types of firms. For firms with enormous sunk costs in old plants, the costs of compliance will be greater than for firms about to construct their factories.

Because of economies of scale in pollution control, the point at which further tightening of standards will increase the output of pollution may be higher for large firms than for small ones. In other words, the environment and the public may be better protected by nonuniform standards. Hence, nonuniformity under enforced self-regulation could be an advantage. More stringent rules could be demanded of firms with lower compliance costs. In some ways, environmental protection agencies already accept this principle by requiring more stringent emission controls on new automobiles than on those already on the road, and by requiring pollution control technology to be installed in new plants, controls not demanded of old ones. Theoretically, enforced self regulation makes possible nonuniform optimal standards that would give greater protection than any (stricter or more lenient) uniform standard. There are a number of ways that a legislature could frame broad statements of what is required of privately written regulations that were not at the same time platitudinous. Consider, for example, an act to set guidelines for the U.S. Mine Safety and Health Administration to follow in approving rules written by coal companies. The Act might recognize in its preamble that the minimum level of safety guaranteed by the Federal Coal Mine Safety and Health Act of 1977 was unsatisfactorily low and instruct the Administration not to approve any corporate safety rules that do not guarantee better safety performance than that ensured by the 1977 Act. Recognizing that American coal miners are three times more likely to be killed at work than British miners (Lewis-Beck and Alford, 1980: 755), the Act might further instruct the Administration not to accept the existing "state of the art" in safety standards. As a third option,[9] the Administration could be directed to structure its approval process so as to halve coal mine fatality and injury rates by a certain year.

The government need not, moreover, adopt this performance target approach to setting overarching standards. In empowering the U.S. Securities and Exchange Commission to ratify accounting rules for individual companies, for example, Congress might list a number of criteria that all sets of accounting rules must satisfy. For environmental rule making, the legislature might define a level of ecological threat that is intolerable under all circumstances. The standards could even specify a range of cost-benefit or cost-effectiveness ratios for proposed rules. These examples are not presented to evaluate the many ways in which the ultimate authority of the legislature might limit private rule making; they are presented only to show that such authority can be exercised in a variety of ways, depending on the circumstances of the regulated industry.

Contracting Around Regulatory Defaults

Instead of mandating that individual firms promulgate self-regulating standards, agencies could allow individual firms to promulgate such standards as an alternative to "backstop" or "default" regulations. Maintaining a regulatory default would still allow regulators to learn from the privately promulgated rules, but would allow some (especially smaller) firms to avoid the costs of rulemaking.

Borrowing from a more general theory of default rules (Ayres and Gertner, 1989), a self-regulatory system of defaults would need to establish not only "the defaults"— what regulations would apply in the absence of private mutation—but also the necessary and sufficient conditions for "contracting around"—what firms would need to do to supplant the default regulations.

In some instances, regulatory defaults would be set at what would be most appropriate for the majority of firms (i.e., what the firms and the state would have negotiated). Such majoritarian rules would allow individual firms to tailor rules to their needs without having to reinvent the wheel for standard provisions. At other times more stringent default regulations should be used even if they may be appropriate only for a minority of firms. For example, if consumers are relatively disenfranchised in the tripartite process, then setting regulatory defaults in their favor (or in favor of any affected, but powerless group) puts the burden on the relatively powerful to justify new regulations. Procedurally this could mean bipartite negotiation of defaults between state and PIG, with the process only becoming tripartite when the firm affirmatively moves to participate in enforced self-regulation. In the extreme case, such nonmajoritarian default rules will act as "penalties" to induce all firms to contract around the unpalatable backstop regulations.

The efficacy of such an approach would also crucially turn on the system of agency ratification—which in a sense would determine the necessary and sufficient conditions for contracting around the regulatory default. Especially when defaults are set to protect the disempowered, it will be appropriate for agencies to apply a higher level of scrutiny to the justifications for individual mutation.

In the United States, insurance regulation displays a default structure in which the status quo represents a default that can be contracted around only by filing before the state insurance commissions (Ayres and Siegelman, 1988). More generally, the corporation statutes of the individual states represent a default form of corporate governance that the individual corporations are allowed to change by filing their corporate charters with the secretaries of state. We envision instances in which regulators should develop different sets of defaults that the regulated firms can choose between as an additional alternative to developing idiosyncratic self-regulation. Indeed, in the United States the diversity of corporate law among the states allows corporations to opt for a variety of forms of corporate governance simply by choosing a state of incorporation, a situation that has a variety of desirable and undesirable consequences (Romano, 1985).

An Illustration: Regulating Corporate Accounting Standards

To illustrate the advantages of enforced self-regulation, let us examine the problems inherent in regulating one important aspect of business practice—corporate accounting. Recognizing that companies can use misleading accounting practices and conceal their assets to evade taxes, most nations provide for the prosecution of firms who fail to report "true and fair" accounts or use "accepted accounting standards" (U.N., 1977). To call such bland admonishments "standards" is to stretch meaning. Their very amorphousness hinders prosecution. Defendant corporations have little difficulty in finding eminent accounting experts to pronounce their practices professionally acceptable because every accountant has a different conception of what is "true and fair" or what constitutes an "accepted accounting standard" (Briloff, 1972).

Unhappy prosecutors can appeal to the legislature for more tightly refined standards, but this may lead to overspecification. No single set of detailed government-imposed standards will satisfy the efficiency requirements of backyard businesses and transnational corporations, banks and manufacturers, holding companies and operating concerns. A company's accounts are a vital tool in evaluating investments and in making other management decisions. Accounts made too subservient to public purposes will be less efficient for private purposes. When required to develop standards to govern accounts, therefore, legislatures around the world have generally opted for the unenforceability of blandness rather than for the inefficiency of overspecification (U.N., 1977).

How can enforced self-regulation resolve this dilemma? Each company would be required to write its own accounting rules in consultation with shareholders and other appropriate stakeholders (perhaps unions, perhaps the Defense Department for a major defense contractor). These rules should enable the company to meet its operational requirements while ensuring public accountability and acceptable comparability with the accounts of other companies. Once these rules have been ratified by the appropriate agency and made available to investors, any violation of them would, by definition, constitute an unacceptable accounting practice and be punishable by law. Tying the specificity of the rules to the unique circumstances of the company for which they were written renders fairness in accounts enforceable. Specificity can replace blandness without the overspecification for the majority of firms inherent in universalistic standards. In addition to the familiar practice of holding outside audits, internal audit groups would be mandated. Enforced self-regulation might, therefore, produce simple specific rules that would make possible both more efficient, comparable accounting and easier conviction of violators.

Strengths of the Enforced Self-Regulation Model

Rules Would Be Tailored to Match the Company

An efficient system of corporate regulation would acknowledge the social risks and social benefits associated with the activities of each regulated company and provide rules appropriate to those characteristics. Under direct governmental regulation, such adaptability over the wide spectrum of business types and sizes is impossible. Government has responded to this problem in two radically different ways: it has either tried to obtain specificity by generating rules that are gargantuan in length and complexity, or written rules for the lowest common denominator of proscribed behavior, as exemplified by the bland platitudes of corporate accounting standards. The resulting universalistic rules often impose unnecessary strictures on some companies and overly lax restrictions on others. Regulations mandating a certain hazard-reducing technology, while forcing less responsible companies to upgrade to this standard, can also cause industry leaders to adopt this fix when, left to their own devices, they would have installed a technology superior in both hazard reduction and economy.[10] Rules that strive for universal applicability cannot avoid some particularistic irrationality.[11]

Legal institutions are designed to be stable and predictable, while economic entities ideally are rapidly adaptable to changing commercial and technological environments. Universalistic laws cannot be quickly altered to reflect changing events lest some critical circumstance be ignored among the infinite array of possible conditions to which the rules might be applied. But enforced self-regulation is by definition tailored to the particular needs of each corporation.[12] The written rules only need to relate to a limited set of economic and structural circumstances rather than to a vast, incoherent range of business activities. The environmental protection regulations to be followed by a self-employed chemicals wholesaler, for example, need not be as complex as those governing a Dow Chemical or a DuPont. Because rules under a system of enforced self-regulation are particularistic, an agency charged with approving those rules need not account for all of the loophole-opening strategies used by different companies to duck their regulatory responsibilities.[13]

In short, under enforced self-regulation, rules could be both simpler and have greater specificity of meaning. The dangers of complexity and blandness may be avoided when rules relate to a finite and known set of circumstances rather than to an infinite and unknowable range of business activities.

Rules Would Adjust More Quickly to Changing Business Environments

A primary reason for the failure of law to control corporate crime is that legal institutions are made to last, whereas economic institutions are designed for rapid adaptation to changing economic and technological realities. Universalistic laws cannot, or at least should not, be rushed through lest they are later found to create more problems than they solve by failing to consider some critical circumstance among the infinite array of possible conditions to which they might be applied. For legislators, many matters take higher priority than attending to matters of business regulation. In every country, the consequence has been that legislators are notoriously slow to enact new regulatory laws when they are needed and even slower at removing such laws when they are no longer needed.

Because particularistic rules have less profound ramifications than universalistic rules, they can be tinkered with more frequently. Consensus can be reached more quickly within one firm than it can across all the firms in an industry. When a new threat is perceived to the public interest (e.g., research discovers a new industrial carcinogen), years of delay can be expected as universalistic rules are drafted and redrafted to meet objections from the disparate types of industries that would be differentially affected by the proposed rule. Lengthy consideration must be given to the now almost inevitable pleas by some firms that they would be forced out of business by the new rules. In contrast, under enforced self-regulation, as immediately as the threat was perceived, all companies would be required to write new, more stringent rules to meet the threat. Of course, companies that feared the financial repercussions of the new controls could be expected to write rules insufficiently stringent to satisfy government and PIG demands. A lengthy process of redrafting and negotiation would commence with those firms. But while this was going on, the majority of firms that were willing and able to introduce satisfactory protections would be following their new rules. Under traditional regulation, these firms would be waiting until the final form of the regulations was decided before investing in new controls. Even those firms that chose to write rules insufficiently stringent might be giving improved protection during the negotiating period if they were following their improved, but still inadequate, standards.

Probably the most important factor enabling particularistic rules to be adjusted more rapidly is that precedent would not be as important as it is under universalism. A pharmaceutical company that abandoned a quality control test in favor of a completely new, more effective, in-process approach to building in quality could be permitted to change its rules immediately to accommodate this innovation under enforced self-regulation. Under traditional regulation, in contrast, the regulatory agency would be slow in deliberating whether allowing this company to abandon the old test would lead to a flood of demands from other concerns that they too be allowed to do away with it (although they had not introduced any alternative controls). The regulatory agency would have to consider whether any pending court cases turning on the validity of the old rule might be lost if the defendants could show that the agency had selectively waived the rule. Under enforced self-regulation, where companies are prosecuted only for violations of their own rules, this kind of precedent would not be an issue.

Regulatory Innovation Would Be Fostered

It has already been implied that governments freed of anxiety over allowing dangerous precedents would be more permissive of radical new approaches to the control of harmful practices or processes. Regulations written in 1992 will tend to ossify control techniques, be they environmental or financial, at the state of the art as of 1992. Enforced self-regulation, in comparison, would tap the managerial genius within top corporations to design custom-made regulatory systems. At all times it would be possible for cheaper and more effective risk management strategies to emerge. Ultimately, more effective approaches to such problems as reducing pollution and assuring product and workplace safety will result from depending on the creative expertise of the private sector, rather than on the more limited reservoir of talent in the bureaucracy. If innovation is encouraged, however, there is also a price to be paid: some technological and managerial "improvements" will prove less effective than existing techniques. A combination of regulatory vigilance, tripartite accountability, and civil liability for damages to victims would have to be counted on to control the excesses of experimentation.

Rules Would Be More Comprehensive in Their Coverage

A series of empirical studies of internal rulemaking and enforcement in over fifty large companies have convinced Braithwaite that internal corporate rules tend to cover a much wider range of industrial hazards and corporate abuses than do governmental regulations (Clifford and Braithwaite, 1981; Fisse and Braithwaite, 1983; Braithwaite, 1984, 1985). While large companies manage to write rules regulating a substantial proportion of the most serious harms or wrongs that could occur in their businesses, governments simply do not. They fail to do so because they lack the time, research resources, and political will necessary to build consensus around a comprehensive set of rules. Instead of dealing forthrightly with their failure to achieve broad regulatory coverage, governments trust firms to regulate themselves voluntarily under the tens of thousands of nongovernmental standards written by trade associations, professional and technical societies, and similar bodies (Hamilton, 1978; Page, 1980; Cheit, 1990). By giving public recognition to private corporate rules, enforced self-regulation could extend the law to cover a wider range of dangerous practices.

The failure of government consensus-building to reconcile conflicts over rules can also subject companies to the demands of two agencies with conflicting goals. This can be demonstrated by the dilemma faced by some Australian meatworks. The companies are trapped in a dispute over how often floors should be washed. Health authorities, concerned only with the cleanliness of the food being processed, require regular wash-downs. Occupational safety officials, worried about the safety of workers carrying sharp instruments on wet floors, want the surfaces kept dry. While the agencies bicker over their regulatory authority, the resulting stalemate benefits neither the consuming public nor the workers. Under enforced self-regulation, each meatworks could be given wide discretion to write (in consultation with employee representatives) its own floor-washing and floor-surfacing rules. Although the respective agencies could still disagree on the relative importance of dry floors versus clean floors, less political will would be required to grant the company discretion to suggest its own way out of the stalemate than would be needed to force consensus between the agencies. As mentioned earlier, regulatory agencies at present have no choice but to guard vigilantly against compromises that set dangerous precedents; under enforced self-regulation firms can be more flexible because precedents will not come back to haunt them. In too many areas, necessary regulations gather dust in the "too-hard" basket because of the consensus-building demands of the command and control model.

Companies Would Be More Committed to Rules They Wrote

As John Kenneth Galbraith (1967: 77) has noted, "[N]othing in American business attitudes is so iniquitous as government interference in the internal affairs of the corporation." If business is responsible for writing and enforcing its own code of conduct, the notion of regulation may become more palatable.

Many corporations are currently alienated from a sense of social responsibility. In highly regulated industries, there can be an attitude of unconcern about corporate abuses that government inspectors do not discover. A senior Australian executive of an international drug company, for example, claimed that "it is the responsibility of the Health Department to work out whether research results have been cheated on. Maybe if we do fudge some result, it's the job of the Health Department to find that out. It's not our responsibility. That's their job." Or, to quote an American counterpart:

> Often our people use the FDA [Food and Drug Administration] to get out of making a decision themselves on a drug. We find it very hard to reach consensus among ourselves on the safety of a product and often there are strong disagreements among us. So sometimes we get out of making our own decision by putting it to the FDA and letting them decide for us.

Irresponsible companies are frequently pleased to hand over incomplete facts to facilitate the government's regulatory decision; if the agency gives them a green light, they delightedly claim, "It's within the rules, so let's go ahead."

Such abdication of responsibility could be minimized by the joint participation of company, government, and stakeholders in a rulemaking program. When the company writes the laws it is more difficult for it to rationalize illegality by reference to the law's being an ass. Moreover, considerable evidence indicates that participation in a decision-making process increases the acceptance and improves the execution of the decisions reached (see Vroom [1969] for a review). Of course, commitment to self-generated rules will be less pronounced when an agency vetoes the initial rules proposed by a company and ultimately approves regulations that the company views as less than optimal.

The Confusion and Costs That Flow From Having Two Rulebooks (The Government's and the Company's) Would Be Reduced

Under enforced self-regulation, it would be no longer necessary for a company to undergo the costs and confusion of having to follow two rulebooks—the government's and its own. This problem is particularly acute in transnational subsidiaries, where the host government's rules may be framed in fundamentally different terms from the rules imposed by corporate headquarters. Obviously the fusing of corporate and host government rules is rarely painless; in many situations governments insist that corporate regulations be modified to conform to local requirements.

But governments should concede the validity of totally different approaches to control developed in other countries. For example, Japanese pharmaceutical companies have adopted an approach to toxicology testing for dangerous side effects of drugs that differs radically from the Western toxicology tradition. Enforced self-regulation might permit a Japanese company operating in the United States to follow its worldwide drug safety standards instead of Western requirements that are thoroughly incompatible with its corporate rules. By allowing the company to preserve the integrity of its total quality assurance and safety testing package, enforced self-regulation might better protect the public.

Business Would Bear More of the Costs of its Own Regulation

Enforced self-regulation, by placing the principal inspectorial burden on internal compliance groups, also allocates most of the costs for such regulation to industry. This is only equitable. If industry profits from its misdeeds, why should it not bear the costs of controlling them? Economic efficiency is also furthered by forcing companies to internalize regulatory costs. If such costs are not included in the price of their products, the price will not reflect fully the social cost of producing them, and the demand for the products will exceed that which would optimize social utility.

More Offenders Would be Caught More Often

In the previous section on "The Theory of Self-Regulation" multiple reasons were advanced to explain why self-regulation results in broader inspectorial coverage by inspectors with a greater capability of discovering violations. Although internal compliance groups can be expected to catch more offenders than government inspectors, they cannot be counted on to send the offenders to courts of law for prosecution with the frequency that we expect of government inspectors. Reasons exist, however, to believe that enforcement would not be less effective. These reasons are considered in the next two sections.

Offenders Who Were Caught Would be Disciplined in a Larger Proportion of Cases Than Under Traditional Government Regulation

Under enforced self-regulation, companies with strong records of disciplining their employees would be rewarded as showing up well in government audits of the toughness of internal compliance systems; existing public enforcement, in contrast, gives companies incentives to cover up and protect their guilty employees. Internal discipline is in many ways more potent than government prosecution because internal enforcers do not have to surmount the hurdle of proof beyond reasonable doubt, and do not have to cut through a conspiracy of diffused accountability within the organization. Corporations in the past have protected their individual members from prosecution by presenting a confused picture of the allocation of responsibility to the outside world. Braithwaite's (1984) research on the pharmaceutical industry concluded that companies have two kinds of records: those designed to allocate guilt (for internal purposes), and those for obscuring guilt (for presentation to the outside world). When companies want clearly defined accountability they can generally get it. Enforced self-regulation would compel firms to use this capability in the public interest. Direct government regulation provides disincentives for nominated accountability, because nominated accountability puts heads on the prosecutor's chopping block; enforced self-regulation provides incentives for nominated accountability because corporations that cannot demonstrate that they are conducting their own executions would be singled out for inquisition.

It Would be Easier for Prosecutors to Obtain Convictions

It has been concluded in the previous two sections that the greatly increased number of discovered violations under enforced self-regulation would be regularly the subject of internal disciplinary action but rarely of public prosecution. Although internal compliance groups would not "call the cops" in normal circumstances, there are other features of the enforced self-regulation approach that would make it reasonable to expect more potent public as well as private enforcement. Essentially, there are three reasons for predicting that more suspects would be convicted under enforced self-regulation than under direct regulation:

1. Because bland and meaningless rules (e.g., that accounts be "true and fair") would be replaced by precise and particularistic rules, acquittals would be more difficult to secure by appeal to the vagaries of the wording.
2. Universalistic rulemaking tends to complexity because the rules must evolve to deal with the infinity of circumstances encountered throughout the entire economy. The more complex the law becomes, the more powerful organizations will exploit that complexity by finding loopholes, protracting proceedings, and otherwise evading the spirit of the law.[14] Under simple particularistic rules, this capacity of company lawyers to exploit complexity would be diminished.
3. In cases where the recommendations of the internal compliance group were defied this fact would be communicated to the regulatory agency. Compliance group reports would then be powerful ammunition for the prosecutor to put before the court. The contents of the compliance group report would also direct the prosecutor to the most valuable insiders to subpoena.

Compliance Would Become the Path of Least Corporate Resistance

Requiring compliance directors to report management refusals to heed their recommendations would pressure executives to comply with those recommendations. For most offenses, the cost of yielding to the compliance director would be less than the costs of fighting the investigation, prosecution, adverse publicity, and exposure to civil litigation that would likely follow rejection of the compliance group's recommendations. And if the agency succeeded in its action, the courts would compel the company to comply with the recommendations originally suggested by the compliance unit. Large corporations have an almost obsessive desire to prevent their dirty linen from being washed in public (Fisse and Braithwaite, 1983). Even when top management believes that it could prevail in court, it might still yield to the compliance group rather than display a rift between the two sections of the company in full view of shareholders, financial institutions, and other key reference groups. On the debit side, then, the compliance directors' statutory obligation to report a failure to rectify could conceivably give them so much clout as to lead to an "over-compliance" whereby management allowed itself to be pushed further than the rules ever intended. To translate into the prisoner's dilemma jargon of Chapter 3, the compliance director might get so much clout that the firm is effectively powerless to retaliate when the compliance director seeks the temptation payoff. Through the agency of the compliance director, the firm might be inefficiently captured by the state.

Incipient Manifestations of the Enforced Self-Regulation Model

Two key elements underlie the enforced self-regulation concept: (1) public enforcement of privately written rules, and (2) publicly mandated and publicly monitored private enforcement of those rules. Each element already exists in a variety of regulatory areas, but there is no manifestation of both in a comprehensive enforced self-regulation scheme.

Every country in the world publicly enforces private rules in its regulation of civil aviation safety. Before an airline flies a new route, the altitude of its approach, the flight path, survival equipment to be carried on board, and other operating procedures must be approved by the national civil aviation authority concerned. The rules are not universal but are tailor-made for the particular flight; the company writes them, and the government ratifies them and punishes deviation from their strictures. Violations of such rules in Australia, for example, are punishable by imprisonment as well as by fines or license revocation. [15]

Perhaps the most highly developed version of this aspect of enforced self-regulation can be found in the U.S. Mine Safety and Health Act of 1977. [16] Section 101(c) of the Act provides:

> Upon petition by the operator or the representative of miners, the Secretary may modify the application of any mandatory safety standard to a coal or other mine if the Secretary determines that an alternative method of achieving the result of such standard exists which will at all times guarantee no less than the same measure of protection afforded the miners of such mine by such standard, or that the application of such standard to such mine will result in a diminution of safety to the miners in such mine. [17]

During its first 5 years, this provision resulted in about 600 petitions for modification (some of them involving packages of standards) being granted by the Mine Safety and Health Administration. In a few instances, civil fines have been assessed against companies that violated the particularistic standards approved under a petition for modification. The program is not without regulatory cost; each petition consumes roughly three-person days for investigation and approval. [18]

The Mine Safety and Health Administration regulations[19] also permit mine operators to submit their own plans for ventilation,[20] dust control,[21] and roof support[22] for the agency's approval. The last is particularly significant since roof falls are the leading cause of fatal accidents in mines.[23] In setting down the criteria to be followed in approving roof control plans, the regulations separately define standards for seven different types of roof support techniques.[24] In addition, mine owners are free to devise their own unique roof control plans.[25] These regulations constitute an impressive example of how criteria to guide administrative discretion can be designed in the face of a variety of technologies, the appropriateness of which depends on the circumstances of a particular mine.

Companies have been criminally convicted in several cases that turned in part on deviations from approved roof control plans.[26] In one of these cases, a mine official of the Vanhoose Coal Company was sentenced to 60 days imprisonment for failing to comply with a roof control plan that the Labor Department had approved.[27] This offense was responsible for a roof fall in which one Vanhoose miner died and another was injured. It is the only case we know of in which an executive has been imprisoned for noncompliance with privately written, publicly ratified rules.

The appropriateness of enforced self-regulation to coal mine safety is patent. As one American coal mining official suggested, "The last four major disasters in this country could be attributed to a weak plan." While violations of specific standards were a problem, the more fundamental cause of the disasters was poor execution of a total safety plan (Braithwaite, 1985). Enforced self-regulation would focus attention on the overall plan, and not simply on the quality of single standards.

Some of the U.S. Environmental Protection Agency's (EPA) enforcement activities also approach the enforced self-regulation model. Indeed, in one important respect, the agency has gone beyond the approach envisaged by this chapter. The Clean Water Act[28] authorizes civil penalties of $5,000 per day for deviations from privately written oil spillage rules that have *not* been publicly ratified.[29] The EPA regulations require companies involved in the production, distribution, or storage of oil to prepare a Spill Prevention Control or Countermeasure Plan.[30] The companies must follow agency guidelines in preparing their plans, but their plans are reviewed by the EPA only if a spill actually occurs. In normal circumstances, the plan need only be certified by a professional engineer who must attest that the plan is in accordance with good engineering practices.[31]

In another area of EPA regulation, the District of Columbia Circuit has upheld civil penalties imposed on the Chrysler Corporation for violating the terms of a certificate of conformity with emission controls under the Clean Air Act.[32] The certificate is, in effect, a license to sell vehicles issued after approval of an application listing vehicle parameters and specifications that reasonably may be expected to affect emissions. Chrysler was penalized for violating some of these specifications. The corporation appealed, claiming that regardless of the breach of the certificate's terms, the emissions of its vehicles remained within federal standards. In finding against the corporation, the court upheld an important principle: The integrity of particularistic standards must be sustained even when full compliance with them proved unnecessary to attain the overarching standards that gave them birth.

In short, then, there are already powerful examples of public enforcement of privately written rules (see further Bardach and Kagan, 1982: 237). But the full enforced self-regulation model requires more; it also mandates governmentally monitored internal enforcement of the internally written rules. The closest incipient approximation is governmentally monitored internal enforcement of *externally* written regulations. The leading illustration is the enforcement of Good Laboratory Practices (GLP) rules imposed on pharmaceutical companies by the FDA.

GLPs were first promulgated in 1978,[33] after it was alleged that pharmaceutical companies replaced animals that developed unhealthy conditions during drug-testing experiments. The regulations seek to render fraud more difficult by requiring strict record keeping[34] and unswerving adherence to scientific protocols.[35] Most interestingly, the GLPs require each drug testing laboratory to have a Quality Assurance Unit (QAU) that acts as an internal compliance policeman.[36] This feature was designed to shift the financial burden of regulation from government to the companies. QAU status reports must routinely be placed before the study director and management of the company.[37] This ensures that management cannot plead ignorance when it fails to act on reports of violations. If management does not know about the discovered violations, the company is guilty of an offense for not knowing. The regulations thus enforce a self-regulatory mechanism to prevent underlings from filtering bad news before it reaches responsible ears.

The decision to throw the major burden of regulation onto an internal QAU raised some thorny issues, however. Industry argued that if QAUs had to make their findings available to the FDA, then their effectiveness as a management tool to ensure the quality of research would be undermined. A QAU which knew that its comments would be read by FDA officials (and by consumer groups, which could get the comments from the FDA under the Freedom of Information Act) would be less than frank in its reports to management. QAU reports would become a public relations function of the company rather than a compliance function. The FDA was persuaded by this argument and decided that, as a matter of administrative policy, inspectors would not request reports of findings and problems uncovered by the QAU or records of corrective actions recommended and taken and would immunize QAU reports from freedom of information access.[38] FDA inspectors still audit the QAU to ensure that it has effective compliance systems in place and to check certain objective compliance criteria. But the records available for regular inspection are separated from reports of findings and problems and corrective actions recommended. Although the latter QAU reports are treated as confidential company documents by the FDA, this does not prevent a court from requiring the disclosure of any report, just as a judge can demand other types of company documents that are confidential for routine inspectorial purposes.

In this chapter, a different resolution to this very knotty problem has been suggested. Under the enforced self-regulation model, the routine reports of internal compliance groups would not be available to regulatory agencies. However, when the compliance group discovered a violation of law and management decided to continue the violation or to ignore a recommendation that the offenders be disciplined, this fact would be put before the agency (and PIGs). The company would be granted the privilege of secrecy only as long as it followed the advice of its internal compliance group. Unrectified violations that were kept secret would not be immune from government prosecution. If these offenses were independently discovered by government inspectors, they could and should be prosecuted. The retention of a limited direct government inspection capacity is important under enforced self-regulation to keep internal compliance groups on their toes. Nevertheless, governments face an ethical dilemma in deciding to treat as confidential compliance group reports that may reveal violations of law. But the need for frank reporting of offenses by compliance groups, the fact that most offenses would rarely become known to anyone (let alone prosecuted) in the absence of such frankness, and the government's retained ability to investigate and convict independently, all suggest that our solution to the dilemma is reasonable.

Government-mandated internal enforcement procedures are used in other areas as well. Under the Mine Safety and Health Act regulations, specially designated miners conduct pre-shift examinations of the mine for safety hazards.[39] Pre-shift examiners are required to record violations of mandatory health and safety standards and in fact do so regularly. But in practical terms, they are not expected to audit systematically the mine operators' compliance with the law. Rather, their goal is to check quickly every working section of the mine for serious hazards. Inspection practice is to check the violations recorded in the pre-shift examination book and to cite the violation if it still exists but ignore it if it has been rectified. There do not seem to have been any prosecutions of pre-shift examiners for failure to report serious violations, although this would seem to be theoretically possible. Similarly, the Toxic Substance Control Act[40] authorizes the Administrator of the EPA to order manufacturers to test suspect chemical substances,[41] to monitor internally compliance with Act procedures,[42] and to indicate proposed quality control protocols.[43] The Administrator can also order revisions of protocols that he or she finds inadequate.[44]

Courts and commissions have also imposed monitored internal enforcement on single companies. Solomon and Nowak (1980) have reviewed a number of Federal Trade Commission (FTC) cases in which companies guilty of consumer misrepresentation have been ordered to (1) institute certain new policies to prevent a recurrence of the offense; (2) establish an internal monitoring function to ensure compliance with these new policies; and (3) establish a record-keeping system for this monitoring so that the FTC could review and verify future compliance. Similar interventions have also been common in consent decrees negotiated by the SEC (Herlihy and Levine, 1976; Sommer, 1977; Reed, 1980). The Swedish Market Courts (and the Market Court in the Australian State of Victoria) are also empowered to impose special rules on individual companies to protect consumers; failure to comply with these particularistic rules is a criminal offense (Duggan, 1980: 220–221).

In addition to monitored internal enforcement of externally imposed standards, there is at least one example of monitored internal enforcement of *unspecified* standards, as demonstrated by the Federal Communications Commission's interesting solution to the problem of regulating the broadcast of popular records whose lyrics promote illegal drug use. Instead of writing rules to specify what constitutes an unacceptable insinuation that drug use is desirable, the Commission required broadcasters to ensure that a responsible station employee reviewed all questionable records before they were aired (Stone, 1980: 44–45).

These examples serve two useful purposes. First, they illustrate that the enforced self-regulation model proposed here is not so radical; instances of all key elements of the model can be found in current enforcement practices. Second, they can provide the raw data for much of the empirical research needed to answer troubling questions about the model. By studying examples of elements of the model in operation, investigators may be able to evaluate its efficacy and to increase its effectiveness and practicality.

Weaknesses of the Enforced Self-Regulation Model

Regulatory Agencies Would Bear Costs of Approving A Vastly Increased Number of Rules Each Year

The actual process of rule making involves considerable costs. It might be objected that what is being suggested is a multiplication of these costs by the number of companies that participate in an enforced self-regulation scheme. Such an objection must be scrutinized carefully. Government rule making is at present such an agonizing and costly process primarily because of the difficulties of writing universalistic rules that do not hinder efficiency. Particularistic rule making would be cheaper because the environmental contingencies to be considered would be finite rather than infinite and the number of interested parties would be smaller. The regulatory agency would no longer have to undertake such steps as playing simulation games to assess how different industries might use the same set of rules to open different loopholes. A rule to close a gap for one company opens a loophole for another. Every word in every regulation must be carefully vetted lest the agency leave itself open to new and dangerous precedents. As we have argued, precedent would not be a worry with particularistic rule making because each set of company rules would be, by design, unique. In short, the factors that are crucial to making universalistic rule making such a time-consuming business are absent from particularistic rule making. This claim could be tested empirically by observing particularistic rule making in action with air safety[45] and other regulatory areas.

There is already some evidence to suggest that particularistic rules may not demand a much greater effort by regulatory officials. In the area of roof control, dust control, and ventilation plans written by coal mining companies, Mine Safety and Health Administration officials indicated that while the approval process was time consuming when first introduced, most plan approvals now can be finished with only a couple of person-days of agency time. With dust control plans, the process has become so routinized that about 90 percent of submissions are simply agency-supplied questionnaires completed by the company. Innovative plans, of course, require a lengthy narrative submission as well, and approval of these may consume up to 30 person-days of time. Plan approval has certainly not turned out to be a bureaucratic nightmare; company representatives hold informal discussions with government officials to ascertain whether a new approach is likely to be acceptable before formally submitting it.

Company rules need only be as individualized as the companies themselves choose. One would undoubtedly find that companies participating in enforced self-regulation would adopt large blocks of rules from other companies, or would adapt model rules suggested by their industry trade association or the regulatory agency. Much of the ratification work of the regulatory agency would be routine. Even so, it must be conceded that the increased costs of scrutinizing thousands of sets of rules might outweigh the savings from the greater simplicity of particularistic rules. Our guess is that they would not, given that the ratification of routine particularistic rules could be entrusted to relatively junior civil servants following guidelines handed down to them, whereas universalistic rules of necessity must be debated by many senior civil servants and politicians.[46] Even if the rule-making costs were greater, this would be more than counterbalanced by the reduced costs of monitoring compliance pointed to earlier. Since monitoring compliance with a rule always costs more than writing it, enforced self-regulation would save taxpayers more money in the monitoring area than it would cost them in the rulemaking domain.

State Monitoring Would Sometimes be More Efficient Than Private Monitoring

The problem with the last point is that although it clearly saves the government money to privatize monitoring, is it socially cheaper overall? In effect are we not imposing an additional tax on the corporation by having it hire the self-regulator? Might it be more efficient to impose the tax directly and have government hire the self-regulator? In some cases we believe it would. When the regulatory problem is concentrated among small companies that do not find it easy to mobilize independent expertise internally, government regulators are likely to be more efficient than self-regulators. More on this later. When one of the most useful things regulators can do is spread ideas—from the companies that are successful innovators in risk management strategies to the companies that are laggards—then government regulators who move from firm to firm will be more efficient than self-regulators confined to one firm. Both these efficiency arguments apply to nursing home regulation, for example, and are convincing grounds for the superiority of direct government monitoring in this arena.

We have seen, however, that there are many efficiency arguments that cut the other way—the superior capacity of insiders to discover where the bodies are buried, to get cooperation, to understand the firm's unique technologies, and so on. The more fundamental reason that enforced self-regulation will often be more efficient overall, however, is that the regulations themselves will be more efficient—being tailor-made for and by the firm.

Finally, we must add an air of political reality to the discussion of this issue. Our political prejudice is to accept the hypothesis that the realities of power in capitalist societies are that business regulatory agencies (unless they are totally captured) will continue to be chronically and inefficiently underresourced. Regulators know that if they can get the industry to pay some of the costs of their own regulation, this inefficient resource deficit can be attenuated. They also know that if they succeed in getting more public resources to regulate say the chemical industry, these costs will not mostly be paid by corporate taxes from chemical companies. So the community loses the efficiency that it gets under enforced self-regulation by including the costs of chemical industry externalities into the price of chemicals.

Cooptation of the Regulatory Process by Business Would be Worsened

Universalistic rule making, it might be argued, draws out broader resistance to the will of business than could be expected of particularistic rulemaking. Ralph Nader or the Friends of the Earth are more likely to organize against a more lax nationwide effluent standard than they are to oppose an effluent permit for one factory. On the other hand, local citizens who would never be activists at a national level might protest effluent standards that allowed discharges into their neighborhood fishing hole.

One of the issues to be considered in weighing the relative advantages of particularism and universalism for a given problem is the extent to which the prospects of popular participation are national versus local. With regulation of mine roof control plans, for example, more interest can be expected from the miners who will be covered by a particular roof plan than from any national activism over coal mine roof safety. And in fact, American mine safety officials told Braithwaite of examples where protests by local miners had forced the Mine Safety and Health Administration to reverse its approval of roof control plans. In certain circumstances, particularism can harness democratic participation more effectively than universalism.

In other cases, national debate is obviously more appropriate in determining regulatory goals. For example, in setting maximum allowable limits for dust concentration in coal mines, not only should mine owners and miners have a say, but also insurance companies, epidemiologists, and others. Here, the dangers of cooptation at a local level are too immense to be countenanced; we simply do not want a situation where local agreements are being negotiated. The maximum allowable coal dust level should be national and nonnegotiable, and any mine that cannot meet that requirement should go out of business.

There are many areas where the dangers of cozy local agreements would be intolerable. However, cooptation can be controlled in many cases by a particularism severely constrained by overarching standards that were themselves products of national debate.

Companies Would Bear Increased Costs in Delay and Paperwork From Getting New Company Rules Approved

At the outset, it must be noted that requiring companies to write the private rules that would be the basis of public enforcement should not impose new costs on them. If companies are not presently writing and enforcing their own rules on safety, environment, accounting, and other regulatory areas, then there is something very wrong. The only new costs to a reputable company would come in the delay and paperwork required in submitting these rules for government approval. As with governmental costs, the costs to business of enforced self-regulation could be counterbalanced by savings from having to learn, communicate, and follow one set of rules instead of two (government and corporate); from following rules that were simpler than existing government regulations; from being able to innovate in new and cheaper control methods; and from no longer having to follow universalistic rules that were particularistically irrational or cost ineffective.

Western Jurisprudence Might not be Able to Accommodate Privately Written Rules Being Accorded the Status of Publicly Enforceable Laws

A detailed legal feasibility study would be premature for a new model such as this, which has barely begun to be evaluated and criticized by others for its conceptual flaws. While broadly drawing attention to the fact that legal tradition could pose some practical difficulties for the implementation of enforced self-regulation, it must also be pointed out that the proposal runs with the tide of growing judicial recognition of privately written rules. William Evan (1962: 165,176) has described the increasing tendency

> for the norms of private legal systems to be judicially recognized, as for example, in a medical malpractice suit in which the code of ethics of the American Medical Association is invoked; in a suit involving the internal relations of a trade union in which the union's constitutional provisions are accorded legal status by the court; or in a suit by a student against a college or university in which the institution's disciplinary rules are judicially recognized. . . . The adoption, as it were, of the norms of private legal systems by public legal systems is functionally equivalent to the conferral of rights on private legal systems.

Moreover, we have seen that quite developed examples of enforced self-regulation have evolved already in the United States without constitutional challenge. Indeed, we have discussed one instance where a person was imprisoned under public enforcement of privately written law. Imprisonment being provided for violations that are particularistic rather than universalistic is not novel. Permits under the U.S. Clean Water Act regulating the amount of effluent that can be discharged from a source vary enormously in stringency, depending on the part of the country in which the source is located, whether the plant is new or old, the economic viability of the industry, and whether pollution reduction is being achieved at a particular time. Although this is a law that is applied in a calculatedly unequal fashion, there is provision for imprisonment for any person who willfully or negligently violates a permit condition.[47] The American legal system is not alone in demonstrating that it will tolerate a law enforcement mode that rejects universalism in favor of particularism.

Particularistic Laws Might Weaken the Moral Force of Laws That Should be Universal

Allowing companies to write their own rules could replace absolute standards with a moral relativism, making the rule of law seem an arbitrary matter. Whether the authority of law would be enfeebled would depend on how firmly regulatory agencies insisted that important absolute standards be reflected in *all* sets of particularistic rules. It would depend also on how firmly the legislature dealt with regulatory agencies that ignored the overarching standards governing self-regulation plans.

Ultimately, however, the law derives much of its moral force from the shame of conviction. More shame would attach to corporate crime if more corporate criminals were prosecuted and convicted. If, as this chapter has suggested, enforced self-regulation would improve the current dismally low conviction rate of corporate criminals, then adoption of the concept could strengthen, not weaken, the moral authority of corporate criminal law.

The Model Would Encourage the Trend to "Industrial Absolutism"

Sixty years ago, Justice Louis Brandeis testified to the Commission on Industrial Relations that as corporations became larger and more powerful, the threat of "industrial absolutism" became more profound (Eells, 1962: 210). Corporations can be as powerful as governments, yet lack the checks and balances against abuses of that power to which governments are subject. Employees do not vote in the private government of corporations. When the corporation sanctions an employee, there is no obligation for a public hearing, no observance of a right to silence, little due process. Giving the corporation power over law making, it could be argued, would surely take us one large step closer to the industrial absolutism Brandeis warned us against.

This line of attack on enforced self-regulation can be easily dismissed. It is not as if corporations do not already have policies under which employees are dismissed, demoted, and sanctioned in other ways. Enforced self-regulation would in some measure control industrial absolutism by requiring that corporate policies be made subject to veto by a democratically constituted government.[48] This is not to deny that industrial absolutism is a problem; it is simply to say that enforced self-regulation would not contribute to it. Indeed, it should be hoped that the formalization of corporate compliance policies, which would come with enforced self-regulation, would be accompanied by a formalization of due process protections for employees.[49] Furthermore, we hope enforced self-regulation would become a catalyst for local grassroots tripartite democratization of the corporate policy process. Indeed in many domains (e.g., occupational health and safety), mandated tripartism is the best hope for making enforced self-regulation work.

Companies Would Write Their Rules in Ways That Would Assist Them to Evade the Spirit of the Law

Companies have a long history of deviousness at finding ways of evading their public responsibilities (Green, 1978; Clinard and Yeager, 1980). By giving them control over the rule-writing process, one might give full reign to their ingenuity at pulling the wool over the eyes of governments. For a start, companies could evade liability by simply failing to write required rules (although this could be dealt with by making the penalties for not having rules more severe than those for breaking them or by making the default rules stringent). Many companies would surely manage to sneak provisions into their rules without the regulatory agency realizing the full implications of the provisions. One can be assured that company lawyers would spend more time working over their rules with a fine tooth comb than would any government employee.

There can be no satisfactory answer to this criticism of enforced self-regulation except to say that, in one way or another, the business community's resourcefulness at law evasion will be cause for weakness in any system of control. As has been argued previously, the opportunities for evasion and exploitation of loopholes are endemic in universalistic laws controlling business practices. We strongly suspect that simple, particularistic rules over which business had considerable control would not be more susceptible to evasion than complex rules over which business had less control,[50] because the whole inherited wisdom from the study of corporate crime is that it is complexity that makes conviction so often impossible. Ultimately, however, this question can only be answered empirically.

Companies Cannot Command Compliance as Effectively as Government

Although most of the other objections to enforced self-regulation turn on the presumed capacity of the corporation to control its environment in ways that would evade the impact of regulation, this objection looks to the ineffectiveness of control in large organizations. In a provocative essay, Thomas Schelling (1974) has argued that the managers of large organizations are rarely in a position simply to issue instructions and expect that they will be carried out. Moreover, in some cases the only way that executives can secure compliance with their instructions is when government backs those instructions. Hence, the board cannot fight resistance from the ranks to affirmative action until the government mandates affirmative action and the directors can plead that the matter is beyond their control. Similarly, corporate policies that require the wearing of safety helmets or air-filter masks are notoriously hard to enforce; compliance works best when management can say that the government insists on it (Schelling, 1974: 86).

The Schelling argument does not pinpoint a weakness of enforced self-regulation, but of voluntary self-regulation. Corporate power and the sense of legitimacy needed to command compliance may be weak when such orders do not have the force of law. Because self-generated rules have legal force under enforced self-regulation, however, the state can be seen as backing the corporate command. In fact, a strength of enforced self-regulation is that it summons the legitimacy of both state and corporate power to entice compliance while the alternative regulatory models rest on the legitimacy of corporate power alone or of state power alone.

The Independence of the Compliance Group Could Never be Fully Guaranteed

An independent internal compliance group is essential to the success of an enforced self-regulation scheme. There are two principal threats to the compliance unit's independence. The first is internal. The group, through a sense of corporate loyalty, might itself subordinate regulatory zeal to the attainment of the firm's productivity goals. Braithwaite (1984) concluded from his study of the pharmaceutical industry that this threat may be somewhat overstated. In that industry, prestige, promotion, and job satisfaction for compliance group personnel were generally a function of their competence at discovering and correcting regulatory problems. Their professional commitment was aimed at ensuring compliance rather than at making profits, and their careers were oriented more to their subunit's goals than to the overall profit goals of the company. Indeed, companies themselves encouraged the compliance groups to strive uncompromisingly for excellence in ensuring compliance lest defective products slip through, creating legal problems and professional and consumer dissatisfaction.

In the field of occupational safety, moreover, the divided-loyalties problem can be somewhat reduced by including worker or union representatives in the compliance group. Presumably, union members or nonmanagement personnel would generally be less willing to subordinate their personal safety to profit goals. To minimize further the chance of cooptation by management, contestable tripartite representation can be introduced as discussed in Chapter 3.[51]

The second threat to the compliance group's independence emanates from the corporation itself; despite an overall commitment to regulatory goals, the compliance group would be compromised when management determined that the unit's recommendations were not in the company's long-run best interests. Here, independence can be strengthened by having directors of compliance report directly to the chief executive or a board audit committee. Braithwaite's interviews with pharmaceutical industry executives revealed the importance of such independence from middle-management pressure. There are occasions when it is economically rational to suspend commitment to quality standards temporarily. If a product is in short supply and major customers are complaining to the marketing manager, that executive may pressure the quality control manager to pass an almost-acceptable batch as acceptable. This pressure can be particularly acute when major customers threaten to switch to a competitor unless continuity of supply is guaranteed. An individual plant manager can also request the quality control director to reverse a regulatory decision, as when the plant had to achieve certain production goals.

These opportunities for meddling can be limited if the corporation is structured so that the quality control director does not have to answer to manufacturing or marketing executives. In some American pharmaceutical companies, the quality control director makes an independent written decision on each drug batch, which he then signs. Only the chief executive can overrule this judgment, and she must do so in writing. The potential for chief executive overruling is far lower than it would be for a veto by a marketing or manufacturing manager. People become CEOs in part because they exhibit a modicum of caution. Imagine the consequences for a CEO if customers are seriously injured because she personally overruled a quality control decision. No matter how low the chances of this event occurring were perceived to be, it would be a foolish risk for a CEO to take for the sake of one batch of product. While the destruction of a batch might be a major aggravation to the marketing or manufacturing manager, to the CEO it is a minor matter. Effectively then, organizational structure lessens the chances of quality control being formally overruled.

In multiple-division corporations, compliance heads within each division or subsidiary, in turn, should have only a dotted-line reporting relationship with the chief executive officer of their subsidiary and a firm line to their immediate superior within the compliance group. It should be their compliance boss who hires and fires them, and who determines their yearly bonuses, not the subsidiary chief executive.

Their future should be linked to their performance in securing compliance, not to their success in pleasing a chief executive. It might be desirable to require companies to notify the regulatory agency of the dismissal of a compliance director and to give reasons for such dismissal.

The best guarantee of compliance group independence is external: making the failure to report unrectified violations a crime. Regulatory agencies would continually audit to determine whether the group was discovering and reporting violations as it should. Once an offense had been discovered, the agency would subpoena the relevant compliance unit reports and uncover any failure of the compliance director to report an unrectified violation. Even a small number of prosecutions for this offense would probably be sufficient to encourage compliance directors to put the company's head on the chopping block—instead of their own. The directors could be further required to sign a quarterly declaration that all violations of law uncovered by the compliance group during that quarter had been rectified or reported to the government, and that all compliance group recommendations for disciplinary action against culpable individuals had also been acted on or reported.

Under any set of independence guarantees, however, top management could still find subtle and not-so-subtle ways to bend the will of the compliance staff. End top management control through reporting relationships, and executives would try to control the compliance unit through budget allocations. If budgetary controls were removed, fewer travel approvals, poor allocation of offices, staff reshuffles, and similar steps to make the work life of employees miserable could be attempted by management to assert its control. This is not to denigrate independence-giving strategies such as granting control of budgets for subsidiary and divisional compliance units to the corporate compliance group rather than to subsidiary or divisional chief executives. It is just to say that eliminating all threats to compliance group independence is impossible. Nevertheless, if the major incentives (promotion and budget allocation) are controlled by other compliance people, then, in spite of residual disincentives, compliance executives will derive the *greatest* rewards from success at ensuring that the rules are obeyed.

The impossibility of assuring independence for the compliance group was the greatest concern of readers of earlier drafts of this essay. The response to them was at two levels. The first response is empirical; Braithwaite has seen many companies in the pharmaceutical industry, the coal industry, and the nursing home industry with tough independent compliance groups that frequently won internal battles against executives who wished to put profits ahead of safety. Cynics can go to any coal mine in the United States and read pre-shift examiners' reports that regularly record serious violations of law for further consideration by government inspectors. Undoubtedly pre-shift examiners fail to report all they should, but they do report a lot.

The second response goes to what we believe are mistaken presumptions as to corporate structure. The assumption that internal compliance groups will be impotent is based on too monolithic a conception of corporations, one that assumes that they are totally controlled from the top down. If subunits, such as compliance groups, develop enough momentum within the organization, in practical terms it can be difficult for the chief executive officer to bend them to her will. Chief executives are, in many senses, politicians who cannot afford to antagonize continually significant corporate constituencies, lest they refuse to cooperate with the CEO when their help or loyalty is really needed. This is true whether one is talking about the president of a university trying to restructure the geography department or the president of a coal company trying to trim the safety staff. Politicians, in short, are never omnipotent. And if internal compliance groups are set up in a way that gives them organizational clout (e.g., with a senior vice president at the helm or direct access to an audit committee of outside directors), their effectiveness will rarely be totally compromised.

For a Mix of Regulatory Strategies

Not all of the foregoing problems with enforced self-regulation can be lightly dismissed. Certainly there is consolation in comparing them to the even more profound pitfalls of voluntary self-regulation and government regulation. Enforced self-regulation can never be a panacea to the well-documented problems encountered under the other two models. To regulate effectively and efficiently the widest spectrum of corporate behavior, the state must be able to show that it can have recourse to a range of regulatory options. Then industry is given reason to make the status quo work for fear that the state will escalate to a more intrusive form of control (see Chapter 2). A pyramid of enforcement strategies also creates an opportunity for industry to persuade agencies to opt for graduated reduction of regulation. As in the GRIT (Graduated Reduction in Tension) strategy in international relations, industry can rise to the challenge of proving to its adversaries that it can provide *better* protection to the community when intervention is de-escalated (Osgood, 1985).

Enforced self-regulation has more bite than voluntary self-regulation organized by a trade association. But the latter still has an important place, particularly in areas of business regulation where the public interests threatened by corporate conduct are not great and where industry does not have a lot to lose, or something to gain, by toeing the line. Voluntary self-regulation is the most attractive option here because, lacking government–industry adversariness, it is the cheapest option. Even in areas where the consequences of corporate misconduct are devastating, voluntary self-regulation can usefully supplement governmental control (though never be a complete alternative to it). Had a self-regulation program run by the Pharmaceutical Manufacturers Association complemented direct regulation by the FDA, for example, the MER/29 drug disaster might have been averted (Braithwaite, 1984: 60–65). Here, two competitors of Richardson-Merrell, the makers of MER/29, had conducted tests on the drug and found it dangerous. Since there was no industry self-regulatory body to which test results could be forwarded, these companies were content merely to report their warnings to Richardson-Merrell, which promptly ignored them. In highly competitive industries, the desire of companies to prevent competitors from gaining an edge can be harnessed to serve the public interest by a voluntary self-regulation program run by a trade association.

Although enforced self-regulation would be more cost effective than direct government regulation in many areas involving the conduct of big business, it could never totally replace the latter. For smaller businesses, a viable and independent compliance unit is impossible. Direct government inspections must be retained for small businesses. In particular, government inspectors would continue to have a vital role in catching fly-by-night operators who calculatedly operate on the fringe of the law. Medium-sized businesses could perhaps be given a choice of opting in or out of enforced self-regulation. Small and medium-sized businesses, which could not sustain a viable and independent compliance unit, would have to be monitored directly for law observance by government inspectors. Nevertheless, the laws being observed could still be laws privately written and publicly ratified according to the enforced self-regulation model. Smaller companies, which could not be bothered writing their own rules, could choose one of a number of standard packages for companies of different types made available by the regulatory agency. Or, more simply, they could copy another company's rules from the public register of company rules.

Even for big business, a modicum of direct inspection must be retained. This would keep the internal compliance group on its toes. At this point, we can envision business people throwing their hands up in horror, and exclaiming, "So the bottom line is to keep the old government inspections while adding just another regulatory layer onto them" (see also Bardach and Kagan, 1982: 237). Not so. What is being suggested here is a reallocation of regulatory resources, not a multiplication of them, a shift from expenditures on direct inspection to expenditures on audits of corporate compliance groups. It happens to be our belief that in general, governments should increase their budgets for business regulation, but such a belief is not relevant to the present proposal.

A fundamental principle for the allocation of scarce regulatory resources ought to be that they are directed away from companies with demonstrably effective self-regulatory systems and concentrated on companies that play fast and loose. In addition to providing incentives for self-regulation, such a policy would tend to channel enforcement toward the companies most likely to offend. Regulatory agencies often provide disincentives for effective self-regulation. SmithKline executives drew one example to our attention. In 1979, the company conducted a detailed in-house examination that discovered contaminants in two of its nasal sprays. Instead of hushing up the problem, SmithKline treated the employee who discovered the contaminant as something of a hero. Her efforts were held up as an example of the kind of vigilance required for the sake of product purity. SmithKline notified FDA that 1.2 million bottles of nasal spray were being recalled from drug stores and supermarkets across the country. According to the executives, they felt terribly discouraged when the government issued a press release that created the impression that the FDA had discovered the problem and forced SmithKline into the recall.

The Corporate Case Law Approach

Rules have their limits. In a technologically complex industry, rules cannot be written to cover every environmental contingency that poses a risk of social harm. To be sure, an advantage of self-regulation is that the rules can more quickly adapt to changing environmental realities or newly perceived threats than can laws imposed by the state.

Even so, however, Braithwaite's (1984) research on the pharmaceutical industry suggests that an accumulation of many minor acts of social irresponsibility (or of many technical breaches) all too frequently does greater harm than grossly illegal acts.

The most effective method of combating minor acts of irresponsibility is through a corporation's identitive power—the use of symbols of pride, shame, and acceptance to control behavior.[52] The culture of a corporation more than anything else determines the safety of its products and the extent to which workers are needlessly injured or the environment needlessly harmed (Stone, 1975: 228–248). If top management tolerates an atmosphere in which the quick fix is accepted, in which rule bending and corner cutting are not frowned upon, then both socially irresponsible and illegal acts will flourish. The strength of identitive power is that it reaches beyond compliance with written rules. Corporations that indoctrinate their employees with an attitude that "the responsible way is the company way," that "the spirit of the rules is as important as the letter of the rules," should be rewarded by regulatory agencies with lower levels of governmental intervention.

The most effective way to inculcate a socially responsible corporate identity may not be through rule making, internal or external, but rather through the development of a corporate case law. A senior executive of one of Australia's largest companies indicated in an interview with Braithwaite and Bill Clifford that his firm was moving toward a "corporate case law approach." In the executive's view, rules could not be codified to cover the ever-changing situations that confront executives with ethical dilemmas. His company, therefore, was beginning to attempt to formalize "corporate case law." The fundamental requirement of the concept is that when executives encounter an ethical dilemma, the problem should be written down. It should then be passed up through the organization until it reaches a person who knows the existing case law with respect to this class of problems. If existing case law decides the issue, the problem goes no further. But if an important precedent could be established, it could go to the "supreme court": the firm's chief executive officer.

A second fundamental requirement of the concept is that any decision be put in writing and sent back down the line.[53] A senior executive must take responsibility for collating, conceptualizing, cross-referencing, and drawing out general principles from the case law. Communicating corporate case law to employees is not a greater problem than communicating case law handed down by state courts. Corporations have coped admirably with disseminating in digestible form the case law in such complex areas as antitrust. Anyone who has read the antitrust compliance guides provided to employees by some large American corporations must be impressed by the lucid use of examples to inculcate the "do's and don'ts" of competitive conduct.

When the corporate case law becomes widely communicated and understood within the organization, the need to pass ethical dilemmas up the line decreases because they are simply no longer dilemmas. The case law can build a corporate culture in which gray issues become black and white. Minimizing the incidence of ethical dilemmas is important because of the potential for delay. Corporations often make the right decisions at the wrong time because they dither while dilemmas are passed up the line. Authority must be devolved if corporations are to maximize their capacity to seize on opportunities when they present themselves.[54] Hence, it is essential that corporate case law be proactive rather than simply reactive.

The formalized organization and reporting of corporate case law would benefit both the regulators and the regulated. A formalized case law would render corporate decision-making processes more vulnerable to criticism. Criticizing unexplicated rules is of less value than reading and responding to actual key decisions. The corporate case law approach could never do away with the need for rules. It could, however, reduce their number and diminish the perennial bureaucratic problem of rules hamstringing action when they are not really apposite to the specific situation. For top management, formalized corporate case law can tighten management control and reduce the risk of wild, idiosyncratic decisions. Costs would not be great. Executives do not encounter significant ethical dilemmas every day of the week; when they do, a more senior person who has encountered problems of this type before should be able to resolve the dilemma rapidly. If the company is criticized for the ethical stance it has taken on a particular issue, the board of directors can be provided with a definitive summary of the relevant case law. The cases are in the files for them to inspect. Criticism can be directed not only at the wording of rules, but also at the managerial judgments underlying the resolution of specific dilemmas that set important precedents.

How would enforced self-regulation be adapted to a compliance system based more on case law than on statute law? It would work by giving the regulatory agency direct access to the written case law. Instead of devoting their time to monitoring rules, regulators would read the cases to ensure the critical ethical dilemmas were not being decided without recourse to this case law. The inspectors would also be charged with ensuring that the decisions reached were in accord with governmental standards.

Persuading jurists to recognize private case law in public courts could be an even greater task than obtaining such recognition for privately written rules. Under enforced self-regulation, however, the case law would be ratified by the state and would thus, in essence, be only semi-private. Periodic review of the case law by the regulatory agency could result in the overturning of decisions and principles that failed to conform to the government's overarching standards. Aggrieved consumers, competitors, or employees could also appeal to the agency for such relief.

In conclusion, let us state that we do not advocate the corporate case law approach, at least not in any immediate or practical sense. Important details must be worked out before the concept can be seriously considered. It does, however, present an alternative or complementary method to rule-based enforced self-regulation that bears further study.

Conclusion

This chapter has suggested that enforced self-regulation could play an important role in a fundamental redeployment of governmental expenditures for regulating business. Under enforced self-regulation, each company would write its own rules. Once these rules had been ratified by the government, a violation of them would be an offense. The company would be required to establish an internal compliance group to monitor observance of the rules and recommend disciplinary action against violators. If management were to fail to rectify violations or to act on recommendations for disciplinary action, the director of compliance would be statutorily required to report this fact to the relevant agency (who in turn would make the information available to PIGs). The role of the regulatory agency would be to determine that the company rules satisfied all of the guidelines set down by government policy, to ensure that the compliance group was independent within the corporate bureaucracy, to audit the performance of the compliance group, to conduct occasional spot inspections of operating units as an independent check that the compliance unit was detecting violations, and to launch prosecutions, particularly against companies that subverted their compliance groups.

Many very important details of how enforced self-regulation might work in practice have not been discussed here. How would the legislature set penalties for offenses? How would legislation deal with the question of intent? Should companies also be able to write their own *mens rea* standards? How would an enforced self-regulation scheme pass constitutional muster? Again, it must be emphasized that our purpose is not to present a packaged legislative proposal ready for implementation.

The ideas presented here may sound complex. They are not. We have attempted to show that one of enforced self-regulation's virtues is greater simplicity than direct governmental regulation. Approaches that are new always seem more complex than they in fact are. Should the reader be asked to explain how the existing American regulatory system works to a Martian (or even an Australian), it too would seem extremely complicated.

Whether the strengths of enforced self-regulation outweigh its weaknesses depends on what area of regulation is being considered and on the history of industry cooperation with the existing level of intervention. A message of this book is that there can be strength in the convergence of weakness. The challenge is to find a mix of self-regulation and governmental regulation—a mix that will cover the gaps left by one approach with the strengths of another approach. By exploiting the advantages and recognizing the weaknesses of enforced self-regulation, voluntary self-regulation, and direct governmental regulation, we might strike a mix that is more effective and less expensive than any one- or two-dimensional approach.

In the search for this mix, the intermediate options are many (Rees, 1988: 8–10). Gerber (1990) has shown how the control of abusive marketing practices by the infant formula industry during the 1980s can be understood as an adaptation of the enforced self-regulation model. Here we had privately written rules that in effect were ratified and enforced (through adverse publicity and consumer boycotts) by PIGs. With an international regulatory problem and in the absence of an international regulatory agency, PIGs acted as a proxy for the state to give effect to enforced self-regulation. Rules can be written publicly, privately by industry associations, privately by firms or in a tripartite forum. Privately written rules can be ratified publicly, by an independent professional or by a tripartite committee. Enforcement can be public, private (industry association), private (corporate compliance group), or any combination of these. Enforced self-regulation is just one of a challenging range of possibilities.

5

Partial-Industry Intervention

The current debate about whether or not to regulate often considers implicitly only two regulatory alternatives: government must either impose industry-wide regulations or allow unconstrained markets to determine the allocation of scarce resources. Regulators must regulate either all members of an industry or none. The regulatory literature has identified significant costs associated with each alternative. Laissez-faire policies that leave unchecked monopoly or oligopoly power in private hands might allow industry members to raise their prices above the competitive level (Bain, 1959). But industry-wide regulation can have the same effect. Regulators may be "captured" by the very firms they attempt to regulate (Stigler, 1971; Peltzman, 1980). Captured regulators can organize a cartel and legally mandate that firms in the industry sell at an inflated price. For those who fear these costs of capture, the only thing worse than letting market power coalesce in private hands is to give a corrupt Leviathan power to define the parameters of market transactions. Even uncaptured regulators face significant informational hurdles in promulgating efficient regulations. Regulatory agencies may have great difficulty ascertaining the "competitive" price. If the agency guesses too low, firms may not recoup their costs; if the agency guesses too high, again consumers may be forced to buy at cartel-like prices.

In this chapter, we explore a middle path between the Scylla of full-industry regulation and the Charybdis of laissez-faire policies. We propose that in some situations "partial-industry" regulation may be superior to either all or nothing regulatory policies. In its broadest sense, partial-industry regulation means that government regulates only a part of the industry, leaving another part unregulated. Under partial-industry regulatory schemes, government purposefully treats firms in an industry differently.[1]

In some regulatory settings, regulating only an individual firm (or a subset of the firms) in an industry can promote efficiency by restraining monopoly power without giving rise to the evils of either captured or benighted regulation. Especially in a dynamic or evolutionary sense, partial-industry regulation may be more resilient against the viruses of private and public market power abuse. Our theory derives its power from both camps of the regulate/deregulate debate. Like advocates of regulation, we accept that unregulated markets sometimes fail to produce competitive prices. But like advocates of deregulation, we accept (not only the costs of capture but more importantly) that unregulated competitors have strong incentives to chisel on cartel agreements and thereby destabilize collusion. Unlike full-industry regulation that extinguishes many forms of interfirm competition,[2] partial-industry regulatory strategies try to harness and foster the welfare-enhancing effects of competition.

Partial-industry regulation takes as its starting point that the existence of a single (or a few) competitive firms can dramatically affect the competitive conduct and performance of an entire industry. The central insight of partial-industry regulation is that government can accomplish many regulatory goals by maintaining the competitive performance of a subset of the firms in an industry. Far from denying the powerful effect of competition, partial-industry regulation uses the regulated firms to affect other firms in the market. Unlike across-the-board industry regulation, however, mistaken or captured government decisions do not need to affect adversely the unregulated firms. Instead of completely displacing the market, partial-industry regulation maintains a structure of ''checks and balances'' between the two extremes of regulation.

Like tripartism and enforced self-regulation, partial-industry regulation may be seen as a form of regulatory delegation. The regulated firms in the industry bear the burden of ensuring that the unregulated firms comply. The compliance of unregulated firms is assured because competition forces them to match the offers of the regulated firm. Unlike other strategies of delegation, however, the regulated firms do not need to appreciate their disciplining function.

A major thesis of this chapter is that government should adopt a ''monopsony standard'' for consumer protection interventions. Under this standard, government should only intervene upon consumers' behalf to improve the workings of a market when a monopsonist buyer would. The monopsony standard provides strong indications of when and how government should intervene. Monopsonists represent the quintessentially empowered consumer. By studying how consumers with market power protect themselves, government can better target and tailor interventions on behalf of less powerful consumers. We argue that a monopsony standard provides particularly strong evidence for the use of partial-industry regulation because monopsonists and oligopsonists (a small set of buyers) often privately undertake partial-industry interventions or their private analogs.

A monopsony standard for consumer protection is also attractive because it provides a limiting principle for when government should intervene. As discussed below, the private practice of second-sourcing—subsidizing second sources of supply—shows not only that treating sellers differently can be individually rational but also points government toward those situations when government sanctioned disparate treatment is likely to be rational and those where it is not. The monopsony standard thus provides a powerful source of necessary (but not sufficient) conditions for intervention. Even when a monopsonist would intervene, particular costs of government intervention may preclude the use of partial-industry regulation. The monopsonist standard more concretely provides a limiting principle to government actions, by suggesting that if a monopsonist would not intervene to change a market outcome nor should government.

From the entrenched mind-set of all or nothing regulatory strategies, many forms of partial-industry regulation may seem radical. This article provides a theoretical justification for further exploring partial-industry regulation and bolsters its theory with examples of both private and public interventions that disparately regulate the sellers in particular markets.

The remainder of the chapter sets out both a theoretical and practical typology of partial-industry regulation. By analyzing both the costs and benefits of such intervention, we show that a diverse range of possible partial-industry interventions exist that government might use to promote competition. We end by discussing a series of applications in which single-firm or partial-industry regulation is currently in place or may be justified.

For the most part, our arguments are directed toward regulatory attempts to promote competitive pricing in industries. But our larger argument is that partial-industry regulation may also be a useful policy tool to correct other types of market failure as well.[3] Government intervention directed at a subset of the firms in an industry, for example, may spur the provision of additional safety, innovation, or information without completely foregoing the checks and balances of private competition.[4]

Throughout, our argument is not that partial-industry regulation is costless or that it should be pursued on an economy-wide basis. As we make clear, there are significant costs to partial-industry regulation that will clearly preclude its use in several regulatory contexts. But, to be viable, partial-industry regulation must only succeed in doing better than the all or nothing alternatives. In some circumstances, we prefer the rifle to the shotgun or no gun at all.

Theory

A Typology of Partial-Industry Regulation

Although partial-industry intervention can take numerous forms, analytically one can distinguish among interventions that are directed at three different types of firms: dominant firms, fringe firms, and oligopoly firms. Analytically it is useful to divide regulation by its objects because partial-industry interventions focused on these three types of firms have different goals and take on different forms.

In many industries there is a pronounced dichotomy between dominant and fringe firms. Dominant firms are larger and seem to take the lead in setting price and other competitive variables, whereas the smaller fringe firms are followers, more passively matching the competitive decisions of the dominant firm(s). The most important decision of the competitive fringe often is, given the prevailing market price, to decide how much to produce (Scherer, 1980).[5] Other markets are more easily characterized as "oligopolies" in which a small number of firms of relatively equal size choose competitive variables in a much more interdependent and strategic fashion. In oligopolistic industries, there are no clear followers or leaders, instead it is through the iterated history of firm interaction that a market equilibrium is fashioned.[6]

Dominant-Firm Intervention. Regulatory policies that affect only the dominant firm in an industry will often be similar to traditional forms of industry-wide regulation. Dominant-firm intervention will generally attempt to constrain the dominant firm from exercising its market power to the detriment of consumers. Most basically, dominant-firm intervention would often establish the price at which the largest firm in an industry must sell its product.

Potential Advantages Over Laissez-Faire Governance. The benefit of dominant-firm regulation vis-à-vis no regulation is twofold. First, like industry-wide intervention, setting a maximum price for a dominant firm can restrict the market power it commands in an unregulated market. Especially if fringe competitors have limited capacities, an unregulated dominant firm may have incentives to raise its price above its (marginal) cost.[7] Fringe firms, however, will have difficulty raising their prices above the restrained price of a dominant firm. By setting the dominant firm's maximum price, a regulatory agency can effectively set an industry's maximum price. Thus, regulating a dominant firm can benefit consumers directly (by lowering the dominant firm's price) and indirectly (by lowering the prices of its competitors).

Second, regulations that in the short run set a dominant firm's minimum price may facilitate additional competition in the market and ultimately benefit the consumer. Although a binding minimum price restriction in the short run increases the amount that consumers would have to pay for the dominant firm's goods, a minimum price restraint can actually facilitate entry that may ultimately inure to the consumer's benefit. Entry into an industry may be deterred by the fear that a dominant firm will reduce its price to make any entry unprofitable. By prohibiting such price decreases, temporally limited minimum price standards may induce entry that will ultimately increase competition.

An extreme form of post-entry price cutting is predatory pricing—where a dominant firm prices below its production cost to drive out fringe competition. Currently, there is a lively debate whether such predation would ever be a profitable strategy for dominant firms.[8] But even nonpredatory price cuts can deter beneficial entry. Consider, for example, an industry in which a dominant firm without competition sets price above its marginal cost. New entrants initially have higher cost (but ultimately because of a "learning curve" effect will have the same costs of production as a dominant firm). As depicted in Figure 5.1, a dominant firm may be able to deter entry by threatening to drop its price just slightly below a new entrant's cost if there is entry.

Because the dominant firm has an initial cost advantage, this price reduction need not be predatory (in the sense that its price is still above its cost). But the price reduction would mean that a new entrant would not be able to recoup any of its start-up costs and accordingly would be deterred from entering. By restraining the ability of dominant firms to respond immediately to entry, minimum price regulation could ensure nascent entry limited protection. If minimum price regulations were then relaxed, the new entrants could compete on an equal footing and consumers could benefit with lower prices. This rationale for minimum price regulation is similar to the use of import tariffs by developing countries to protect temporarily fledgling domestic industries from international competition that might have an exclusionary effect. Although neither company import tariffs nor temporary minimum price regulation are policies with general appeal, we can see that it is theoretically possible for them to be strategically responsive to specific structural contexts. Thus, dominant-firm regula-

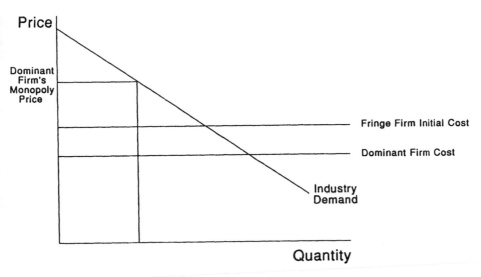

Figure 5.1. The possibility of deterring fringe entry without predatory pricing.

tion may be superior to laissez-faire policies because it can (1) restrain supracompetitive pricing by all the firms in an industry, and (2) facilitate entry by temporarily limiting dominant firm price cuts in response to entry.

Potential Advantage Over Industry-Wide Regulation. Dominant-firm regulation may also be superior to industry-wide regulation because it preserves the independence of fringe firms as a competitive check on the decisions of regulatory agencies. Although fringe firms will rarely have incentives to price above a dominant firm, fringe firms may have strong incentives to undercut dominant firm prices. By maintaining this potential for fringe price cutting, dominant-firm intervention may engender more competition than industry-wide intervention.

Industry-wide price regulation can allow the coercive power of the state to police anticompetitive collusion. As analyzed earlier, regulators can be "captured" by the firms they are supposed to restrain. Firms wishing to collude successfully must overcome four distinct "problems" (Osborne, 1976; Ayres, 1987). A cartel must be able to:

1. Reach agreement,
2. Detect breaches of the agreement,
3. Punish breaches of the agreement, and
4. Deter entry.

A captured regulatory agency can dramatically facilitate collusion by helping firms to overcome each of these obstacles to collusion. Regulators can openly promulgate regulations stating the agreed price; regulations can mandate that firms disclose the prices at which they sell. Perhaps most important, industry-wide regulations can punish any price chiselers that undercut the supracompetitive price. Finally, many regulatory agencies have the discretion to limit new entry. In most countries, public regulation limits the number of taxi licenses and controls the difficulty of passing the bar to practice law (Peltzman, 1980).

By leaving fringe firms completely unregulated, dominant-firm regulation undermines the ability of "captured" regulators to organize a cartel. To be sure, an agency can still facilitate reaching a collusive agreement by holding meetings and announcing a collusive price. But partial-industry intervention gives the unregulated firms greater opportunities to undermine the three other prerequisites for profitable cartelization. Fringe firms cannot be made to disclose publicly their prices so that it will be more difficult for a cartel to detect breaches of the collusive agreement. Fringe firms will not be bound by the dominant firm's regulated price, so that price cutting will not be subject to legal sanctions. New entry by nondominant firms cannot be legally proscribed; and, as argued earlier, entry may even be encouraged if dominant firms must wait before lowering their regulated price. Our argument is not that dominant-firm regulation eliminates the potential abuses of regulatory capture—only that it mitigates them.

To restrict dominant firm price, the public agency would need to undertake the same factual inquiry as is currently conducted in many industry-wide regulatory regimes. Namely, what price will provide the regulated firm with a fair return on capital. Initially then, dominant-firm intervention in the form of setting price will not reduce the informational burden of regulatory agencies. The agencies will still need to undertake the same estimation of cost in determining a reasonable price.

The freedom of unregulated firms to undercut the dominant firm's regulated price, however, may also provide information for the uncaptured, but uninformed regulator. The persistence of price cutting by fringe firms provides strong evidence for uninformed regulators that the dominant firm's price has been set too high. Indeed, price cutting by fringe firms may even lead the dominant firm to lobby the agency for lower regulated prices.[9]

Our theory of dominant-firm regulation gains its strength from the critiques of both laissez-faire and industry-wide policy perspectives. Dominant-firm regulation acknowledges the dangers of both private and public supracompetitive pricing and proposes an alternative in which the regulated and unregulated portions of an industry serve to check each other's abuse. Under dominant-firm intervention, the portion of the market that fails least will, in a sense, determine the level of competition. If either the regulators or the unregulated firms want to set a competitive price, then competition will prevail.[10] The law of one price will tend to drive the market price toward the price generated by the more competitive portion of the industry. In a world where either portion can fail to produce a competitive price, it may be best to let consumers have the benefit of both a regulated and an unregulated market presence.[11]

Fringe-Firm Intervention.   An alternative partial-industry regulatory strategy is to focus government attention on fringe producers. To implement a fringe-firm strategy, regulators would leave the dominant firm or firms in the industry unregulated and "intervene" to affect the behavior of fringe firms. Whereas dominant-firm intervention seeks to restrain the behavior of dominant firms, fringe-firm interventions seek to create or maintain the existence of additional competitors. Instead of directly regulating the behavior of firms in an industry (as with the price regulation of dominant-firm intervention), fringe-firm intervention seeks to change the structure of the industry and thereby induce more competitive behavior.[12]

A broad range of regulatory strategies could promote the existence of additional competitors. The government could implement a variety of subsidies to small competitors. It could directly subsidize new entry or preserve existing fringe firms with loans at favourable rates.[13] The government in its capacity as a consumer might also promote the competitive presence of fringe firms by patronizing fringe firms. For example, many U.S. state governments attempt to promote the economic viability of smaller banks by placing government deposits with them.[14] Alternatively, a progressive corporate tax system might give smaller competitors a competitive advantage. The global nature of such taxes makes them poor instruments for targeted competitive strategies. Nevertheless, the idea may not be lacking merit for more limited application, such as progressive taxation of profits from newspapers. In the extreme case, the government itself can enter a market as a producer of the good in question. A flavor for the diversity (of partial-industry regulation) is provided in more detail in the next section of applied case studies.

Efforts to increase the number of competitors in a market by such fringe-firm interventions may structurally serve to improve the laissez-faire performance of an industry. Both theory and practice offer strong support that in many contexts increasing the number of competitors will engender more competitive behavior.[15] Stigler's seminal *Theory of Oligopoly*, for example, presents a model showing why larger cartels will have more difficulty detecting breaches of their agreements (Stigler, 1964). The result is replicated in simple models of tacit collusion (e.g., the noncooperative Cournot model). The robust result in such models is that as the number of firms increase, the market price falls toward the competitive level (e.g., Rasmusen, 1989).

Empirically, several studies have validated this intuition. Paul MacAvoy's detailed study of railroad cartels dramatized that the existence of even a third competitor can significantly destabilize efforts at cartelization (MacAvoy, 1965). Studies of the airline industry replicate this result (e.g., Ayres, 1988). Cross-sectional studies that must aggregate data crudely from disparate industries have generated more varied results, but as Frederick Scherer has summarized, "[T]here is a rather robust tendency for a positive association to emerge between seller concentration and profitability" (Scherer, 1980: 278). Again, the preponderance of evidence supports the conclusion that a smaller group of sellers has a greater ability to raise price above their costs.

Moreover, empirical studies indicate that government ownership of businesses does not necessitate inefficient production. For example, in Canada the publicly owned railroad has achieved the same efficiency as its private rival (Caves and Christensen, 1980). Vickers and Yarrow (1991) have similarly concluded that competition rather than ownership per se was the key to efficiency.

The possibility that fringe-firm interventions can promote competition is also confirmed directly by private interventions in contiguous markets. In a number of contexts the downstream purchasers of products willingly subsidize the entry and continued existence of additional upstream competitors. This practice of "second sourcing'' is commonly used, for example, by governments in procuring defense contracts and by automobile manufacturers seeking the production of specialized inputs (see Riordan and Sappington, 1989).

Even the name second sourcing indicates that the presence of a single additional producer can significantly improve the performance of the upstream market. The theory behind second-sourcing strategies is relatively simple. Downstream firms willingly incur the costs of subsidizing additional upstream competitors because the presence of such competitors will constrain the market power of the incumbent producers and ultimately lower the downstream input prices.

The effectiveness of second sourcing in reducing upstream market power can also be gleaned from the resistance of upstream incumbents to this strategy. For example, in *Barry Wright Corp. v. IIT Grinnell Corp.*,[16] a downstream purchaser of mechanical snubbers (pipe shock absorbers for nuclear power plants) contracted to subsidize the entry of a new upstream producer. The incumbent snubber producer reacted immediately by cutting its downstream price and attempting to enter into a long-term arrangement that effectively mandated exclusive purchases from the incumbent.[17]

Upstream incumbent producers resist second sourcing for the same reason that downstream consumers undertake the strategy—additional competition will limit the ability of upstream producers to extract monopoly rents from downstream consumers. A striking prerequisite for private second-sourcing strategies, however, is a concentrated downstream demand for a given product. Because second sourcing often entails subsidization, downstream firms have great incentives to free ride on the second-sourcing efforts of their competitors. Since all downstream firms benefit from the competitive presence of additional upsteam firms, downstream rivals would prefer to free ride on the investments of their rivals in establishing these upstream competitors. Due to this free riding effect, only concentrated downstream industries may be able to overcome the underinvestment problem. Second sourcing is a public good to downstream competitors and the more diffuse the downstream competitors the less they will invest in subsidizing the public good—upstream entry. It is not surprising then that leading examples of second sourcing occur when the downstream firm is a monopsonist of specialized products (for example, in defense procurement or automobile inputs).

The fact that second-sourcing strategies are not undertaken in industries with more diffuse downstream demand does not indicate, however, that such strategies could not efficiently improve competitive performance. Instead, because of the free riding problem, industries with diffuse downstream demand are unable to overcome the collective action problem of optimally investing in second sources. With diffuse demand, the transaction costs of reaching such subsidization agreements are prohibitive. Yet, the fact that second sourcing is cost justified when demand is concentrated is strong evidence that it may be cost justified when demand is diffuse. The revealed preference of concentrated buyers to incur the costs of subsidization in expectation of lower input prices is strong prima facie evidence of its efficiency.[18]

The possibility that second sourcing is efficient in markets with diffuse demand is a forceful argument in favor of fringe-firm intervention. Fringe-firm intervention is simply a public form of the second-sourcing strategy. Regulators, acting as the agents of diffuse downstream consumers, can overcome the collective action problem of free riding and subsidize additional entry.[19]

Fringe-firm interventions as public attempts at second sourcing also generate two informational advantages over industry-wide interventions. First, efforts to promote the continued existence of fringe firms will not put the same informational demands on regulators as imposing, for example, industry-wide prices. "Existence" subsidies require less detailed information about production costs and reasonable returns.[20] Second, the subsidized fringe firms may themselves provide regulators with information that lets them assess and regulate more effectively the performance of other firms in the industry. Especially, for example, when government engages in the extreme strategy of government ownership, the process of producing the good itself may provide regulators with more reliable cost data about other firms in the industry. In the 1970s, the Australian government bought a pharmaceutical company, partly to inform government price-setting decisions under its Pharmaceutical Benefits Scheme. Data generated from fringe-firm intervention might then be used to set more precisely the dominant firm's price. Thus, fringe-firm interventions may be informationally superior than industry-wide intervention by both demanding less information of regulators and supplying regulators with more useful information.

Therefore, the pervasive use of private second-sourcing strategies by concentrated buyers argues in favor of public fringe-firm strategies that replicate the benefits of increased upstream competition. Government is especially well placed to provide the public good of increased competition by inducing and maintaining the structural conditions for such competition.

Oligopoly Tournaments. The dichotomy between dominant firms and fringe firms breaks down in a number of industries in which there is a small number of firms of relatively similar size. In such oligopolies, it may be beneficial for the regulator to employ either dominant- or fringe-type interventionist strategies. That is, even when all the firms serving the industry are relatively homogeneous it may be desirable (1) to restrain the anticompetitive behavior of part of the industry or (2) to subsidize entry by additional firms. In some contexts it may even be desirable to pursue a combination of these strategies. For example, government could intervene to promote new entry and then regulate its prices. The arguments in favor of dominant- and fringe-firm intervention, therefore, do not require that the regulated firm be necessarily large or small.[21]

There is, however, a third class of regulatory interventions that may be most especially appropriate when the firms in an industry are of equal size. In such instances, the very similarity of the firms may make "tournament" regulation an effective policy tool. In a regulatory tournament, an agency's treatment of individual firms depends on their *relative* performance.

The use of grading curves in teaching is a classic example of a tournament ("game") that makes the grades ("payoffs") of individual students ("players") depend on the performance of others in the class (Rasmusen, 1989). Hosts of current regulations similarly establish tournaments among firms in an industry. In the United States, affirmative action guidelines that set hiring targets for federal contractors based on average minority employment in the market create a similar interdependence.[22] Alternatively, the due care standards in medical malpractice often depend on the prevailing customs of doctors in a relevant geographic market.[23] The use of diagnostically related group reimbursement by Medicare also exemplifies tournament competition. Medicare reimbursement is tied to the average costs of treating patients within a particular diagnostic group (Shleifer, 1985). And game theorists have paid particular attention to "patent race" tournaments, in which the first firm to innovate gains the enhanced profits of patent protection (see Barzel, 1968; Gilbert and Newbery, 1982; Reinganum, 1985).

Tournament regulation can be distinguished from dominant-firm or fringe-firm intervention by its timing. The essence of dominant-firm and fringe-firm regulation is disparate treatment. Different firms in an industry are treated differently: some are regulated; others are not. But the disparate treatment of tournament regulation only attaches *ex post*—at the end of the play. From an *ex ante* perspective, firms competing in a regulatory tournament are treated the same: they have an equal opportunity to "win" a tournament. For example, any firm has an opportunity to invest resources in research and development; the disparate treatment of patent protection attaches only after the patent race has been won. From this *ex ante* perspective then, tournament interventions are a form of industry-wide regulation that makes the payoffs of the individual firms interdependent. Tournament regulation strives to induce enhanced competition for a tournament's prize, thereby increasing the efficiency of the market.

A particularly effective class of tournaments, analyzed in the game theory literature, involves a form of "yardstick competition" (Shleifer, 1985; Farrell, unpublished).[24] Regulators of public utilities can engender such yardstick competition by basing each utility's price on the average costs of *other* similar utilities. Such a regulation can give the individual utilities optimal incentives to reduce the cost of their own production because their regulated price is independent of their own cost-saving efforts. Accordingly, yardstick competition creates a tournament in which a firm's profits are determined by its ability to generate lower costs than its competitors. Yardstick competition puts the utilities in a type of prisoner's dilemma in which, although they collectively prefer not to undertake the effort of reducing cost, individually they are driven to keep ahead of their competitors. In equilibrium, yardstick competition can induce efficient behavior in which the utilities, striving to gain a competitive advantage, are all driven to the competitive optimum.

Like fringe-firm intervention, yardstick competition has distinct informational advantages for regulators. The crucial aspect of utility regulation is finding the appropriate cost benchmark to induce efficient behavior and assure a sufficient return. Yardstick competition is especially attractive because utilities in otherwise distinct geographic markets compete in a sense to provide regulators with such a benchmark.

In sum, partial-industry regulation can seek (1) to restrain anticompetitive behavior (or dominant-firms); (2) to promote additional entry (by fringe firms); or (3) to engender tournament competition for an interdependent prize. In contrast to traditional forms of industry-wide regulating, partial-industry regulation retains an unregulated market presence that can mitigate corrupt or misguided government regulation. In Chapter 3, we suggested that tripartism could be used to promote cooperation without falling prey to the costs of capture. Here, we seek to restrain the private exploitation of monopoly power without substituting the public exploitation of capture. Both public and private market governance can fail to provide efficient resource allocation. Partial-industry regulation creates dual governance of individual markets. The competition between these public and private systems of economic governance can serve as a check on both forms of market failure. We are not suggesting that a governmental presence is appropriate in all or even a majority of industries. Instead, rational regulation will assess when the types of partial-industry regulation discussed earlier will produce better results than the more traditional regulatory alternatives.

A Monopsony Standard for Government Intervention

These theories of partial-industry intervention gain support from an analysis of monopsonist behavior. The conduct of single buyers (monopsonists) or concentrated buyers (oligopsonists) provides a unique vantage point for consumer protection advocates. Because monopsonists have market power,[25] they are often able to effectively protect themselves.[26] In a broad variety of contexts, monopsonists will improve market efficiency by inducing more competitive conditions of supply. Put simply, governments interested in promoting consumer welfare should often emulate what a monopsonist consumer would do.

This monopsony standard for government intervention can support a wide variety of partial-industry regulations discussed above. Most directly, a monopsony analysis underscores the potential usefulness of fringe-firm intervention. One way to reconceive of the regulator's decision about whether to use a particular form of fringe-firm intervention is to ask whether a downstream monopsonist would be willing to subsidize upstream entry. The decisions of a hypothetical monopsonist would replicate a consumer welfare standard because such a downstream consumer fully internalizes the costs and benefits of the second sourcing strategy.[27] In short, government should consider second sourcing where a monopsonist would.[28]

The monopsony standard also supports the limited use of "excessive consumption" by government (Romano, 1991). In industries with large fixed costs (and declining average costs), it is possible that average costs will everywhere be above the consumer demand curve. In this situation, no producer can profitably supply a point on the demand curve and there may be no entry—even though the foregone consumer surplus on infra marginal purchases would make production efficient. Romano has shown that consumers may engage in excess consumption (that is, consumption beyond their nonstrategic demand curves) to make production profitable. Thus, Romano is able to explain why residents of Lake Wobegon would be willing to buy their toaster at a local Hardware store—even though it could be purchased more cheaply at an out of town K-Mart (Keillor, 1985: 95–96).

Just as second sourcing may promote the entry of second (or third) sources of supply, excessive consumption may be thought of as a form of "primary sourcing" that seeks to encourage an initial source of supply. But as with second sourcing, excessive consumption of this type is unlikely to be a successful fringe firm intervention if there is a diffuse group of consumers—who would prefer to allow others to bear the subsidization costs of excessive consumption. As before, the government, under the monopsony standard, might act on behalf of more diffuse groups to affect this form of excessive consumption.

The minimum price regulation of dominant firms can have an analogous second-sourcing effect. As discussed previously in the *Barry Wright* opinion, incumbent producers are likely to cut prices to undermine second-sourcing strategies to foster new entry. A monopsonist can retain the benefits of these price cuts and the competitive benefits of second sourcing by continuing to buy a certain proportion of its demand from higher-priced new entrants. When demand for a product is diffusely distributed among several competitors, however, it may be difficult to organize individual buyers to continue to buy a proportion of their sales from higher-priced entrants. Individual buyers, while wanting the increased competition, will prefer that their competitors pay the second-sourcing subsidy. Minimum price regulation of incumbents facing new entry is an indirect way of recreating the behavior of a monopsonistic or oligopsonistic buying group—by removing the incentive of individual buyers to chisel on a second-sourcing strategy.[30]

Maximum-price regulation of dominant firms and oligopoly tournaments can also be seen as public analogs of private monopsony behavior. The market power conveyed by monopsony will, like maximum price regulation, constrain the ability of dominant firms to sell at supracompetitive prices. Monopsonists wishing to retain the pro-competitive effects of fringe suppliers would rationally negotiate individualized prices related to the costs of the individual sellers. Like partial-industry intervention, the maximum prices negotiated by monopsonists with dominant firms are likely to be lower than the prices negotiated with higher-cost fringe suppliers. The monopsony standard harmonizes so well with partial-industry regulatory strategies because monopsonists often find it in their interest to negotiate individualized deals with their suppliers. Disparate treatment is often the essence of monopsonists' attempts at consumer self-protection.[31]

Finally, the private use of explicit and implicit tournaments, which make suppliers' profits dependent on the conduct of their competitors, argues for greater attention to public interventions of this form. Buyers with market power routinely use not only explicit bidding but in dynamic contexts often place repeat business depending on the relative service of suppliers. Firms buying services from employees often resort to contests that reward employees on their relative marketing success or performance.

A monopsony standard not only provides a powerful tool for analyzing how government might intervene to protect consumers, but also a limiting principle for analyzing when intervention is appropriate. For although the private practice of second sourcing provides powerful evidence that public second-sourcing or fringe-firm intervention might benefit consumers, the fact that second sourcing is not undertaken by all monopsonists suggests that there will be many situations in which fringe-firm intervention is not appropriate.

The monopsony standard provides a sufficient condition for non-intervention but only a necessary condition for intervention. By these we mean, that if a monopsonist would not intervene say to second source then that should be sufficient to deter government from intervening on behalf of a more diffuse group of consumers. But the converse does not hold. The fact that a monopsonist would second-source does not imply that government should. The costs of administering public second sourcing—including the possibility of captured partial-industry regulation—may militate against government intervention even in those situations when monopsonists would act. Thus, the monopsony standard at once holds out the possibility of beneficial partial regulation but at the same time provides a one-tailed test to circumscribe its use.

The industrial organization literature contains a rich analysis that can inform the application of this hypothetical standard. In attempting to analyze how a hypothetical monopsonist would behave, consumer protection advocates might begin by assessing the degree to which additional competitors are likely to reduce an industry's prices. Monopsonists will tend to second source when the gains from lower input prices exceed the costs of the second sourcing subsidy. As is generically the case, the final analysis will turn on an empirical assessment of the costs and benefits of the regulation.

Because the forms of partial-industry regulation are so diverse the specific administrative detail of such intervention is largely beyond the scope of this chapter—although the same particulars are discussed in the next section's industry studies. Our goal here is to point to the possibility of a new genre of regulatory possibilities that is largely being ignored by the public sector but has been a staple of private consumer protection. The possibility of fringe-firm intervention—or public second-sourcing on consumers' behalf—is anathema to the current collective mind set. But even authorizing government agencies to disparately subsidize fringe-firm production is less invasive than many traditional forms of industry-wide regulation—such as prevailed in airline fare regulation for several decades prior to deregulation. The fact that consumers with market power often protect themselves with analogs to partial industry intervention argues that government power might emulate these strategies to protect less powerful groups of consumers.

Equal Protection Impediments to Partial-Industry Regulation

The potential benefits stemming from the various forms of partial-industry regulation generate unique problems of administration and enforcement. This section highlights an important equitable difficulty inherent in partial-industry regulation. A chief complaint among industry participants concerns the fundamental fairness of treating firms differently. Under dominant-firm intervention, for example, those firms subject to price regulation will argue that it is unfair that their competitors go unregulated. Under fringe-firm intervention, those firms not subject to government subsidies will argue that it is unfair that they are unregulated. Yet, it is important to stress that the equal protection principle only mandates that similarly situated entities be treated equally (Tribe, 1988). In fact, the theory of equal protection is violated when dissimilar entities face equal treatment. Of course, much turns on what counts as a relevant similarity.

The arguments of the previous section have suggested that dominant and fringe firms are dissimilar in terms of their competitive impact on an industry and that their dissimilarities provide a rational basis for the disparate treatment of either form of partial-industry regulation. In legal terms, a partial-industry regulatory scheme that made distinctions based on size would surely pass the modest rationality standard of U.S. equal protection analysis.[32]

As argued previously, however, there may be times when society may benefit from applying dominant-firm or fringe-firm regulatory strategies to individual firms within a fairly homogeneous oligopoly. In such oligopolies, there still may be competitive advantages from restraining the pricing of individual firms. However, the very similarity of the firms increases the equitable claim of the restrained firm being treated unfairly. Regulators can respond to these equitable concerns in two ways without forfeiting the benefits of single firm intervention.

First, it may be possible to turn the government's choice of regulation into a tournament itself. For example, if the government decides that it should restrain the pricing of an individual firm within an oligopoly, it might choose to single out the firm that has behaved least competitively in the past. Individual firms trying to avoid the price regulation could then compete to avoid the regulatory constraint by pricing more competitively in the preregulation periods.

Second, the government might randomly choose the firm that is to be the object of the price regulation for a finite period and different firms could be chosen in each successive period. As discussed earlier, such a decision rule would put the similar firms in the same *ex ante* position, therefore, from at least one perspective there would be no disparate treatment.[33]

The more substantive risk with this decision rule concerns the possibility that firms would be singled out nonrandomly in a systematic effort to exclude them from the market. Regulators that were captured by certain firms in an industry might purposefully seek to regulate other firms to put them at a competitive disadvantage. If individual firms could cause regulators to force their rivals to increase their price or undertake inefficient modes of production, then the regulated rivals might be effectively excluded from the market. While mitigating industry cartelization, partial-industry regulation might facilitate the raising of a rival's costs (Krattenmaker and Salop, 1986). Even more perniciously, regulators might threaten targeted burdensome regulation as a way of extracting "rents" from competitors in an industry (McChesney, 1987). The appropriateness of partial-industry regulation would turn on the ability of society to control these deleterious forms of capture and rent seeking.[34]

In summary, we would say that there are no serious equal protection concerns with the two most important types of partial-industry intervention: (a) where the dominant firm suffers the cost of regulation while less powerful fringe firms escape that cost; and (b) where a weak fringe firm enjoys a benefit that keeps or brings it into existence, a benefit denied to its stronger competitor(s). In the case of regulatory costs being imposed selectively on equally matched firms, however, equal protection concerns can be profound. We have suggested tournaments, lotteries and turn-taking as equitable solutions to this dilemma. More than this is needed, however, to guard against capture and corruption in decisionmaking about selective regulation. Openness, accountability and rights of appeal are vital. Our own strongest preference for special measures to guard against capture and corruption in the exercise of regulatory discretion is the explicit involvment of PIGs in the regulatory decision-making.

Applications

The theories elaborated have been implemented to varying degrees in a variety of regulatory contexts. In this section, we explore the actual and potential use of single-firm or partial-industry regulation by examining in more detail four industry case studies: (a) oil, (b) airlines, (c) news media, and (d) long-distance telephone service.

Destabilizing OPEC

After 13 years of successful collusion, the oil cartel of the Organization of Petroleum Exporting Countries (OPEC) disintegrated in 1986. Price chiseling by individual nation states brought on a price war that more than halved the price of oil from its high of more than $30 per barrel. The instability of OPEC was in part brought on by the downturn in demand for oil in the United States. Individual OPEC members could not raise the revenue requirements for domestic programs and were led to cut price to increase their shares of total production (Ayres, 1987). But some analysts fear that OPEC may be on the verge of reestablishing its ability to raise the price of oil.[30] World consumption has returned to the higher pre-OPEC rates of growth and the member states may have lowered their domestic revenue requirements after more than 3 years of price wars.

In the wake of Iraq's unsuccessful invasion of Kuwait, some analysts fear that OPEC may be on the verge of reestablishing its ability to raise the price of oil. With Iraq and Kuwait's production capacity limited by the war's destruction and with world consumption having returned to the higher pre-OPEC rates of growth, OPEC's recent success in agreeing to modest reductions in production quotas may be the harbinger of a tighter cartel in the future.

It is natural to ask whether the United States, the primary importer of energy and consequently the primary victim of the OPEC cartel, could do anything to prevent the resurgence of a cartel that sent seismic shocks through the world economy for 13 years. We argue that enlightened use of partial-industry intervention could achieve this objective.

Individual members of OPEC have a powerful incentive to break OPEC price or production limits. For example, by slightly cutting price, a producer might sell much more oil at a still highly inflated price. In deciding whether to engage in such price chiseling, OPEC members must weigh the gains from price chiseling against the possibility of lost future profits if a price war ensues. If enough members choose to chisel, the cartel will disintegrate. Thus, the presence of even a few cartel chiselers can drastically reduce the effectiveness of a cartel.

As OPEC's experience in the 1980's suggests, these destabilizing forces are by themselves very powerful. When oil-exporting debtor nations, such as Nigeria and Venezuela, began routinely to exceed their production limits to increase their oil revenues, Saudi Arabia (the dominant OPEC producer) retaliated in kind, driving the price of oil to less than half its former level. But the history of OPEC also suggests that these incentives to chisel do not always preclude collusion—after all, the inherent instability of cartels did not keep OPEC from gouging oil consumers for more than a decade, and it cannot guarantee competition in the future. Although the OPEC ministers seem to be in disarray now, there is no guarantee that a new Sheik Yamani will not forge another cohesive Arab alliance, or that in the future demand will not again outstrip non-OPEC supply.

Partial-industry strategies might have been used in the past (or might be used in the future) however, to undermine the ability of OPEC to raise price above its cost. Intervention strategies cannot take the form of direct regulatory fiat—as, for example, with dominant-firm price regulation—because any nation's regulatory power does not encompass the pricing decisions of separate sovereign states. But we argue that structural incentives directed at individual member states can induce a competitive market for oil. Simply stated, the United States and its allies could destabilize OPEC by giving individual producer nations greater incentives to breach the OPEC agreement. An optimal strategy of destabilization would combine a mixture of carrots and sticks to achieve this end. Debt forgiveness, favored nation trading status, additional foreign aid to specific oil-producing nations and promises of diplomatic and military support in the event of attack could thus be conditioned on the excess production of oil. Linking badly needed economic development loans and their refinancing to OPEC betrayal might be especially effective. After all, the need of oil revenues for maintenance of existing debts is what induced Nigeria and Venezuela to cheat in the first place. The International Monetary Fund has been conditioning loans for years on such factors as the borrower's fiscal deficit or money supply. Destabilization would simply make assistance responsive to a different action of the borrowing state.

This form of partial-industry regulation would be akin to dominant-firm price regulation because the goal would be to restrain the anticompetitive behavior of individual firms. The example of OPEC is useful because it demonstrates the wide variety of policy options that may be available to implement partial-industry regulatory strategies.

Such a policy is feasible. The inefficiency of cartelization implies that consumers lose more than producers gain. Supracompetitive pricing produces a dead-weight loss that represents this amount. In Figure 5.2 the gain from cartelization is represented by the area in rectangle 1, but the consumer losses from cartelization equal the area in rectangle 1 and the dead-weight loss triangle 2 (Posner, 1976).

Theoretically there exists, therefore, a lump-sum bribe that consumers could pay a cartel to produce the competitive quantity. This is a theoretical possibility for all cartels, but as before, diffuse consumers of oil are foreclosed from reaching this hypothetically beneficial agreement by the tremendous collective action problem of such multilateral contracting. The United States, however, is well positioned to overcome the tendency of individual oil consumers to free ride on the bribery investments of others. An efficiency bribe of this type would represent a kind of "industry-wide" intervention. The government would negotiate a lump sum bribe to all of OPEC to increase its production.

Partial-industry strategies are, however, likely to achieve the same results at a fraction of the cost. By exploiting the inherent destabilizing incentives for cartel cheating, regulators could achieve the same result at a fraction of the cost. The U.S. government would not need to take on all of OPEC to maintain competition in the oil

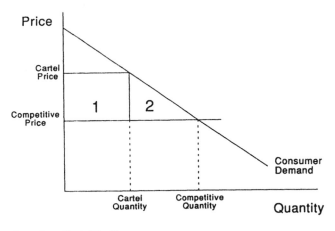

Area 1 = Cartel Profits

Area 1 + Area 2 = Consumer Loss (Potential size of bribe to increase
output to competitive quantity)

Figure 5.2. The possibility of efficient cartel bribes.

market. As argued previously, the presence of a small number of competitive firms can have a dramatic procompetitive effect on a market. And the costs of targeted destabilization could be further reduced because the threat of U.S. punishment (in reduced credit financing or aid) could be just as effective as the promise of a bribe in encouraging individual countries to defect from OPEC production limits. Moreover, OPEC's recent instability demonstrates that several nations have been choosing to chisel of their own accord, therefore, the size of the prizes or punishments would not need to be great to make it in an individual country's interest to breach the cartel agreement.[35]

An overt policy of targeted destabilization might, however, have other costs—for example, affecting diplomatic relations with Middle Eastern nations. Liberals might criticize punishments that inequitably target Third World countries like Nigeria; conservatives might disdain bribes as a type of ransom for economic terrorists. Moreover, consumers, like that sometimes Texan, President Bush, might decide that they really do not want lower domestic oil prices.[36] Policy makers should at least realize that targeted, partial-industry strategies represent a powerful tool to ensure competitive oil prices, if politically the United States has such a goal.

The OPEC cartel would be a criminal conspiracy under the Sherman Antitrust Act if it operated in the United States. Yet the U.S. response to date has been an attempt to hide from the criminal—by making itself less energy dependent. Reduced energy dependence is something we must support if we are to be more responsible citizens of the global village. However, energy independence is a blunt industry-wide instrument for combating cartelization. The unregulated market provides strong incentives for price chiseling that can eventually cause cartels to disintegrate. But as OPEC has shown us, "eventually" can be a painfully expensive period. Partial-industry intervention in the forms of targeted incentives (both carrots and sticks) for individual nations to cut price or increase output can transcend blind faith in cartel instability to the more rational policy perspective that we can enhance these very destabilizing forces to ensure competition.

Bailing Out People's Express

In October 1986, the Justice Department's antitrust division, in a decision that was broadly consistent with the Reagan administration's antitrust enforcement, approved the merger between People's Express and Texas Air. People's Express has been a price cutter—charging sometimes as little as a third of the going fare. People's presence dramatically changed the nature of competition on the routes it served, forcing other airlines to engage in fierce price competition (Ayres, 1987). The loss of People's Express as an independent market force almost immediately was followed by fare increases on the routes that People's had serviced, just as transatlantic fares increased after Sir Freddie Laker's financial demise.

Under the Reagan administration's antitrust policies, however, even the forseeability of higher prices did not mean this merger was likely ''to lessen competition substantially.'' The merger's approval in part stemmed from the losses that People's had been sustaining. People's Express was classified as a failing firm that was likely to join its subsidiary Frontier in bankruptcy. The Justice Department reasoned that if the choice was between People's loss through merger or bankruptcy, preventing the merger would not preserve competition.

Regulatory choices, however, need not be this restrictive. The failing firm doctrine is flawed because it does not take seriously the possibility of intervention to keep People's Express as an independent market force, the possibility of fringe-firm intervention. This intervention might take any one of a number of forms—from a bailout to an outright purchase. Single-firm interventions to maintain the existence of individual firms have occurred in the past; the bailout of Chrysler is a notable example. Past interventions have been primarily motivated by labor or banking concerns (e.g., the Amtrak bailout). Yet, as discussed earlier, competitive concerns might also justify a bailout. As the experience of People's Express illustrates, the continued presence of a single price-cutter can beneficially discipline an industry.

Single-firm intervention is by no means a panacea. Chief among its weaknesses would be the problem of how to keep the price-cutting mentality intact after intervention. The costs of erroneous intervention are sufficient to restrict the policy to those industries in which market forces fail to engender a competitive price. But increasing the number of competitors can by itself undermine the ability of dominant firms to charge supracompetitive prices.[37] When the prices in a market have been persistently and disproportionately high, or when a merger is likely to generate such high prices, then taking over or subsidizing a failing firm might promote competition most effectively. Once again, we do not have to believe that the firm intervention is without cost, only that it is better than the alternatives of doing nothing or intervening on a larger scale (with dismemberment or regulation).

The claim that public ownership of an individual firm falls outside the proper domain of government conduct is easily refuted by the previous analysis of second sources. In markets that have consistently failed to produce competition, competition is itself a public good that should be government's "business" to provide. When People's Express cut price (to increase its sales), there were many benefits that People's did not capture—not only did People's passengers pay lower fares but the passengers of other airlines paid lower fares also because of the People's-inspired competition. Subsidizing People's Express might have paid big dividends by keeping all airline fares low.

Critics also argue that People's Express failed because it was inefficient and that subsidizing its continued existence would only have prolonged this inefficiency. But this argument ignores the realities of private second sourcing. The core of second sourcing is a subsidy from downstream firms to an upstream firm with higher costs that attempts to maintain its competitive presence in the upstream market. Not only is it a theoretical possibility that the inefficiency of maintaining a higher cost upstream producer is outweighed by the increased competition in the upstream market, but also the prevalence of second sourcing by monopsonist buyers is strong evidence that subsidizing failing firms can be efficient in markets with less concentrated demand. The government is, as with the OPEC example, well positioned to act on consumers' behalf to make this subsidy.

Competition could be fostered even further by the very fact that a single-firm subsidy discriminates against other firms in the industry. As argued in the previous section, the government might purposefully create a tournament in which the firms in an industry compete for the privileged position. The subsidy would be awarded on the basis of competition itself, that is, who was the biggest price cutter. People's Express easily met this standard. Subsidizing price cutting could create dramatic incentives to defect from collusive cartel arrangements, either tacit or explicit.

The current era of airline deregulation complicates the analysis. The new threat of potential competition may keep the fares low on some of People's routes, but study after study reject the hypothesis that airline routes are contestable (see e.g., Ayres, 1988a; Call and Keeler, 1985). Nor will People's Express be the last price cutter to end in bankruptcy or merger. Price cutting is a risky business and it may be socially desirable to provide some insurance for this strategy from which consumers are bound to benefit. The People's Express example is not a curiosum. Although we do not argue that the government should frequently bail out failing firms, competitive bailouts deserve reassessment. In the end, one might conclude that it is administratively too difficult for government actors to identify the worthy recipients of an "efficiency" bailout. But the fact that downstream consumers are often willing to buy or subsidize failing upstream suppliers is at least sufficient evidence to shift the burden to those who would dismiss such interventions out of hand.

A final, more recent example involves the Supreme Court's decision of November 1989, to allow the Detroit News and the Detroit Free Press to merge (Greenhouse, 1989). The two papers had been fierce competitors in past years and had claimed losses in recent years. Industry analysts predict, however, that the merger (technically called a joint operating agreement) will generate profits of up to $100 million a year. The merger, by eliminating competition, will almost certainly increase the advertising rates in the city. Even if the Detroit market is a natural monopoly, in the sense that two competitive firms cannot recoup their fixed costs, it may be in the government's interest to subsidize one or both firms to engender an unnatural duopoly. If the two firms were only losing $5 or $10 million a year, the investment in a subsidy of this size to keep them both viable competitors might be cost justified if it ensured more competitive advertising and newspaper prices, as well as higher employment and a more competitive marketplace for ideas.

Since 1969, Sweden has undertaken such selective intervention with continuing multimillion dollar subsidies of newspapers "to counteract further concentration of ownership and to facilitate the establishment of additional newspapers." (Swedish Institute, 1988.)[38] Again the comparison with the observable second-sourcing practice of private downstream firms is compelling. It can be in consumers' interest to subsidize failing firms if their continued presence will significantly constrain supra-competitive pricing.

The Disparate Treatment of Broadcast and Print Media

Although this chapter has focused on regulatory strategies to constrain supracompetitive pricing, the partial-industry interventions analyzed have potential for enhancing the competitive performance of industries on other policy dimensions as well. A striking example of the use of partial-industry regulation in other contexts comes from the current regulatory structure for the market place of ideas in the United States (Ayres, 1988b). In two seminal cases,[39] the U.S. Supreme Court has established that the government could regulate the broadcast media in ways that would be unconstitutional if applied to print media. Specifically, these cases allowed the Federal Communications Commission (FCC) to impose "equal time" regulations on radio and television broadcasters while striking down the application of such regulations for newspapers.[40] The Supreme Court based its disparate treatment on what it perceived to be a difference in the technological capacities for multiple speech. The Supreme Court felt that the scarcity of the broadcast spectrum could justify regulation that would be inappropriate to nonscarce speech opportunities.

The Supreme Court's scarcity distinction has been roundly criticized by academics who have shown, for example, that the economic opportunities for multiple newspapers in small towns may even make the print media a more difficult environment for multiple voices. Some commentators, perceiving no difference between the two types of media, argue for industry-wide regulation (Barron, 1967), others, perceiving no difference, have argued for laissez-faire policies (Powe, 1987).

Lee Bollinger, however, has proposed an innovative theory that acknowledged that print and broadcast media were similar, but suggested that partial-industry regulation might be advantageous (Bollinger, 1976). Bollinger's article (which for our purposes was suggestively subtitled *Toward a Theory of Partial Regulation of the Mass Media*) proposed the provocative thesis that "the very similarity of the two major branches of the mass media provides a rationale for treating them differently" (Bollinger, 1976: 36). Lucas Powe summarized Bollinger's thesis:

> The separation of broadcasting from print provides the nation with "the best of both worlds": "access in a highly concentrated press and minimum government intervention." Access and balance are important goals, but governmental regulation always brings with it the risk of censorship, either private or public. The fact

that print is unrestrained, however, provides a check on those risks: information not disseminated by broadcasters will be available in newspapers, and the very existence of an unregulated press will provide a competitive spur to offset any tendency of broadcasters to be excessively timid.[41]

Bollinger's apology for the disparate treatment of print and broadcast speech is strikingly similar to the preceding arguments for partial-industry regulation. Bollinger's theory is a form of dominant-firm intervention that leaves the competitive fringe unregulated. The regulated and unregulated portions of an industry can create a system of mutual checks and balances, where each checks the potential abuses of the other and provides a competitive backstop for a society that does not know which mechanism of market organization (public or private) to trust.

Dominant-Firm Regulation of Long Distance Telephone Service

Dominant-firm regulation currently governs the U.S. long distance telephone industry. Under the present regulatory regime, only the dominant firm, AT&T, must submit its rates to the FCC for approval.[42] Fringe long distance firms, such as MCI and Sprint, can legally cut price.[43] As discussed in the preceding section, the maximum price aspects of AT&T regulation can constrain supracompetitive pricing. The minimum price aspects of the rate regulation can restrain price-cutting aimed at excluding its new competitors from the market. Moreover, partial-industry regulation can do this without foregoing the disciplining effects of having a price-cutting fringe.

The presence of price-cutting firms in the long distance telephone industry has had a dramatic effect on the market. It is not surprising, therefore, that 1 month after MCI announced plans for nationwide long distance service in selected cities, AT&T sought permission to lower its long distance rates in many of those cities. The success of dominant-firm (relative to industry-wide) intervention in this industry at least argues for increased scrutiny of its application in other regulatory settings.

Conclusion

In this chapter we have argued that partial-industry regulation may more adequately organize industrial competition than industry-wide regulation or laissez-faire policies. Partial-industry regulation can take a wide variety of forms:

1. Dominant-firm strategies seek to restrain anticompetitive behavior of dominant firms (while leaving fringe firms unregulated)
2. Fringe-firm strategies seek to promote or preserve the existence of fringe firms (but then allow the structurally improved market to set its own price)
3. Oligopoly tournament strategies seek to reward firms for their relative performance (as with patent races and yardstick competition)

These strategies might be used individually or in conjunction to enhance the competitive environment of an industry. An example of combining all three could be where the fringe-firm strategy of bailing out People's Express was conditioned on its sustained price-cutting, this condition resembling a dominant-firm price restraint.

Another such example would be (1) where dominant-firm prices must be submitted for approval, (2) where a fringe firm gets a tax break for research and development expenditure, and (3) where this tax break is targeted to the fringe firm with the best record of developing innovations that open new export markets.

In responsively searching for optimal regulation, here as before it may be useful to employ an pyramid of regulatory intervention (Fig. 5.3). The dimension of regulatory choice varies by the proportion of the industry targeted. For many markets that are reasonably competitive, laissez-faire policies will suffice. For industries where laissez-faire organization fails to produce competitive behavior, the government might move first to fringe-firm interventions. Fringe-firm interventions are minimalist in the sense that they do not demand that an agency mandate particular market behavior (for example, a regulated price). When the structural impact of fringe-firm strategies is insufficient, regulators might explore the use of dominant-firm intervention. Although dominant-firm intervention demands that regulators investigate and proscribe market behavior, it leaves part of the industry unregulated and thereby creates a competitive check if the regulations are anticompetitive or benighted.

As discussed, oligopoly tournaments represent a form of *ex ante* industry-wide regulation. Accordingly, such strategies represent in one sense a higher form of intervention. But as our discussion of yardstick competition indicated, tournaments might allow regulators to set price based on rivals' behavior instead of independent investigation. Finally, industry-wide regulation would remain an option for industries that remain resilient to the milder forms of partial-industry intervention.

Beyond the plausibility of laissez-faire being at the bottom of the pyramid in Figure 5.3 and industry-wide regulation at the top, there is a certain arbitrariness about the ordering of the interventions. This does not matter. Our key idea is that

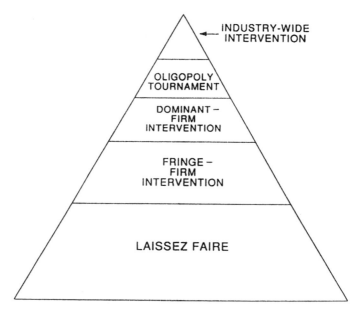

Figure 5.3. A pyramid of partial-industry interventions.

regulation must be responsive to the reality of the industry. In some industries a dominant firm will have good reason to fear entry of an aggressive fringe firm more than it will fear dominant-firm regulation; in other industries dominant-firm regulation will be a greater threat than fringe-firm intervention. The challenge for the regulator is to project a pyramid of escalations in intervention that is responsive to such contingencies. The trick of successful institutional design is to have industry believe that the consequence of monopolistic or oligopolistic abuse at one level of the pyramid will be escalation to a level of intervention that will be more painful in their eyes. It follows that pyramids must be painted to be responsive to just what is most feared in the eyes of the key participants in the particular industry.

Some levels of the pyramid in Figure 5.3, such as fringe-firm bailouts, may appear shocking to libertarian economists. For them, we wish to reassert the paradox of the pyramid: when the state signals a capacity and willingness to escalate to the most meddling of interventions in response to laissez-faire market failure, then laissez-faire efficiency will be nurtured. The range of domains where laissez-faire is left free to deliver competitive prices is expanded. The invisible hand of the market gains strength when the alternative to it is made visible as the boot of the state.[44]

Beyond this, the present chapter has enabled us to see an important limitation of the benign big gun theory as outlined in Chapter 2. Chapter 2 portrays escalatory moves up the pyramid of regulatory strategies as occurring *sequentially*. In this chapter, we have seen how strategies at different levels of the pyramid can be deployed *simultaneously*. At the same time as one firm is subjected to the most intensive intervention, the rest of the industry can enjoy a strategy of laissez-faire. Even moving up a notch in abstraction, we have seen that at the same time a dominant-firm intervention is implemented, fringe-firm and tournament strategies can also be played. Hence, the astute regulator can display to the industry a complexly responsive capacity to escalate simultaneously to different levels of the pyramid to affect differentially firms that are differentially competitive. The degrees of strategic freedom this gives the regulator may indeed motivate the firm to see playing the game at the base of the pyramid as the simplest, best and most proper course.

Our characterization of partial-industry regulation also intersects with our earlier discussion of tripartism and the beneficial uses of PIGs. The unregulated portion of a partially regulated industry can serve much the same function as a PIG. Both provide a competitive check on captured regulators. The unregulated firms, like PIGs, can blow the whistle on anticompetitive or benighted regulation by, for example, cutting price significantly below the regulated price or adopting alternative forms of technology. Fringe-firm strategies especially resemble tripartism because capture is impeded by the proliferation of either PIGs or unregulated fringe firms.

Dominant- and fringe-firm intervention can also impose disparate regulatory *processes* on firms within an industry to investigate, promulgate, and enforce regulatory standards. For example, regulators could mandate that dominant firms undertake special programs of enforced self-regulation (as discussed in Chapter 4)[45] or that third parties be empowered to participate in the regulatory process. An incipient form of this latter strategy has been adopted with British and Australian Telecom having been required by their national governments to consult with Consumer Councils. An approximation to fringe-firm tripartite intervention occurs with nursing home regulation. Consumers have little market power in this industry; they are mostly too frail to vote with their feet by leaving the nursing home. An alternative route to consumer sovereignty is via participation on Residents' (and Relatives') Councils, as discussed in Chapter 3. Historically, the way regulators have sought to achieve this in Australia and the United States has been by encouraging sympathetic fringe firms to innovate (the state of Michigan, for example, paid bonus Medicaid rates to nursing homes that established effective Residents' Councils). The result of this intervention in both countries was first to establish a Residents' Council as an emblem of high standards. Then, large nursing home chains decided that they wanted this reputational emblem worn by the fringe innovators. And now *not* having a Residents' Council is an emblem of low standards.

Our proposal that partial-industry regulation be studied as a plausible regulatory alternative should draw some support from both sides of the deregulation debate. For conservatives that are fighting industry-wide regulation, partial-industry regulation is less interventionist. For social democrats trying to overcome laissez-faire market failure, it offers a public response. Indeed, the political lines of support will often be drawn in terms of the current regulatory benchmark. If the benchmark is industry-wide regulation, conservatives are likely to argue that partial-industry regulation is "market compatible." If the benchmark is deregulation, partial-industry regulation will be anathema. A similar "shoe on a different foot" phenomenon will likely characterize the response from the left.

We suspect, however, that there may be cases where say consumer groups on the left and industry on the right will be willing to contemplate "doing a deal" to avert respectively the worst excesses of industry-wide regulation and the worst abuses of unrestrained laissez-faire market governance. In some situations partial-industry regulation will be superior to either full regulation or laissez faire—and will leave both sides better off than the status quo.

In this article we have argued for the plausibility of beneficial partial-industry regulation—a plausibility that is bolstered not only by a handful of instances in which such regulations are already used but by the targeted use of analogous strategies by monopsonists. A government interested in acting on behalf of its consumer constituents should begin the job by studying and at times emulating the practices of these quintessentially empowered consumers.

Our message is that if these consumers with market power protect themselves by strategies such as second-sourcing, we should consider the use of government power to second-source on behalf of less powerful consumers. At the same time, the behavior of monopsonists can provide a limiting principle on the use of such government power: if it would not be efficient for a private monopsonist to do it, the government should not do it. Even more circumspectly, we have argued that meeting the monopsony standard should be a necessary but not a sufficient condition for partial-industry regulation.

Although we have argued that partial-industry regulation imposes much lower information demands on government regulators than industry-wide price regulation, information demands on any form of economic regulation are so considerable as to caution bureaucratic humility. Hence, we would not counsel even the consideration of partial-industry regulation in markets for this or that widget. Where it should be considered is in markets that are so fundamental to the infrastructure of the economy—energy, transport, telecommunications—as to justify concerted deliberation of the risks and information costs involved in regulatory intervention. Moreover, there are special reasons to contemplate partial-industry regulatory strategies with the media. The economic significance of the media is compounded with a significance for democratic freedoms in averting monopolisation of the markets for ideas and news.

The history of economic thought since Keynes has been a period of emphasis on the need for government intervention to correct market failure followed by a period of emphasis on government failure in its efforts to correct the market failures. Public choice theorists, for example, have argued that government intervention can deliver worse outcomes than failed markets. Today the economic policy debate proceeds as a battle between those on the left who want governments to implement industry policies to correct market failure and those on the right who think that the propensities of governments to incompetence, capture, and empire-building ill equip them for industry regulation.

In the terms of our analysis, this is a debate between those who favor regulatory shotguns and those who advocate no guns at all. We contend that by selecting the right rifle, it is theoretically possible to restrain the private exploitation of monopoly power without substituting the public exploitation of capture and bureaucratic empire-building. Partial-industry regulation uses public regulation as a check on private monopoly power and private competition as a balance against regulators being captured. The state is restrained from acting as a cartel ringmaster when there remain unregulated firms that can provide competition. If the state gets it wrong in controlling the price or facilitating the survival of a single firm, the error may not be fatal because the unregulated firms in the market are not constrained by the error. Conversely, when the market fails, the market failure will not necessarily be fatal because of the attempt at a fail-safe intervention by the state. Admittedly, both market and government will sometimes fail simultaneously. But when that happens, consumers only have to put up with the worst of the two failures. And moreover, each institution (the market and the state) is less likely to fail when it is put under pressure from the other.

The insight of the partial regulation idea is that we do not have to choose between siding with the regulators or the deregulators. Creative policy design can put the strengths of each analysis to work in guarding against the weaknesses of the other.

6

Delegation and Participation in a Responsive Regulatory Order

The deregulation debate stems in large part from dissatisfaction with the efficacy of the contemporary regulatory state. On the right, critics claim that regulation is an inefficient and stifling force that drives them to laissez-faire prescriptions. The political left, however, often views contemporary regulation as ineffectual or coopted. The resulting crisis in confidence leads these camps to strongly divergent proposals for reform. This book is an attempt to transcend the stalemate by proposing alternative modes of regulation that take each criticism seriously.

Our proposals center on regulatory delegation that is underwritten by escalating (and increasingly undelegated) forms of government intervention. We propose that certain regulatory tasks might be delegated to private parties but that this delegation be reinforced by traditional forms of regulatory fiat—if delegation fails. By delegating certain regulatory tasks to private parties, government can more closely harmonize regulatory goals with laissez-faire notions of market efficiency. The delegated aspects of responsive regulation hold out the prospect of a regulatory equilibrium that retains many of the important benefits of competition while the potential for escalating intervention maintains the integrity and pursuit of regulatory goals to correct market failure.

The contingent nature of the escalating forms of government intervention—the enforcement pyramid—is especially important. If the government's ''big gun'' threats are effective, regulatory compliance will arise out of a quasi-laissez-faire governance structure. In equilibrium, the delegated private enforcers will carry out many of the regulatory functions. Under effective responsive regulation, government need not be large as long as it credibly commits to ''largeness'' if delegation fails.

Regulatory tasks might usefully be delegated:

1. To public interest groups
2. To the firms themselves or to their industry associations, and
3. To the firm's competitors

Although we have not discussed the option in this book, others have considered the delegation of regulatory tasks to independent professionals such as financial auditors, insolvency practitioners or environmental engineers (Halliday and Carruthers, 1990; Grabosky, 1991). Empowering these private actors to promote compliance with regulatory standards can provide distinct advantages over the traditional choices of either regulatory fiat or laissez-faire capitalism. In analyzing tripartism (Chapter 3), we argued that empowering PIGs could avoid the perils of corrupt or captured regulation, while preserving the potential for cooperative dispute resolution and collective commitment to public interest objectives. Our analysis of enforced self-regulation (Chapter 4) showed how delegating compliance responsibility to the firms themselves could at times more effectively engender compliance. Finally (in Chapter 5), government can effectively delegate regulatory tasks to a firm's competitors by forcing unregulated firms to compete with regulated ones. In an industry where only some of the firms are regulated, the regulated firms can induce indirectly unregulated firms to "comply" with nonbinding standards by the lash of competition.

The Appropriate Form of Delegation

Delegated strategies will not always be appropriate and the particular form of delegation will necessarily turn on the industry structure and especially on the nature of market failure. Partial-industry regulation, for example, is only likely to be appropriate when the market failure at issue injures someone in contractual privity with the firms in the industry. Competition will force the unregulated firms to match the regulated contractual offers of the regulated firms. Thus, partial-industry regulation might force an entire industry to supply a wider selection of goods, with higher quality or a better price. Alternatively, partial-industry regulation might force an entire industry to treat employees better if unregulated firms are to attract employees from a dominant firm whose working conditions are regulated. Partial-industry regulation will not, however, be effective in engendering industry-wide compliance with regard to pollution standards. Since the people who are injured by industrial pollution are often not (or not exclusively) in privity with the offending corporations, competition will not force the unregulated firms to match the behavior of the regulated firms. Forcing a subset of oil companies not to spill oil will not force unregulated firms to take more care.[1] Indeed, the regulated firms that bear additional costs of regulatory compliance will put less competitive pressure on their unregulated rivals.

In contrast, delegation of regulatory tasks to PIGs will be particularly effective to assure the participation of those who are not in contractual privity with the corporation but are injured by externalities. Thus, it is not surprising that some of the most visible PIGs—such as the Sierra Club, the National Wildlife Federation, and the Australian Conservation Foundation—are concerned with market failures that are external to the corporation's nexus of contracts. To be sure, tripartism also holds out the potential for improving industrial performance regarding workers and consumers (who are contractually related to the firm).

Tripartism will be an especially effective form of regulatory delegation when empowerment of responsible and responsive PIGs is possible. As we have argued, effective tripartism requires protection against oligarchy; it requires that constituent members of PIGs are free to contest effectively for better leadership. As with the market for corporate control, vigorous contestability can discipline PIGs to represent faithfully their constituent interests. But neither PIG activism nor PIG contestability are easily secured. They may require state intervention to nurture the creation of empowered PIGs, but this nurturing needs to be contingent on democratic constitutions that render PIG politicians vulnerable to being deposed by a membership that is open to all relevant communities. Even so, contestability of PIG influence will sometimes be impossible. In regulating the production of chemical weaponry, the inherent secrecy of the industry would obviously impede outsiders from robustly contesting the judgments of a PIG leadership that was given access to regulatory decision making.

The possibility of empowering PIGs in a tripartite regulatory scheme is supported most directly by the continued existence and lobbying efforts of what in many industries are relatively disempowered PIGs. The very fact of empowerment could make it more worthwhile for rational parties to invest in their own protection. At the very least, the pessimistic conclusion of Mancur Olsen (1965)—that diffuse public interests will not find it worthwhile to spend money in promoting their public interest—is continually falsified by the history of community mobilization. Not only do people go to the trouble of voting, but they invest significant resources to protect spotted owls and discourage drunken driving. Collective action problems in the purely economic arena are overcome in part through the transformation of economic wrongs into moral wrongs. Activists devote (what seem from the public choice perspective) irrational amounts of time lobbying to protest the abuses of a powerful corporation because they invest in the issue normative importance that transcends the narrow utilitarian impact on them. It is difficult to organize the collectivity to lobby against artificially inflated prices on canned fruit. Yet empirically, we sometimes find that an organization like Consumers' Union—because of its ideological commitment to empowering consumers with information in mass-circulation magazines such as *Consumer Reports,* and to checking the abuses of organized producer interests—does organize on exactly such issues. If we understand private voluntary groups as no more than "roving bands of self-interested Hobbesian rent-seekers" (Sullivan, 1988), we will never comprehend the republican citizenship that can protect a spotted owl or expose a conspiracy to fix the price of canned fruit.

In the end, the choice of a specific form or forms of delegation is likely to be highly contextual. Enforced self-regulation, for example, is only likely to be beneficial when regulators and/or PIGs are able to verify cheaply the success of delegation. In many instances, our varying forms of delegation are needed to reinforce one another. Tripartism may be able, for example, to spur the effectiveness of partial-industry regulation—because informed PIGs can magnify the competitive forces that would cause the unregulated firms to match the enhanced quality of the regulated producer.

In the previous chapter, we mentioned the rapid spread in recent years of the innovation of nursing homes having a Residents' Council to air resident grievances. Most nursing homes in both the United States and Australia have these. The spread of this innovation can be accounted for by regulators, PIGs, and professional leaders persuading the best nursing homes to introduce the innovation (de facto partial regulation) and as a consequence of the top places doing it, lesser institutions regarding a Residents' Council as a badge of excellence in the industry.

A similar process is under way in the American nursing home industry on the issue of restraints. Compared with other nations, the United States has a shocking level of physical and chemical restraint of residents. Some industry and professional leaders (most notably at the Kendal Corporation), following the example of British restraint-free nursing homes, have established restraint-free nursing homes in America. The National Citizens Coalition for Nursing Home Reform (NCCNHR) has lionized these pioneer restraint-free nursing homes, through, for example, an "untie the elderly" seminar on Capital Hill (United States Congress, 1989). Expressly recognizing the influence on them of the NCCNHR campaigning, the New Hampshire Health Care Association (the leading industry association in that state) has announced that New Hampshire intends to become the first restraint-free state. In August 1990, NCCNHR reported in its newsletter Vermont's senior state nursing home regulator as contesting New Hampshire's leadership, claiming that restraint use had fallen 50 percent in Vermont in a year. A similar decline occurred in Florida during the same period. This then is a harbinger of the possibilities for republican regulation, where market forces for social improvement are unleashed by a combination of professional leadership, PIG activism, and responsiveness by regulators and industry associations.

The Appropriate Enforcement Pyramid

The optimal structuring of responsive regulation will have two components: (1) choosing the appropriate form of delegation, and (2) choosing the right kind of escalating (nondelegated) regulation. Choosing the appropriate form of delegation focuses on what the base of the pyramid should be. The choice of specific forms of contingently escalating responses is the issue in the design of an appropriate enforcement pyramid. Delegation is only credible if it is backed up with various forms of more traditional regulatory fiat. Where delegation is successful, the upper reaches of the escalating interventions will seldom if ever be activated. However, the very success of the regulatory delegation will turn on the existence of a credible government response if the delegation fails to engender compliance and problem-solving.

We have given examples of how enforcement pyramids could be structured. Our analysis is not intended to completely describe all or any possible pyramids. Our hope is that in a fully participatory regime, the regulatory creativity of a republic in designing win–win regulatory solutions would be unleashed, so that all manner of hybrid regulatory forms would appear on the scene. Indeed, it seems to us a mistake to prescribe an optimum enforcement pyramid for any regulatory arena in any country at any point in history. This is because we favor enforcement pyramids that are a product of tripartite negotiation within particular regulatory communities at particular historical moments. We do not see our theory as laying the analytical foundations for the design of optimum enforcement pyramids derived from an abstract theory of regulatory effectiveness. Rather we see our work as providing theoretical foundations for why it is important to think responsively. Furthermore, we hope to have provided some policy heuristics—ideas for regulatory communities to toss around as they debate the shape of their unique regulatory institutions.

Participation

Our analysis has been grounded both normatively and instrumentally in the tradition of civic republicanism. Instrumentally, we aspire to participatory rules that transmit information, aggregate preferences, and shape preferences in aid of controlling abuses inherent in regimes of delegated regulation and/or concentrated power.

While "delegation" connotes a top-down orientation in which power devolves from a concentrated Leviathan, we in fact envision the form of delegation to result from a public discourse that flows both up and down. And in particular, our proposals for tripartite regulatory forms directly cede regulatory power to broader groups of the affected polity.

Normatively, we view the republican emphasis on participatory democracy as a valued end in itself. Yet, even readers with other political preferences might find the delegated strategies of regulation analyzed in this book to be pragmatic ways of dealing with some regulatory failures. Although we would prefer substantive standards to grow out of a rich republican dialogue, appropriate delegated strategies that are reinforced with escalating government intervention instrumentally can beget improved compliance with regulatory standards at lower cost—no matter how one politically decides what the substantive standard should be.

The delegated strategies analyzed in this book find support from disparate forms of analysis. In our treatment of tripartism (just as with tit-for-tat) we found convergence from radically different methodologies: delegation of regulatory authority to PIGs gained plausibility from both the perspectives of republican empowerment and rational choice. Convergence on a common prescription from divergent methodologies as strongly as anything else argues for further empirical analysis of regulatory delegation. Responsive regulation can help transcend the deregulation debate because in equilibrium regulatory tasks are privatized and carried out in a practical sense by markets—but the community does not need to cede judgments about welfare wholly to the unconstrained forces of the market.

NOTES

Chapter 1

1. The quotation is found on New Hampshire License plates, but was originally made by General John Stark in 1808 (*World Almanac and Book of Facts*, 1990: 643).

2. Source *Corporate Crime Reporter*, 18 April, 1988. There is some question that quite a bit of this increase may be due to more consistent reporting of lower-level officials who abused their offices. (But see further *Corporate Crime Reporter*, 16 April, 1990: 20–21.)

3. Abolafia (1985) provides an outstanding case study of how the commodity futures market was constituted by self-regulation under the auspices of the Chicago Board of Trade starting in 1848. Among other things, the market is constituted by a formalization of contract terms, standardization of times and methods of trading, centralization of the release of price information, and emergency power to limit or halt trading in any contract. Abolafia shows how the last of these powers can be necessary to preserve the market—to protect competition, competition sometimes has to be suspended or limited.

4. The Trade Practices Commission is Australia's national antitrust and consumer protection agency.

5. Re: Media Council of Australia (2) (1987) Australian Trade Practices Reporter 40 774.

6. For example, with the deregulation of telecommunications, the TPC has been involved in setting up compliance and training programs within the Overseas Telecommunications Commission to ensure that employees are having their obligations under the Trade Practices Act brought to their attention by training and internal discipline.

7. The Law Council of Australia, for example, has expressed the view that the Commission's initiative in proactively promoting the self-deregulation of the professions oversteps the commission's legal mandate, which the Law Council sees as to enforce reactively the Trade Practices Act (see also Pengilley, 1989).

8. Our lack of sympathy for these individual views stems not from our disbelief in them (that the state can pose a threat to freedom, or that the unregulated market can exploit), but, on the contrary, from our belief that each is true. Because unchecked power in any one of these institutions inevitably leads to abuse, we prefer empowering competing institutions to best ensure social welfare.

9. Examples of the associations we would regard as vital for exercising countervailing power are free trade unions, civil liberties groups, women's organizations, and the consumer and environmental movements.

10. These dangers are, respectively: the majoritarian tyranny of the community order; the poverty, pollution, and other externalities of the market order; the totalitarianism of the state order; and the oligarchy of the associational order.

11. The limits of pluralism are well captured by Silbey's (1984) attack on responsive regulation, which is really an attack on liberal pluralist responsiveness. Just as liberal legalism involves an individuation of grievances that denudes them of their political content, so a regulatory regime will be impotent when it relies solely on complainants spontaneously and individually coming forward to have their disputes with business mediated. Silbey (1984)

discusses a case of such an agency, the Massachusetts Consumer Protection Division. The risks of such an approach are that: (1) preexisting power and information differentials between atomized consumers and collectivized producers make domination of producer perspectives likely; (2) the structural content underlying disaggregated individual grievances is not addressed by structural reforms; and that (3) amoral calculators in the business community can secure good returns by compensating the tiny fraction of individuals who have the persistence to assert their rights, while pocketing the returns from denial of rights to all noncomplainers. As we discuss in Chapter 3, the solution to this impotence of liberal pluralism is political struggle to aggregate the interests of diffuse individuals with common grievances and to empower them organizationally in tripartite regulatory forums. When diffuse interests acquire some power through organization, they sometimes clamor for the addressing of structural problems that victimize their members. They also usually demand that complaint-driven reactive regulation be complemented by proactive regulation. In very few parts of the world, for example, are trade unions satisfied by occupational health and safety regulation that involves no more than mediation of complaints that come across the inspector's desk. The kind of regulatory agencies described by Silbey (1984), which Braithwaite et al. (1987) labeled "conciliators," are not uncommon, but nor are they among the most common types of regulatory agencies (at least not in Australia where we have the most systematic data [Braithwaite et al., 1987; Grabosky and Braithwaite, 1986]). Interestingly, at the time Silbey undertook her research, most nursing home regulatory agencies in the English-speaking world would have fitted a description rather similar to that of the Massachusetts Division of Consumer Protection. But, today, many nursing home advocacy groups are well organized; they monitor regulatory regimes that are more proactive than reactive, and that increasingly begin to grapple with structural sources of poor quality care.

12. This is not meant to imply that the policy ideas we develop would necessarily be congenial to Sunstein. Sunstein (1990) is in fact wary of the associational order, giving much higher prominence to the courts and lesser prominence to tripartite forums as arenas for settling questions of law to implement regulatory laws. In this respect, we are sympathetic to the critiques of Sunstein and Michelman's (1988) court-oriented republicanism by Abrams (1988), Brest (1988), and Sullivan (1988).

Chapter 2

1. "Speak softly and carry a big stick." (Theodore Roosevelt, speech at Minnesota State Fair, 2 September, 1901).

2. This dichotomy has even earlier antecedents: "The law is not made for a righteous man, but for the lawless and disobedient" I. Timothy, i, 9.

3. Indeed, even economic analysts of tax compliance have been driven (in trying to capture reality) to construct models with sizeable proportions of the population who (irrationally) choose not to cheat regardless of the chances of detection (e.g., Graetz and Wilde, 1985).

4. Alternatively, Robert Frank (1988) has argued that rational economic actors may try to precommit to moral behavior to gain greater *future* rewards. If one cannot keep from blushing when telling a lie, then employers concerned about embezzlement may be willing to pay a higher salary (and hire fewer auditors). Pinocchio might end up with a higher (after tax) income after all. But then Pinocchio might end up poor should he decide to become a used car dealer, politician, or lawyer.

5. By deontological reasoning, we mean reasoning that constrains the actor to do what is right regardless of the consequences for her or for others.

6. Brennan and Buchanan (1985: 59) make a similar point, when following Hobbes and Hume they suggest that "an appropriate behavioural model will have to reckon with the fact that the harm inflicted by those who behave 'worse' than the notional average will be proportionately greater than the 'good' done by those who behave 'better' than the average." However, they assume that these worst cases will be actors who are rational and bad (and therefore, can be deterred), while we raise the spectre of the "pathological" actor who is not even rational.

7. A similar tendency of regulators to favor the most charitable interpretation of the regulated is identified as a "rule of optimism" by Dingwall et al. (1983) in their study of welfare workers dealing with the problem of child abuse and neglect.

8. We are indebted to Geoffrey Brennan for this point.

9. Consider, for example, U.S. Secretary of State Dulles' (1957) discussion of this topic (more generally, see Mearsheimer, 1983):

> In the future it may thus be feasible to place less reliance upon deterrence of vast retaliatory power. . . . Thus, in contrast to the 1950 decade, it may be that by the 1960 decade the nations which are around the Sino–Soviet perimeter can possess an effective defense against full-scale conventional attack and thus confront any aggressor with the choice between failing or himself initiating nuclear war against the defending country. Thus the tables may be turned, in the sense that instead of those who are non-aggressive having to rely upon all-out nuclear retaliatory power for their protection, would-be aggressors would be unable to count on a successful conventional aggression, but must themselves weigh the consequences of invoking nuclear war.

10. The possibility of a range of sanctions will induce more deterrence than the expected certain sanction if the regulated are risk averse (Rasmusen, 1989: 53).

11. "The *commitment* process on which all American overseas deterrence depends—and on which all confidence within the alliance depends—is a process of surrendering and destroying options that we might have been expected to find too attractive in an emergency. We not only give them up in exchange for commitments *to* us by our allies; we give them up on our own account to make our intentions clear to potential enemies. In fact, we do it not just to display our intentions but to *adopt* those intentions. If deterrence fails it is usually because someone thought he saw an "option" that the American government had failed to dispose of, a loophole that it hadn't closed against itself" (Schelling, 1966: 44).

12. Kaiser et al. (1985: 291) express this claim in the following terms: "The longest period of peace in European history is inconceivable without the war-preventing effect of nuclear weapons. During the same time span more than a 100 wars have taken place in Asia, Africa, and Latin America, where the numbers of dead, wounded, and refugees run into the millions."

13. Mistaken resort to severe regulatory penalties, however, will not lead to such dire consequences. The regulatory use of big guns would, for example, at most destroy individual firms. We should stress, indeed, that in making this analogy to nuclear weaponry, we are not trying to explain or justify the maintenance of a nuclear arsenal. Nuclear deterrence is used as no more than an heuristic to stimulate our thinking about regulatory deterrence.

14. In the extreme case VTFT becomes the "grim" strategy of infinitely reiterated punishments (Tirole, 1988). Grim strategies in theory generate larger punishments and, accordingly, greater deterrence. However, the "grim" practical consequence of infinitely lived punishments provides a strong rationale for shorter-lived vindictiveness or for "partial restarts."

15. We are not interested in how this is accomplished in terms of the genetic endowments, rational calculation, or human training of the dog. Rather, we are interested in the strategic effects through which it is accomplished.

16. We are indebted to Philip Pettit for discussions that helped clarify this point and the consequential distinction between economizing on virtue and economizing on motivation.

Chapter 3

1. This differs from the role that Scholz (1984a: 216–217) considers for interest groups—influencing regulators as factors in the external environment.

2. Few markets in modern economies could be characterized as "contestable." For example, although some commentators have suggested that American airline routes might be contestable markets (Bailey and Panzar, 1981), several studies have rejected the empirical implications of contestability (Call and Keeler, 1985; Ayres, 1988).

3. This contestability phenomenon can be illustrated by the way the Australian Federation of Consumer Organizations (AFCO) exercised responsibility for putting representatives on Standards Association of Australia (SAA) committees during the period of one author's tenure at AFCO in the early 1980s. AFCO trusted SAA to warn it when a consumer representative might be needed on a particular committee because the standard being written involved product safety or other issues of concern to the consumer movement. The trust was based on a realistic perception that if AFCO was not told up front, it would be likely to find out later and cause political grief for SAA. AFCO accepted invitations onto only about fifty standard setting committees at any time for reasons of resource limitations. For many other committees, however, it would decline representation "for the time being" and ask to receive draft standards and minutes of meetings to "see how things develop." Such a posture signals contestability at the same time as participation is declined. This concept of contestability is at odds with the view that "what really matters under the interest group theory of administrative law is who actually participates, not who theoretically could." (Cheit, 1990: 214).

4. This is the idea of the *qui tam* suit relied upon heavily in England during the fourteenth and fifteenth centuries. *Qui tam* private prosecutions continue to be available under a number of American statutes. The U.S. Congress has recently revitalized the idea under the False Claims Act (31 U.S.C.A.§§3729–3731 [West. Supp 1989]). The result has been a rash of private prosecutions largely of defense contractors suspected of defrauding the Federal Treasury (Caminker, 1989). Crumplar (1975) has supported the *qui tam* idea in the domain of the Securities and Exchange Commission and Fisse and Braithwaite (1983: 250–254) have done so more generally. More broadly, on the concept of the private attorney general, see Garth et al. (1988).

5. The process of selecting the PIGs to be privileged in negotiation raises difficult issues of the legitimacy of exclusion. Cohen and Rogers (forthcoming 1992) have argued that the proper solution to this moral dilemma is to make decisions about which PIGs will be accorded a quasi-public status under conditions in which the views of each citizen are accorded equal weight. This can be accomplished by making the choice of PIGs, the criteria of their selection, and the accountability rules PIGs must satisfy, themselves the object of popular political choice through democratic institutions. That is, political parties would be expected to include in their election platforms policies about which PIGs or PIG peak councils would be privileged as representatives of labor, environmental, and consumer groups, and how and under what conditions they would be privileged. An alternative arises from Schmitter's proposal for a voucher system of state support for PIGs. All citizens would get vouchers, representing a promise of funds to be paid out of consolidated revenue to PIGs. The state could then be considered to privilege the PIGs who received most vouchers. (See Phillipe C. Schmitter (1988) "Corporate democracy: Oxymoronic? Just plain moronic? or a promising way out of the present impasse? Unpublished manuscript).

6. The initiatives of U.S. Environmental Protection Agency Administrator Rucklehaus in

introducing "regnegs," tripartite regulatory negotiation over standards, have been generally well received as an advance over litigious rule making, but have been criticized for their "closed shop" features (Boyer, 1989; Harris and Milkis, 1989: 304–305).

7. Cheit (1990: 77) gives a number of illustrations from the United States standard-setting domain: insurance industry representatives pushing for tough standards that control losses; vendors of safety equipment with obvious interests in safety; respresentatives of gas utilities whose employees must confront the victims of product injuries.

8. A related solution, analyzed in Chapter 5, is partial-industry regulation, where a dominant firm in an industry is regulated, whereas other firms are free to compete as they like. The theory here is that regulation of say the prices of the dominant firm will be designed to protect the public interest from abuse of market power, while price competition from the unregulated sector will threaten any benefits the dominant firm could obtain by capturing the regulator. The unregulated fringe firms, under this theory, would be the best placed PIGs to guard the workings of the industry from the harms of regulatory capture.

9. Scholz's model implicitly assumes that the agency and the regulated firm move simultaneously. Although simultaneity abstracts from real-time enforcement, this assumption is standard in the literature (see Axelrod, 1984). For the single-period game, joint defection would ensue if either the agency or the firm were given the opportunity to move first. In the capture model, one can think of the firm lobbying and choosing to cooperate or defect before the agency moves. Capturing then besides changing the agency's payoff, also gives the firm a first-mover advantage.

10. We imagine in many regulatory contexts that agencies would not have the temptation incentives to deviate from joint cooperation equilibria—because the temptation payoff from defection would not in fact be higher than an agency's joint cooperation payoff. In such situations, the regulatory game would change from Scholz's (and Axelrod's) "two-sided" prisoner's dilemma (Rasmusen, 1989: 94–96). In two-sided prisoner's dilemmas, joint cooperation can be undermined by either side defecting (with the resultant retaliation), whereas in a one-sided prisoner's dilemma only one player has an incentive to defect.

One-sided prisoner's dilemma games will still often lead to joint defection equilibria. For example, even if the agency has no incentive to defect from joint cooperation, there will be joint defection by firm defection. The firm may still have incentives to defect from cooperative agency enforcement and the agency will still have incentives to retaliate against such defection. The implications of capture and the evolution of cooperation on such one-sided games arc explored in footnote 19.

Alternatively, we imagine that the agency's defection path to a joint defection equilibrium might be blocked by a firm's reluctance to retaliate. If the firm's punishment payoff (for complying with the letter, but not the spirit, of the law) is less than its sucker payoff, then the Nash equilibrium will become firm cooperate/agency defect. Scholz's implicit claim is that the firm's punishment payoff will exceed its sucker payoff because agencies will not be able to impose large fines on literal (if not spiritual) compliance. When, however, high punishments deter firm retaliation, firms will retain incentives (as discussed later) to capture regulators to move either to a joint cooperation or to a firm defect/agency cooperate equilibrium.

11. As Scholz (1984a: 189) defines it: "The discount parameter is the product of two factors that jointly determine the current value of future payoffs: the first is the standard discount rate used to determine the current value of future rewards, and the second is the perceived probability in any given round that there will be another round."

12. Scholz attempts to extend Axelrod's result by calculating preconditions of stable cooperation if the firm reevaluates its TFT strategy in midstream after evading (Scholz 1984a: 190). This rather convoluted scenario is homologous to an initial TFT strategy that presumes guilt instead of innocence—by choosing to defect until the opponent cooperates (instead of

cooperating until the opponent defects). The game-theory literature is rich with alternative assumptions that place alternative restrictions on TFT stability (see, e.g., Boyd and Larberbaum, 1987). Scholz's and Axelrod's multiperiod formulation is an example of a supergame or metagame that has become a standard way of modeling multiple-period strategic interactions (see Rotenberg and Saloner 1986).

13. Accordingly, joint cooperation will be stable only for sufficiently small discount or interest rates. This makes intuitive sense. If players discount future payoffs (because they have a high discount rate) the threat of future punishment will not deter the temptation of today's defection.

14. The latter assumption implies that:

$$V_{ff}(i,j) = V_{at}(j,i) \text{ for all } i \text{ or } j.$$

The assumption of symmetric payoffs does not affect our results. If the agency and firms have asymmetric payoffs so that, for example, $T_f \neq T_a$, then the captured agency's net temptation to defect, Δ_{tempt}, will be:

$$\Delta_{tempt} = \alpha(S_f - R_f) + (1 - \alpha)(T_a - R_a),$$

which equals the change in the captured agency's payoff for defecting from a joint cooperation equilibrium. Similarly, the captured agency's net incentive to retaliate against firm defection, Δ_{retal}, will be:

$$\Delta_{retal} = \alpha(P_f - T_f) + (1 - \alpha)(P_a - S_a),$$

which equals the change in the captured agency's payoff for retaliating against a firm defect/agency cooperate equilibrium. Under this more general formulation, increasing degrees of capture (increasing α) reduces both the agency's temptation to defect from joint cooperation and the agency's incentive to retaliate against a defecting firm (both Δ_{tempt} and Δ_{retal} decrease). This parallels in all relevant respects the effects of capture in the symmetric model (increasing S' and decreasing T').

15. If repeated joint cooperation is supportable, then an infinite number of less profitable equilibria will also be stable (for example, the symmetric strategies of defecting in the first period and playing TFT thereafter would be stable). This result is ensured by the venerable Folk theorem of game theory (so named because no one can remember who should get credit for it) (Rasmusen, 1989). We restrict our attention to repeated joint cooperation equilibria on the plausible assumption that the players will choose the supportable equilibrium with the highest payoff.

16. As stated earlier, efforts to capture also reduce the agency's temptation payoff. The temptation effect may induce a separate form of capture, which we discuss later.

17. This net improvement would satisfy the Kaldor–Hicks welfare standard. One equilibrium is Kaldor–Hicks superior to another if those receiving more (the "winners") could potentially compensate those receiving less (the "losers"), so that after this hypothetical compensation no one would be worse off and at least one person would be better off (Posner, 1986).

18. At times, the enhanced firm payoffs from zero-sum capture will represent a bare redistribution of wealth from other members of the society, as, for example, when regulation increases a corporation's sales (and profits) by displacing or excluding one of its competitors. Yet this redistribution of profits is likely to be accompanied by production inefficiencies. Moreover, the process of lobbying to change the regulator's payoffs will often entail an inefficient consumption of real resources.

19. Pareto-efficient capture may also facilitate the multiperiod evolution of cooperation. Axelrod demonstrated that TFT strategies could only support a joint cooperation equilibrium if the following inequalities were met:

$$\delta > (T - R)/(T - P)$$
$$\delta > (T - R)/(R - S)$$

Capture can also affect the evolution of cooperation by affecting these inequalities. By decreasing the temptation payoff ($T' < T$) and increasing the sucker payoff ($S' > S$), capture may change the range of δ for which joint cooperation is stable. These inequalities imply critical lower-bound values of δ below which cooperation cannot evolve. As before, reducing the temptation payoff facilitates cooperation, and increasing the sucker payoff restricts the opportunities for cooperation. In the multiperiod setting, decreasing the temptation loosens the first inequality so that at the margin certain discount rates that would not support a joint cooperation equilibrium without capture may be sufficiently small once capture has reduced the temptation payoff. Analogously, the second inequality is loosened by keeping captured S low by social disapproval of regulators who succumb to zero-sum capture. Thus, we can see a second way that social disapproval reductions to T and S can foster joint cooperation: by extending the range of discount rates where joint cooperation will remain stable in multiperiod games.

Axelrod's dual prerequisites for the evolution of cooperation correspond to the "two-sided" nature of the traditional prisoner's dilemma. If the regulatory game, however, more closely represents the "single-sided" prisoner's dilemma game (discussed in footnote 10), then the regulatory players will only need to overcome the first inequality. Accordingly, the evolution of cooperation will be easier to establish in single-sided prisoner's dilemma games because the players need to deter only one path to joint defection (firm defection/agency retaliation). Efficient capture will also be much easier to obtain in single-period games. As long as a firm can gain a first-mover advantage by capture (see footnote 9), then it can choose the higher payoffs of joint cooperation without fear of agency defection.

20. Although reducing the agency's temptation payoff ($T' < R$) can deter agency defection from joint cooperation, joint cooperation will only be an equilibrium if the firm itself is also deterred from defection. This will often be the case because, although the agency may be deterred from defection, it will still retaliate if the firm defects. In these situations, the firm is left only with the choice of joint cooperation or joint defection—and clearly prefers the former. In other instances, the process of capture will destroy both the agency's incentive to either defect ($T' < R$) or retaliate ($S' > P$). In these circumstances capture will not facilitate joint cooperation as the firm will simply choose to defect. The circumstances under which this will occur are discussed in Figure 3.3.

21. See our discussion of discount rates in footnotes 11 and 19.

22. It is interesting that we usually do not think about the possibility of reverse capture—that of the agency capturing the firm to increase the agency's payoffs. Analytically both firms and agencies are controlled by managers who are agents for unconcentrated and rationally ignorant principals. Reverse capture would take three analogous forms—for example, reverse zero-sum capture would lead to a firm cooperate/agency defect equilibrium—in which the agency defects to strict rule enforcement without retaliation from the firm. This conspicuously unanalyzed possibility of reverse capture is especially surprising since in other contexts, such as takeovers, policy makers can easily conceive of managers taking actions that deviate from shareholders' interests. Possibly the moral exhortations of agencies to corporate managers is a subtle way of convincing the board that conversely what is good for America is good for General Motors.

23. See, for example, more than thirty studies cited by Hawkins (1984: 3). A third of the ninety-six Australian regulatory agencies studied by Grabosky and Braithwaite (1986) had not instituted a prosecution in 3 years. Even for the most punitive of regulatory agencies, the overwhelming majority of detected violations are not dealt with by punishment. Moreover, the attitudinal evidence of an ideological predisposition to cooperation is overwhelming (Grabosky and Braithwaite, 1986: 192–193).

24. The issue is whether agencies' current attitude against defecting to the temptation payoff is the by-product of firm lobbying or not.

25. The issue here is whether the uncaptured equilibrium would be one of joint coopera-tion (as implied by inefficient capture) or joint defection (as implied by zero-sum capture).

26. On the other hand, it must be said that because $T - R$ is greater than $T - P$, the incentives for this first form of capture, inefficient capture, are less than the incentives for zero-sum capture. However, the base of cases of joint defection from which the stronger incentives for zero-sum capture can operate is so small that it is implausible that zero-sum capture could ever become more widespread than inefficient capture.

27. Joel Rogers has argued that in a world where people have some basic democratic rights but little other power, they may use those rights in destructive ways. The conservative response to this destructiveness is to urge reductions in the political resources of less powerful groups. Rogers contends, in contrast, that increasing their political resources is at least as plausible a strategy for dealing with these problems. Instead of seeing adversarial PIG zealotry that reduces social product as a sign of their "excessive" strength, Rogers sees it as "a sign of weakness, testimony to the lack of alternative sanctions available to those who would curb the arbitrary exercise of power (people stand on their rights because they have nothing else to stand on)" (Rogers, 1989: 3). When organizations have a solid political foundation with which to extract long-term benefits, they are more likely to show the restraint that eschews short-term punch and grab strategies that undermine the prospects for long-term cooperative benefits. Weak PIGs, in contrast, "have every incentive to free-ride on their future interests, since they may not have a future" (Rogers, 1990: 5).

28. Four years of observation by one of the authors of the ACTU leadership dealing with the leadership of the business community and the Australian government around the table of the Economic Planning Advisory Council leaves little doubt about this, at least for the present ACTU leadership.

29. Bendor (1987) presents a lucid account of how incomplete information (about whether defection has occurred) can undermine TFT strategies and the evolution of cooperation in a two-person prisoner's dilemma.

30. This way of describing litigation regularly recurs in Braithwaite's field notes of interviews with regulators.

31. However, litigation to change the law may be more cost effective for the PIG than either front-end or back-end participation in enforcing the law as it exists. Nevertheless, we then need to go on to consider whether front-end tripartite participation in *writing* the law is more cost effective for the PIG than waiting for back-end litigation to change the law.

32. Forty-two percent of 358 directors of nursing of Australian nursing homes agreed with the statement: "My proprietor has the attitude that the government's standards and regulations must be met no matter what the costs" (Braithwaite et al., 1990).

33. Business executives are frequently captured by regulators for the same reason. To avoid the angst of a confrontation, they may prefer to comply with what they perceive as an unreasonable regulatory demand.

34. An alternative model here is that regulatory laws are usually set at a standard that everyone, including regulators, understands is too high. Agencies seek a level below the standard in the law that the state accepts as normally appropriate. Then the model unfolds in the same way: the industry bargains for less than this, the PIG for more, so that with the PIG playing the game, the result is more likely near the standard the state accepts as appropriate. Similarly, in those situations where the law has lagged behind technological change and the state seeks a standard higher than that embodied in the law, PIG participation will bring the final result closer to that preferred state standard.

35. Baar (1989: 1) says responsiveness "requires a sensitivity to the priorities of others

and to the trade-offs others are prepared and unprepared to accept.'' In commenting on this chapter Baar said: ''I think responsiveness is better because trust assumes that one defines the other as a good apple and I don't think that's necessary.'' Perhaps she is right. We suspect, however, that effective regulation requires that the players are able to view each other as good apples at least in the sense of expecting that they will generally honor their undertakings.

36. Menkel-Meadow (1984: 785) found that most of a random sample of 240 cases taken from federal and state reporters were not zero-sum. Unsophisticated commentators on regulation assume that it is a zero-sum game. Actually, even at the most unusually adversarial phase in any regulatory process—a criminal prosecution—the game is typically non–zero-sum. Mann's (1985) book on the work of white collar defendants' attorneys shows this clearly. When prosecutors and white collar defense attorney trust each other, they are able to strike a variety of types of mutually beneficial deals. The defendant can win immunity by testifying against other participants in the industry. The two can strike a plea agreement that means cost-effective enforcement for the prosecutor (leaving more resources to crack other cases) and lower sanctions for the defendant. Most dramatically, it can be in the interests of both parties for the defendant's attorney to adopt the ''junior prosecutor role'' (Mann, 1985: 84–85), voluntarily collecting for the government investigator the evidence needed to make a case against her client. In the regulatory enforcement arena, where information costs are so high, even in the supposedly paradigm case of adversarial win–lose exchange—the criminal process—joint cooperation payoffs are routinely constituted.

37. Alternatively, we can read the literature on the difficulties that confront business in some Third World countries in enforcing impersonal contractual obligations (Hart, 1988) less as a failure of trust than as a failure of law, a failure of reliance on anything but a limited network of trust. Whatever of these competing readings, they do not trouble our fundamental theoretical position on the mutually constituting quality of the relationship between trust and power. Elsewhere, it has been argued that the power of law constitutes trust (Braithwaite, 1989b). And, of course, if citizens did not trust their lawyers and judges, the law would have no power.

38. More precisely, we should say that trust is not a resource that is depleted if it is used in a trustworthy way; it will most certainly be depleted if it is exploited in an untrustworthy way.

39. This policy choice is similar to the ''Battle-of-the-Sexes'' game, a conflict between a man who wants to go to the ballet and a woman who wants to go the a prize fight. While selfish, they are deeply in love and also prefer to be together (Rasmusen, 1989: 34).

The payoffs for such a conflict could be rewritten in terms of the policy conflict:

PIG

	AB	WX
CD	(2,1)	(−5,−5)
YZ	(−1,−1)	(1,2)

FIRM

Payoffs to (PIG, FIRM)

The compromise policy choice of ABYZ corresponds to the negative "off-diagonal" payoffs of uncoordinated attendance.

Unlike the prisoner's dilemma, there is no dominant equilibrium for the Battle of the Sexes game. Instead, our argument is that tripartism could improve prospects that a coordinated equilibrium will be reached. Tripartism, indeed, might be able to increase the possibility that the PIG's preference is followed. The multiplicity of PIGs might in some contexts constitute a type of precommittment for their preferred strategy. In the Battle of the Sexes, if one party can precommit to picking a certain strategy, the other player will predictably acquiesce. We will not press this line too far, however, because there is a third player involved—the state that will ultimately decide whether to reject ABYZ.

40. In *Edwards* v. *National Coal Board,* "reasonably practicable" was judicially defined by Asquith L.J. as follows:

> 'Reasonably practicable' is a narrower term than 'physically possible,' and seems to me to imply that a computation must be made by the owner in which the quantum of risk is placed on one scale and the sacrifice involved in the measures necessary for averting the risk (whether in money, time or trouble) is placed in the other, and that, if it be shown that there is a gross disproportion between them—the risk being insignificant in relation to the sacrifice—the defendants discharge the onus on them. Moreover this computation falls to be made by the owner at a point of time anterior to the accident. ([1949] 1 K.B. 704; [1949] 1 All E.R. 743 at 747).

41. Of course, this is also consistent with the psychological literature showing that face-to-face contact increases empathy (Latané and Darley, 1970). In one of Milgram's (1974: 34) experiments, for example, subjects were less likely to administer what they understood to be lethal electric shocks when they could see the victim suffer.

42. The resolution to this problem can only be of an institutionally contingent form. We do not see any easy general theoretical resolution. However, one of the authors has certainly participated in Australian regulatory cultures where the problem is solved fairly well by an appropriate mix of opportunities for key players to meet both collectively and in pairs. Indeed, many university departments solve this problem pretty well: there are some issues where constructive communication will best be advanced at a full faculty meeting, others where it is better for smaller working groups to meet, others where it is best for the chairperson to communicate individually with all faculty members. As long as the agreements that are the product of a sequence of private discussions are ultimately tabled in a way that gives all parties an opportunity for open communication about them, tripartite process can be constructively advanced by confidential caucusing (see Olson, 1981, for general information).

43. Scholars of a rational choice bent sometimes persist in a disinclination to accept that trust is a precondition for their explanations based on economic interests. Speaking of economic reform, Elster and Moene (1988) say this of trust:

> Indeed, some amount of trust must be present in any complex economic system, and it is far from inconceivable that systems with a higher level of general trust could come about. It would be risky, however, to make higher levels of trust into a cornerstone of economic reform. We may hope that trust will come about as the by-product of a good economic system (and thus make the system even better), but one would be putting the cart before the horse were one to bank on trust, solidarity and altruism as the preconditions for reform.

But what reform could there be of the securities market, arguably the central institution of a capitalist economy, for which trust was not a precondition? How could a securities market, or its replacement, work efficiently when distrust meant that trades could not be agreed, could not affect prices, until contracts were signed by vendor and purchaser? The very etymology of "security" is grounded in the discourse of trust and confidence; in the Oxford dictionary, a security is a "pledge for the fulfilment of undertaking." Trust is constitutive of a good economic system and a good economic system is constitutive of trust. Sound institutional design is impossible without taking both economic incentives and trust seriously as preconditions for success.

44. Handler (1988, 1990) has eloquently taken up the relevance of the work of these and other postmodern and communitarian scholars to practical programs of reform to strive toward dialogic communities. For a related, although different approach to reform, see Sciulli's (1988) synthesis of Habermas on communicative action and Lon Fuller's preceduralism.

45. Figures supplied by the Health Care Financing Administration from inspections of all nursing homes with Medicare or Medicaid residents in the United States (see also United States Congress, 1989).

46. Together with Valerie Braithwaite, Diane Gibson, David Ermann, and Toni Makkai.

Chapter 4

1. In Chapter 2, however, we did explore the possibility of superpunishments—"stick and carrot" strategies to induce the firm's cooperation in its own sanctioning.

2. Public goods often exhibit characteristics of "nonexclusivity" in consumption, meaning that the enjoyment of the good by one person does not preclude its enjoyment by another (Scherer, 1980).

3. Our analysis in Chapters 3 and 5 follow similar themes. In Chapter 3, the government delegated (or "externalized") some of its regulatory functions to public interest groups. In Chapter 5, we investigate how unregulated competitors of regulated firms could substitute for regulatory supervision.

4. Because enforced self-regulation effectively entails "off budget" government expenditures, a more rational fiscal policy might develop a "tax expenditure budget" (which attempts to estimate how much government spends through tax subsidies). A "self-regulation expenditure budget" would estimate how much government spends by having private industry do its work.

5. This example raises the spectre that self-regulation can be improperly used to end-run procedural limitations on state power. In the United States, for example, constitutional proscription of police entrapment might lead the state to recruit private agents to circumvent certain enforcement constraints. In some instances, however, market forces or the political power of unions may control arbitrary abuse of industry self-regulatory power. Employers who capriciously entrap and discipline their employees may have more difficulty recruiting and retaining quality employees. In sum there may be situations where market checks of private abuse sufficiently substitute for constitutional checks of public abuse to justify private self-regulatory methods that would be unacceptable if imposed by the government.

Civil rights restrictions on how public agencies enforce regulatory standards in a real sense increase the cost of public enforcement. Although, in general we argue that self-enforcement is appropriate when it is cheaper than public enforcement, we stress that there may be instances in which the cost savings of self-enforcement comes with the cheapening of civil rights protections that should be avoided. For this reason, laws are needed to guarantee those rights that are peculiarly vulnerable to private justice systems (such as rights to protection from unreasonable electronic surveillance).

6. One pharmaceutical quality control director showed Braithwaite that his firm had failed a batch of drugs for being slightly overstrength, even though the FDA would have been unlikely to detect the variation. The director said that the batch was sacrificed to stress to employees the importance of unswerving adherence to specifications.

7. Other weaker reporting options exist. The compliance group could be statutorily

mandated to report instances of management overruling to the board of directors or to an audit committee of outside directors.

8. We would stress that there are severe constitutional and moral objections in allowing private firms "to contract" for punishments of imprisonment or corporal punishment. In the United States, however, recent Supreme Court cases have intimated that the outer bounds of criminal insider trading actions may be determined by the nature of the private employment contracts (*Basic* v. *Levinson*, 1988). Judge Easterbrook has argued from the bench that criminal insider trading provisions are defaults capable of private contractual mutation (*Duff* v. *Phelps*, 1983). See also our discussion *infra*, pp. 108–109.

9. Other possible approaches exist. For example, the preamble to the standards might draw attention to the variable performance of different companies to give broad guidance. Westmoreland Coal was found by the President's Commission on Coal to have an injury rate of twenty-one lost workday cases per 200,000 hours in its twenty-nine underground mines. In contrast, United States Steel maintained an injury rate of three in its twenty-eight underground mines. Five of the largest twenty coal producers maintained rates lower than six lost workday injuries per 200,000 work hours (President's Commission on Coal, 1980: 42). Hence, the legislation could point to the safety performance of these five companies as a more appropriate yardstick. The regulatory agency would be instructed to satisfy itself that company rules, and the enforcement of them, were sufficiently stringent to cause it to expect an average attainment of fewer than six lost workday injuries per 200,000 work-hours.

10. Executives of the companies that are leaders in quality control and toxicological methodology in the pharmaceutical industry have complained to Braithwaite that the FDA's Good Manufacturing Practices and Good Laboratory Practices regulations at times forced them to adopt what they considered second-best control techniques.

11. For an account of how the national imposition of a particular pollution abatement technology resulted in some companies switching to high sulfur coal so that their aggregate output of pollution actually increased, see Ackerman and Hassler (1981).

12. See Fisse (1978), for a discussion of various reasons why internal rule making presents advantages in simplicity and enforceability over external rule making. See also Amsterdam (1974), in which Prof. Amsterdam argues that rules of conduct written by police departments themselves are likely to be more refined than rules conferred externally because they are drawn up and modified by people in touch with the day-to-day realities of implementation.

13. For example, legislation rushed through to close one loophole might be used by sharp corporate attorneys to justify a principle that enables them to open a new loophole elsewhere.

14. As the web of law becomes more complex, the more possible it is for lawyers to use the doctrines implicit in one part of the law as a justification of actions that evade other parts of the same body of law (Sutton and Wild, 1978; Braithwaite, 1980).

15. See 1981 Austl. Stat. R., §§ 212–14, 312 (as amended Sept. 4, 1981) (regulations under the Air Navigation Act, 1920: 74) 1 Acts. Austl. P. 143.

16. 30 U.S.C. §§ 801–23, 824–902, 921–924, 925–34, 936–60 (Supp. I 1977, Supp. II 1978, and Supp. III (1979) (as amended).

17. U.S. Mine Safety and Health Act of 1977, Pub. L. No. 95–164, § 101(c) 91 Stat. 1294 (codified at 30 U.S.C. § 811(c) (Supp. I 1977)).

18. Information from interviews conducted by the author with mine safety officials in 1981 and 1982.

19. 30 C.F.R. §§ 70.1–90 301 (1981).

20. 30 C.F.R. § 75.300–.330–1 (1981).

21. 30 C.F.R. § 75.400–.404 (1981).

22. 30 C.F.R. § 75.200–.205 (1981).

23. U.S. Dept. of Labor, Mine Safety and Health Administration, Annual Report and Achievements (pt. 1) 27 (1978).

24. The categories of roof support plans are: full roof bolting, 30 C.F.R. § 75.200–07; conventional roof control, 30 C.F.R. § 75.200–08; combination roof control, 30 C.F.R. § 75.200–09; spot roof bolting, 30 C.F.R. § 75.200–11; special roof control, 30 C.F.R. § 75.200–12; and temporary support, 30 C.F.R. § 75.200–13.

25. Roof control plans that do not conform to these criteria may be approved providing the operator can satisfy the District Manager that the resultant roof conditions will provide no less than the same measure of protection to the miners. 30 C.F.R. § 75.200–06 (1981).

26. *United States* v. *Wyatt,* CR 81–00029 (W.D. Va. plea entered April 29, 1981); *United States* v. *Vanhoose Coal Co. Inc. No. 1 Mine,* CR 81–4 (E.D. Ky, plea entered April 15, 1981); *United States* v. *United Castle Coal Co. No. 1 Mine,* CR 80–00093 (W.D. Va. plea entered April 9, 1981); *United States* v. *J & P. Coal Co.,* CR 80–0060 (W.D. Va. plea entered Sept. 8, 1980).

27. *United States* v. *Vanhoose Coal Co. No. 1 Mine,* No. 81–4 (E.D. Ky. plea entered April 15, 1981).

28. Codified in scattered sections of 33 U.S.C. (1976).

29. 40 C.F.R. § 114.1 (1981).

30. 40 C.F.R. § 112.1–07 (1981).

31. 40 C.F.R. § 112.3(d) (1981). The criteria can be found in 40 C.F.R. § 112.7 (1981).

32. *United States* v. *Chrysler Corp.,* 591 F.2d 958 (D.C. Cir. 1979).

33. See 43 Fed. Reg. 60,013 (1978).

34. 21 C.F.R. § 58.185–.195 (1981).

35. 21 C.F.R. § 58.120–.130 (1981).

36. 21 C.F.R. § 58.35 (1981).

37. 21 C.F.R. § 58.35 (b)(4) (1981).

38. See 43 Fed. Reg. 59,998 (1978).

39. Three hours before the beginning of any shift, and before any miner enters a working area of the mine, the pre-shift examiner checks the atmosphere, roof supports, conveyors and travelways, and other actual or potential safety hazards. If a hazardous condition is discovered, the examiner, a miner himself, posts a ''danger'' sign, reports the hazards to a mine official, and notes the condition in a book kept at the site for inspection. 30 C.F.R § 75.303 (1981).

40. 15 U.S.C. §§ 2601–2629 (1976 and Supp. IV 1980). The inclusion of this example was suggested by Stone (1980:144).

41. 15 U.S.C. § 2603(a) (1976).

42. 15 U.S.C. § 2605(a)(4) (1976).

43. 15 U.S.C. § 2605(b)(1) (1976).

44. 15 U.S.C. § 2605(b)(2)(A) (1976).

45. What one might expect to find from such empirical work is a fairly routine, perfunctory approval of standard rules for common flight paths (e.g., New York–London) and one hopes, very painstaking scrutiny of out-of-the-ordinary routes (e.g., Auckland–Antarctica). It was the failure of this special regulatory scrutiny that was partially responsible for the Mt. Erebus DC-10 crash in Antarctica (see Fisse and Braithwaite, 1983). The problem was that the regulatory costs being shouldered were less than they should have been.

46. It could be suggested that the relatively junior civil servants, to whom power over approving rules would have to be decentralized, would be less formidable adversaries to corporate power than the senior bureaucrats who currently control rule making. Our experience of regulatory agencies, however, is that employees who are antibusiness firebrands tend to remain in junior positions, whereas bureaucrats who have a ''cooperative relationship'' with industry make it to the top. In support of this view, note many of the findings of the Dorsen

investigation into allegations of victimization of adversarial employees of the Food and Drug Administration. See U.S. Dept. of Health, Education & Welfare, Review Panel on New Drug Regulation, Final Report 17 (1977).

47. 33 U.S.C. § 1319(c)(1) (Supp. I 1977).

48. The democratic ideal is strengthened not only by holding the unelected government of corporations accountable to the elected government of the state, but also by grassroots participatory possibilities under enforced self-regulation. Already, American regulatory agencies that have opted to give public recognition to privately written rules have provided for public comment on such recognition. For example, the Mine Safety and Health Administration gives notice to miners and their representatives of agreements it has made with mining companies on ventilation and roofing plans, and of petitions for modifications to the regulations for particular mines.

49. Brent Fisse and John Braithwaite are currently working on this problem for a future book likely to be entitled, *Passing the Buck: Criminal Responsibility in a Corporate Society.*

50. It would also be wrong to assume that business has no control over existing governmental rule making. Joseph Stetler, former president of the American Pharmaceutical Manufacturing Association, once commented, ''As I look back over three or four years, we have commented on 60 different proposed regulations. At least a third were never published in final form. And every one, without exception, picked up a significant part of our suggestions'' (Hughes and Brewin, 1979). An official of the Association of the British Pharmaceutical Manufacturing Industry told Braithwaite that many British government regulations were written in its offices.

51. The leading example of worker participation in OSHA self-inspection programs is the so-called Bechtel plan. At Bechtel Group Inc.'s nuclear power plant at San Onofre, California, OSHA blessing has been given to monthly labor–management safety inspections as an alternative to government inspections. Under this plan, management must explain its reasons for not adopting the recommendations of the inspection team. See Lublin, ''OSHA Head Wants to Cut Regulation, Using Labor-Management Inspections,'' *Wall St. J.,* Mar. 26, 1981, at 8, col. 4.

52. The power is one of three suggested by Etzioni. In addition to identitive power, rewarding with prestige, esteem, and acceptance (pointing out ''that's not the sort of thing an IBMer does''), there are coercive power, the use of physical means for control purposes (e.g., torture, imprisonment, removal from the organization); and utilitarian power, the use of material means for control purposes (e.g., promotion, payment of bonuses, allocating capital for expansion) (Etzioni, 1965: 650–651).

53. Exxon has exemplary policies in this regard. When an individual reports a rule violation up the line, the executive to whom the report is made has an obligation to report back to the person who made the report what action has been taken. If the latter does not receive this feedback, she knows that somewhere the bad news has been blocked. She then has an obligation to report the breakdown directly to the audit committee of the board. This builds in a strong incentive against orchestrated communication blockages to cover up a violation (see Fisse and Braithwaite, 1983).

54. This is particularly true with larger organizations. The larger the organization, the greater the devolution of decision-making power. This was demonstrated empirically by Mileti et al. (1979).

Chapter 5

1. Most broadly, partial-industry regulation would encompass regulatory regimes that disparately affect industry members. Thus, in the United States the piecework regulation of

competitors in the securities markets (equivalent securities face different regulation from the Securities and Exchange Commission and the Commodity Futures Trading Commission) and the regulation of dairy markets set different minimum prices for milk producers in different states. Different levels of judicial or agency scrutiny (including disparate efforts to detect noncompliance) would create a partial-industry regulatory dynamic in that some firms would effectively be less regulated.

Partial industry regulation may be especially important in international markets; the idea intersects with the current "industrial policy" debate. In international markets, where many foreign competitors are beyond the reach of an individual government's fiat, partial industry regulation may in effect be the only regulatory alternative. As discussed below, assuring second sources of supply may be especially important. But in the international context individual states are likely to prefer expanding local production over the improvement of global social welfare.

2. For example, when the United States Civil Aeronautics Board set airline fares, by law, airlines could not compete over price and were left to compete on such nonprice dimensions as nonstop flights and on-time performance to woo customers (Posner, 1986: 257).

3. For example, in Chapter 6, we discuss more explicitly situations in which partial-industry regulation may not be appropriate. In particular, when market failure injures people that are not in privity with the industry (as with pollution) then competition between regulated and unregulated firms will not engender general industry compliance.

4. Spence (1975) has shown that when firms incur fixed costs to produce different types of products competitors will be led to produce the type (or quality) that is valued by the marginal consumer (the consumer who is almost indifferent about buying) and not the average consumer. Social welfare can be sacrificed as the majority of consumers are denied their preferred product type. Partial-industry regulation could, at least theoretically, overcome this market failure by redefining the margin over which unregulated firms compete. By forcing a subset of firms to produce the quality or type preferred by the average consumer, partial-industry regulation could force unregulated producers to produce a more highly valued product. In practice, however, regulators will face important informational hurdles to determine the desires of the average consumer.

5. Even in those markets with a dominant firm and smaller fringe competitors, there are times at which the competitive fringe more actively chooses variables such as price and quantity. The U.S. telephone market might exemplify this situation.

6. These classifications do not, of course, reflect the prevailing organization of all markets. Some markets that consist of numerous small competitors comport more with our notions of perfect competition. Moreover, even highly concentrated industries may be constrained to competitive behavior if the barriers to entry are sufficiently low. As discussed in Chapter 3, when potential competition is great, even a concentrated market may mimic the competitive price because of contestability (Baumol et al. 1988). The analysis of this chapter is accordingly restricted to those markets where sufficient barriers to entry and sufficient concentration of production exist so that anticompetitive outcomes pose a regulatory concern.

7. Fringe firms in such situations may have incentives to follow a dominant firm's price increase. David Haddock, for example, has shown how base-point pricing can be described in terms of such dominant–fringe firm interaction. Under a base-point pricing scheme, the price that customers pay for a good includes a transportation price "as if" the good were shipped from a certain basing point. For example, under the "Pittsburgh-plus" steel system, the price of steel for Chicago purchasers was calculated as if the steel had been shipped from Pittsburgh even when it was shipped from nearby Gary, Indiana. Haddock demonstrates that because Pittsburgh manufacters were dominant suppliers, steel firms in Gary had natural incentives to match Pittsburgh's delivered price (Haddock, 1982).

8. See *Matsushita Electric Industrial Co.* v. *Zenith Radio Corp.*, 75 U.S. 574 (1986); Easterbrook (1984:26).

9. See *infra* discussion of AT&T.

10. This result depends on the ability of the more competitive portion to supply the industry demand at the more competitive price and is limited if there are capacity constraints. Also, as argued previously, the regulators may (reasonably) place minimum price regulations on dominant firms that would constrain their ability to match a lower fringe price.

11. In algebraic terms, if the regulators set a price P_r and the unregulated fringe producers set a price of P_f, then the preference of consumers to buy the cheapest product will tend to produce a market price, P_m: $P_m = \min(P_r, P_f)$. The failure of regulated and unregulated firms is represented by the deviations of their prices above the competitive level, P_c. Heuristically, the potential for public and private market failure could be modeled by having P_r and P_f as randomly distributed variables. In such a crude model, the superiority of dominant-firm regulation is captured in the notion that the expected price under the mixed (partial-industry regulation) regime would be lower than the expected price under either industry-wide or laissez-faire regimes.

12. Fringe-firm interventions might fit into a larger system of "structural" interventions. Structural theories of collusion include a long list of structural variables that might influence the ability of industries to fulfill the prerequisites of successful cartelization (Ayres, 1987). Further research might be directed at explaining other ways that government could structurally intervene to improve the competitive performance of industry.

13. See *infra* our discussion of the Chrysler bailout.

14. Similarly, purchases by the U.S. government at one point accounted for one half of American Motors' sales. It might be possible to justify the minority (and small business) set aside programs on a similar ground (Days, 1987). Many of these measures, however, derive more from government interests in redressing past discrimination than efforts to restrain supracompetitive pricing.

15. An important prerequisite for this result is the existence of some barriers to entry. As discussed earlier, in perfectly contestable markets even a small number of producers may be constrained to behave competitively by the ever-present threat of potential competition.

16. *Barry Wright Corp.* v. *IIT Grinnell Corp.* 724 F.2d.227 (1st Cir. 1983).

17. Judge Stephen Breyer rejected, however, the arguments of the failed entrant that this behavior constituted either actionable predation or acts of monopolization.

18. Downstream consumers are actuated by consumer–welfare and not social–welfare concerns. It is possible, therefore, that second sourcing may inefficiently reduce the upstream price. An upstream monopolist with a lower cost, but higher monopoly mark-up, may be more efficient than a competitive duopoly with higher unit costs. This is another example of the Williamson trade-off (Williamson, 1990). Consumers, however, will prefer lower prices (even if there are inefficiently higher costs).

19. The concepts of second sourcing and fringe-firm intervention can be applied to downstream production as well. Private manufacturers often are willing to subsidize downstream retailers to promote downstream intrabrand competition and reduce the monopsony power of individual retail buyers. Similarly, one could imagine that fringe-firm government intervention to create additional "downstream" copyright distributors (such as BMI or ASCAAP) could be worthwhile to protect the interests of diffuse "upstream" sellers.

20. This point will not always be true. To determine the smallest subsidy that will support new entry, regulators would need to estimate the costs and revenues for the individual firms.

21. However, applying dominant firm price restraints to fringe competitors is less likely to provide a competitive check if dominant firms remain unregulated.

22. See Heckman and Wolpin (1976).

23. See Shapo (1987).

24. See Tribe (1988).

25. The determination of market power is linked to the underlying definition of a relevant market. For example, under the Justice Department Merger Guidelines, relevant antitrust markets are defined so that colluding sellers would have the ability to raise price five percent. Guidelines Section 4.2. Analogously, a monopsonist buyer with market power should have the ability to lower the price (if the industry has an upward sloping supply curve).

26. At times monopsonists have incentives to distort supply by inefficiently depressing their demand to lower of the cost of goods purchased. This is illustrated by the fact that monopsonists will only purchase up to the point at which its marginal cost of the good purchased equals the monopsonist's marginal value. If the production of the good involves the use of scarce resources so that the supply curve is upward sloping, then the monopsonist will restrict the amount it purchases below the competitive level to the monopsonist's lower equilibrium demand. By suppressing the quantity demanded, the monopsonist is able to increase its profits by reducing the price below the competitive level. The possibility that monopsonists will sometimes act to reduce social welfare cautions against a mindless replication of monopsonist behavior.

27. Downstream monopsonists might also engage in second-sourcing to ensure uninterrupted supply of an essential input (which might be disrupted if a single supplier faced a strike or natural disaster). Yet these additional reasons for private second sourcing equally justify government intervention on behalf of diffuse consumers when assurance of an uninterrupted supply is desired.

28. Of course, even when a monopsonist would second source, government may not want to because the cost of implementation/administration may outweigh the benefits.

29. Besides directly buying goods, government could subsidize initial entry or create tax incentives to effectuate primary sourcing.

30. Minimum price regulation substitutes for direct second sourcing strategies, but at a cost. Monopsonists that second source can still buy from incumbents at a lower price than the subsidized entrant. Minimum price regulation forces consumers to buy from even the non-subsidized incumbents at a higher price. Of course, the incumbent dominant firms—knowing that monopsonists may continue to purchase from new entrants at a higher price—will have reduced incentives to cut their price. The amount of price-cutting in response to entry will not be as great when there is monopsonist demand and consequently the relative cost of minimum price regulation will not be as high.

31. The individualized negotiation of price is often referred to as "price discrimination." The practice of negotiating individual prices is often used by sellers with market power to extract consumer surplus, *see* Ayres, (1991), but price discrimination can also be used by consumers to extract producer surplus from the supply side of the market.

32. See Tribe (1988).

33. A random-choice rule seems outlandish. But tax auditing choices are, for example, often made stochastically. In calculating the fairness of random intervention, one should distinguish between "equal protection" arguments and "takings" arguments. Equal protection arguments focus on the disparate treatment of the regulated and the unregulated. Takings arguments, however, would suggest that, irrespective of competitors' treatment, it is unfair to restrain a regulated firm (without just compensation). It would be difficult to imagine that on takings grounds a government would be constrained from regulating a single firm when it could regulate an entire industry. In this instance, the greater takings power includes the smaller (see Epstein, 1988).

34. In some contexts, society may be better off committing (by a quasi-constitutional norm) to an equal protection standard that prohibits partial-industry regulation.

35. Indeed, Iraq's recent invasion of Kuwait and threatened invasion of Saudi Arabia can be understood in part as a form of partial-industry intervention aimed at shoring up oil prices. Saddam Hussein explicitly justified this action as a targeted punishment for Kuwait's violating its OPEC production quota. Moreover, the massing of Iraqi troops on the Saudi border has been interpreted as a threat designed to force Saudi Arabia to curtail its production.

36. An import tariff on oil, however, could maintain high domestic oil prices for Texas and Alaska without foregoing the benefits of lower OPEC prices. With an import tariff, the U.S. government would retain the benefit through tariff revenues. Higher taxes on oil could continue to deliver the environmental benefits of energy conservation while averting the deadweight loss of supracompetitive pricing.

37. Continuing subsidies may also undermine the incentives of regulated firms to undertake cost-saving ventures. Accordingly, regulators should not adopt an attitude of keeping fringe firms in at any cost—but only costs that reflect efficient production. In particular, agencies might create tournaments among potential fringe firms to determine the least cost subsidy.

Although yearly subsidies need to be limited to these cost-justified amounts, it is possible that subsidies be continuing. Returning to our analogy of private second sourcing, one finds that firms (such as GM) are willing to pay direct and indirect subsidies on an ongoing basis to retain second sources for inputs. Government similarly may be advised to bail out repeatedly competitive producers on behalf of its citizenry.

38. The Swedish considered but explicitly rejected industry-wide subsidies: "It is sometimes argued that general measures such as VAT exemption, reduced postal charges, etc., as opposed to selective measures, are neutral as regards competition. The analyses presented by the latest price commissions, however, show that a general system accentuates the market mechanisms, favours the strong papers and accelerates the concentration process" (Swedish Institute, 1988).

39. See *Red Lion Broadcasting Co.* v. *Federal Communications Commission*, 395 U.S. 367 (1969) and *Miami Herald Publishing Co.* v. *Tornillo*, 418 U.S. 241 (1974).

40. A specific type of equal time regulation commonly referred to as the "fairness doctrine" required "that discussion of public issues be presented on broadcast stations, and that each side of those issues must be given fair coverage." See *Red Lion Broadcasting Co.* v. *Federal Communications Commission*, 395 U.S. at 369.

41. Powe (1987: 5) quoting Bollinger, (1976: 27, 36). See also Ayres (1988b: 416).

42. See *In re* Policies and Rules Concerning Rates and Facilities Authorizations for Competitive Carrier Services (CC Docket 79–252), Notice of Inquiry and Proposed Rule Making, 77 F.C.C.2d 308 (1979), First Report and Order, 85 F.C.C.2d 1 (1980). For a discussion of these proceedings, see MCI Telecommunications, 765 F.2d at 1188–89.

43. See Fourth Report and Order, 95 F.C.C.2d at 578–79.

44. This seemingly radical notion has more prosaically been incorporated in proposals to prohibit tacit collusion. State intervention in response to tacit collusion or conscious parallelism changes the firm's payoffs and thereby encourages more independent laissez-faire pricing (Posner, 1969).

45. The dominant firm can be required to write rules to restrain monopoly abuse, which are then publicly approved. It can be required to put in place internal enforcement mechanisms to sustain compliance with those rules, and this self-enforcement can be backed up by public enforcement of the privately written rules.

Chapter 6

1. It is possible that consumers injured by pollution will prefer buying their oil from the regulated firms that take more precautions, but the fairly clear failure of consumer boycotts of Exxon testifies to the attenuated nature of such effects and argues strongly against relying solely on partial-industry regulation to engender compliance when contractual privity is absent.

REFERENCES

Abolafia, Michael Y. (1985) "Self-regulating as market maintenance: An organization perspective," in Roger G. Noll (ed.) *Regulatory Policy and the Social Sciences.* Berkeley: University of California Press.

Abrams, Kathryn (1988) "Law's republicanism," 97 *Yale Law Journal* 1591–1608.

Abreu, Dilip (1986) "Extremal equilibria of oligopolistic supergames," 39 *Journal of Economic Theory* 191–225.

Ackerman, Bruce A., and William T. Hassler (1981) *Clean Coal/Dirty Air.* New Haven: Yale University Press.

Adams, Jan (1977) *Citizen Inspectors in the Soviet Union: The People's Control Committee.* New York: Praeger.

Amsterdam, Anthony G. (1974) "Perspectives on the fourth amendment," 58 *Minnesota Law Review* 349–477.

Anderson, Frederick R., Allen V. Kneese, Phillip D. Reed, Russell B. Stevenson, and Serge Taylor (1977) *Environmental Improvement Through Economic Incentives.* Baltimore: John Hopkins University Press.

Andreen, William L. (1987) "Beyond words of exhortation: The Congressional prescription for vigorous federal enforcement of the Clean Water Act," 55 *George Washington Law Review* 202–258.

Arrow, Kenneth J. (1972) "Gifts and exchanges," 14 *Philosophy and Public Affairs* 343–362.

Axelrod, Robert (1980) "Effective choice in the prisoner's dilemma," 24 *Journal of Conflict Resolution* 3–25.

Axelrod, Robert (1984) *The Evolution of Cooperation.* New York: Basic Books.

Axelrod, Robert (1986) "An evolutionary approach to norms," 80 *American Political Science Review* 1094–1111.

Ayres, Ian (1987) "How Cartels punish: A structural theory of self-enforcing collusion." *Columbia Law Review* 295–325.

Ayres, Ian (1988a) "Determinants of airline carrier conduct," 8 *International Review of Law and Economics* 187–202.

Ayres, Ian (1988b) "Halfway home: On Powe's 'American Broadcasting and the First Amendment'," 13 *Law and Social Inquiry* 413–427.

Ayres, Ian (1991) "Fair Driving: Gender and Race Discrimination in new car negotiations," 104 *Harvard Law Review* 817–872 (1991).

Ayres, Ian, and Peter Siegelman (1988) "The economics of the insurance antitrust suits: Toward an exclusionary theory," 63 *Tulane Law Review* 971–997.

Ayres, Ian, and Robert Gertner (1989) "Filing gaps in incomplete contracts: An economic theory of default rules," 99 *Yale Law Journal* 87–130.

Baar, Ellen (1989) "A balance of control: Defining the risk bearers role in the regulatory equation," Paper to Annual Meeting of the Law and Society Association, Madison, Wisconsin.

Bailey, Elizabeth, and John Panzar (1981) "The contestability of the airline markets during the transition to deregulation." 44 *Law and Contemporary Problems* 125–145.

Bain, Joe (1959) *Industrial Organization*. New York: Wiley.

Bardach, Eugene, and Robert A. Kagan (1982) *Going by the Book: The Problem of Regulatory Unreasonableness*. Philadelphia: Temple University Press.

Barron, Jerome (1967) "Access to the press—A new First Amendment right," 80 *Harvard Law Review* 1641–1678.

Barzel, Yoram (1968) "Optimal timing of innovations," 50 *Review of Economics and Statistics* 348–355.

Baumol, William J., John C. Panzar, and Robert D. Willig (1988) *Contestable Markets and Theory of Industry Structure*. New York: Harcourt Brace Jovanovich.

Baumrind, D. (1973) "The development of instrumental competence through socialization," in A. D. Pick (ed.) *Minnesota Symposium on Motivation* (Vol.7). Minneapolis: University of Minnesota Press.

Bellah, R. N., R. Madsen, W. M. Sullivan, A. Swindler, and S. M. Tipton (1985) *Habits of the Heart: Individualism and Commitment in American Life*. Berkeley: University of California Press.

Bendor, Jonathan (1987) "In good times and bad: Reciprocity in an uncertain world," 31 *American Journal of Political Science* 531–558.

Bernstein, Marver H. (1955) *Regulating Business by Independent Commission*. Princeton: Princeton University Press.

Bernstein, Richard (1983) *Beyond Objectivism and Relativism: Science, Hermeneutics and Praxis*. Oxford: Blackwell.

Berry, Jeffrey M. (1984) *The Interest Group Society*. Boston: Little Brown.

Black, Donald (1976) *The Behavior of Law*. New York: Academic Press.

Bocock, Robert (1986) *Hegemony*. London: Travistock.

Boggiano, Ann K., Mary Barrett, Anne W. Weiher, Gary H. McLelland, and Cynthia M. Lusk (1987) "Use of the maximal-operant principle to motivate children's intrinsic interest," 53 *Journal of Personality and Social Psychology* 866–879.

Bollinger, Lee C. Jr. (1976) "Freedom of the press and public access: Toward a theory of partial regulation of the mass media," 75 *Michigan Law Review* 1–42.

Bowles, Chester (1971) *Promises to Keep: My Years in Public Life 1941–1969*. New York: Harper & Row.

Bowles, Samuel, and Herbert Gintis (1986) *Democracy and Capitalism*. New York: Basic Books.

Boyd, Robert, and Jeffrey P. Larberbaum (1987) "No pure strategy is evolutionarily stable in the repeated prisoner's dilemma game," 327 (no.6117) *Nature* 58–59.

Boyer, Barry (1989) "The federal trade commission and consumer protection," in Keith Hawkins and John Thomas (eds.) *Making Regulatory Policy*. Pittsburgh: University of Pittsburgh Press.

Boyer, Barry, and Errol Meidinger (1985) "Privatizing regulatory enforcement: A preliminary analysis of citizen suits under the federal environmental laws," 34 *Buffalo Law Review* 833–964.

Braithwaite, John (1980) "Inegalitarian consequences of egalitarian reform to control corporate crime," 53 *Temple Law Quarterly* 1127–1146.

Braithwaite, John (1982) "Enforced self regulation: A new strategy for corporate crime control," 80 *Michigan Law Review* 1466–1507.

Braithwaite, John (1984) *Corporate Crime in the Pharmaceutical Industry*. London: Routledge and Kegan Paul.

Braithwaite, John (1985) *To Punish or Persuade: Enforcement of Coal Mine Safety*. Albany: State University of New York Press.

Braithwaite, John (1989a) *Crime, Shame and Reintegration.* Sydney: Cambridge University Press.

Braithwaite, John (1989b) "Getting on with the job of understanding organizational deviance," Paper to Workshop on Organizational Deviance, Harvard Business School, March 9, 1989.

Braithwaite, John, Peter Grabosky, and Debra Rickwood (1986) "Research note: Corruption allegations and Australian business regulation," 19 *Australian and New Zealand Journal of Criminology* 179–186.

Braithwaite, John, Peter Grabosky, and John Walker (1987) "An enforcement taxonomy of regulatory agencies," 9 *Law and Policy* 323–351.

Braithwaite, John, Toni Makkai, Valerie Braithwaite, Diane Gibson, and David Ermann (1990) *The Contribution of the Standards Monitoring Process to the Quality of Nursing Home Life: A Preliminary Report.* Canberra: Department of Community Services and Health.

Braithwaite, John, and Philip Pettit (1990) *Not Just Deserts: A Republican Theory of Criminal Justice.* Oxford: Oxford University Press.

Brennan, Geoffrey, and James M. Buchanan (1985) *The Reason of Rules: Constitutional Political Economy.* Cambridge: Cambridge University Press.

Brest, Paul (1988) "Further beyond the republican revival: Toward radical republicanism," 97 *Yale Law Journal* 1623–1631.

Briloff, Abraham J. (1972) *Unaccountable Accounting.* New York: Harper & Row.

Bronfenbrenner, Urie (1972) "Another world of childhood," 19 *New Society* 278–286.

Call, G. D., and T. E. Keeler (1985) "Airline deregulation, fares and market behavior: Some evidence," in Andrew F. Daugherty (ed.) *Analytical Studies in Transport Economics.* Cambridge: Cambridge University Press.

Caminker, Evan (1989) "The constitutionality of *qui tam* actions," 99 *Yale Law Journal* 341–388.

Carson, W. G. (Kit), and Cathy Henenberg (1988) "The political economy of legislative change: Making sense of Victoria's new occupational health and safety legislation," 6 *Law in Context* 1–19.

Carson, W. G. (Kit), and Cathy Henenberg (1990) "Social justice at the workplace: The political economy of occupational health and safety laws," 16 *Social Justice* 124–140.

Caves, Douglas and Laurits Christensen (1980) "The relative efficiency of public and private firms in a competitive environment: The case of Canadian railroads," 1980 *Journal of Political Economy,* 958–976.

Cheit, Ross (1987) "Administrative procedures and private regulation," Paper to Annual Meeting of Law and Society Association, Washington D.C.

Cheit, Ross (1990) *Setting Safety Standards: Regulation in the Public and Private Sectors.* Berkeley: University of California Press.

Cheyne, J. A., and R. H. Walters (1969) "Intensity of punishment, timing of punishment, and cognitive structure as determinants of response inhibition," 7 *Journal of Experimental Child Psychology* 231–244.

Christie, Nils (1981) *Limits to Pain.* Oslo: Universitetsporlaget.

Clark, Michael (1986) *Regulating the City: Competition, Scandal and Reform.* Milton Keynes: Open University Press.

Clegg, Stewart (1975) *Power, Rule and Domination.* London: Routledge and Kegan Paul.

Clifford, William, and John Braithwaite (1981) *Cost Effective Business Regulation.* Canberra: Australian Institute of Criminology.

Clinard, Marshall, and Peter Yeager (1980) *Corporate Crime.* New York: Free Press.

Coase, Ronald H. (1937) "The nature of the firm," *Economica* 386–405.

Cohen, Joshua, and Joel Rogers (1983) *On Democracy: Toward a Transformation of American Society*. Harmondsworth: Penguin.

Cohen, Joshua, and Joel Rogers (forthcoming 1992) "Secondary associations in democratic governance." Unpublished manuscript.

Comment (1980) "Corporate self-investigations under the foreign corrupt practices act," 47 *University of Chicago Law Review* 803–811.

Cranston, Ross (1978) *Consumers and the Law*. London: Weidenfeld & Nicholson.

Crumplar, Thomas C. (1975) "An alternative to public and victim enforcement of the federal securities and antitrust laws: Citizen enforcement," 13 *Harvard Journal on Legislation* 76–124.

Davis, Kenneth Culp (1969) *Discretionary Justice*. Urbana: University of Illinois Press.

Day, Patricia, and Rudolph Klein (1987) "Residential care for the elderly: A billion pound experiment in policy-making," *Public Money*, March, 19–24.

Days, Drew S. III (1987) "Fullilove." 96 *Yale Law Journal* 453–485.

de Bono, Edward (1985) *Conflicts: A Better Way to Resolve Them*. London: Harrays.

Derthick, Martha, and Paul J. Quirk (1985) *The Politics of Deregulation*. Washington D.C.: Brookings Institution.

Dienstbier, R. A., D. Hillman, J. Lenhoff, J. Hillman, and M. C. Valkenaar (1975) "An emotion-attribution approach to moral behavior: Interfacing cognitive and avoidance theories of moral development," 82 *Psychological Review* 229–315.

Dingwall, Robert, John Eekelaar, and Topsy Murray (1983) *The Protection of Children*. Oxford: Basil Blackwell.

Dix, Theodore, and Joan E. Grusec (1983) "Parental influence techniques: An attributional analysis," 54 *Child Development* 645–652.

Duggan, A. J. (1980) "Consumer redress and the legal system," in A. J. Duggan and L. W. Darvall (eds.) *Consumer Protection Law and Theory*. Sydney: Law Book.

Dulles, John F. (1957) "Challenge and response in U.S. foreign policy," 36 *Foreign Affairs* 25–43.

Easterbrook, Frank (1984) "The limits of antitrust," 63 *Texas Law Review* 63–66.

Eckstein, Harry (1975) "Case study and theory in political science," in F. Greenstein and N. Polsby (eds.) *Handbook of Political Science, Vol. 7: Strategies of Inquiry*. Reading, Mass.: Addison-Wesley.

Edelman, J. M. (1964) *The Symbolic Uses of Politics*. Urbana: University of Illinois Press.

Eells, R. (1962) *The Government of Corporations*. New York: Free Press of Glencoe.

Elster, Jon, and K. Moene (eds.) (1988) *Alternatives to Capitalism*. Cambridge: Cambridge University Press.

Epstein, Richard A. (1988) "Foreward: Unconstitutional conditions, state power and the limit of consent," 102 *Harvard Law Review* 4–104.

Etzioni, Amitai (1965) "Organizational control structure," in James G. March (ed.) *Handbook of Organizations*. Chicago: Rand McNally.

Etzioni, Amitai (1988) *The Moral Dimension: Toward a New Economics*. New York: Free Press.

Evan, William M. (1962) "Public and private legal systems," in W. Evan (ed.) *Law and Sociology: Exploratory Essays*. New York: Free Press of Glencoe.

Farrell, Joseph, and Nancy Gallini (1988) "Second sourcing as a commitment: Monopoly incentives to attract competition," 103 *Quarterly Journal of Economics* 673–694.

Feeley, Malcolm (1983) *Court Reform on Trial: Why Simple Solutions Fail*. New York: Basic Books.

Fisher, Roger, and William Ury (1981) *Getting to Yes: Negotiating Agreements Without Giving In.* London: Business Books.

Fisse, Brent (1978) "The social policy of corporate criminal responsibility," 6 *Adelaide Law Review* 351–412.

Fisse, Brent, and John Braithwaite (1983) *The Impact of Publicity on Corporate Offenders.* Albany: State University of New York.

Frank, Nancy (1990) "Risk and distributive justice," Paper to Edwin Sutherland Conference on White-Collar Crime, Indiana University.

Frank, Robert H. (1988) *Passion Within Reason: The Strategic Role of Emotions.* New York: Norton.

Friere, Paulo (1985) *Pedagogy of the Oppressed.* New York: Continuum.

Fuller, Lon (1978) "The forms and limits of adjudication," 92 *Harvard Law Review* 394–395.

Gadamer, Hans-Georg (1975) *Truth and Method.* New York: Seabury Press.

Galanter, Mark (1981) "Justice in many rooms," 19 *Journal of Legal Pluralism* 1–47.

Galbraith, John K. (1967) *The New Industrial Estate.* London: Houghton.

Gambetta, Diego (1988) "Can we trust trust," in D. Gambetta (eds.) *Trust: Making and Breaking Cooperative Relations.* Oxford: Blackwell.

Garth, Bryant, Ilene H. Nagel, and S. Jay Plager (1988) "The institution of the private attorney general: Perspectives from an empirical study of class action litigation," 61 *Southern California Law Review* 353–398.

General Accounting Office (1983) Wastewater Dischargers are Not Complying with EPA Pollution Control Permits. Washington, D.C.: General Accounting Office.

Gerber, Jurg (1990) "Enforced self-regulation in the infant formula industry: A radical extension of an 'impractical' proposal," 17 *Social Justice* 98–111.

Gilbert, Richard, and David Newbery (1982) "Preemptive patenting and the persistence of monopoly," 72 *American Economic Review* 514–526.

Good, David (1988) "Individuals, impersonal relations and trust," in D. Gambetta (ed.) *Trust: Making and Breaking Cooperative Relations.* Oxford: Blackwell.

Goodin, Robert E. (1983) "Voting through the looking glass," 77 *American Political Science Review* 420–434.

Goodin, Robert E. (1984) "Itinerants, iterations and something in between," 14 *British Journal of Political Science* 129–132.

Grabosky, Peter (1991) "Professional advisers and white collar illegality: Towards explaining and excusing professional failure," Canberra: Australian Institute of Criminology.

Grabosky, Peter, and John Braithwaite (1986) *Of Manners Gentle: Enforcement Strategies of Australian Business Regulatory Agencies.* Melbourne: Oxford University Press.

Graetz, Michael J., and Louis L. Wilde (1985) "The economics of tax compliance: Fact and fantasy," 38 *National Tax Journal* 355–363.

Gramsci, Antoniono (1971) *Selections from the Prison Notebooks of A. Gramsci.* Ed. and trans. Q. Hoare and G. Nowell-Smith. London: Lawrence and Wishart.

Green, Mark J. (1978) *The Other Government: The Unseen Power of Washington Lawyers.* New York: Norton.

Greenhouse, Linda (1989) "Lineup of 2 Detroit papers upheld by court in tie vote," *The New York Times,* Nov. 14 at 29, col. 1.

Grusec, J. E. (1983) "The internalization of altruistic dispositions: A cognitive analysis," in E. T. Higgins, D. N. Ruble, and W. W. Hartup (eds.) *Social Cognition and Social Development: A Sociocultural Perspective.* New York: Cambridge University Press.

Grusec, J. E., L. Kuczynski, J. P. Rushton, and Z. M. Simutis (1978) "Modeling direct instruction and attributions: Effects on altruism," 14 *Development Psychology* 51–57.

Grusec, J. E., and E. Redler (1980) "Attribution, reinforcement and altruism: A development analysis," 16 *Development Psychology* 525–534.

Gunningham, Neil (1984) *Safeguarding the Worker: Job Hazards and the Role of Law*. Sydney: Law Book Company.

Haddock, David (1982) "Base-point pricing: Competitive vs collusive theories," 72 *American Economic Review* 289–306.

Halliday, Terence C. (1987) *Beyond Monopoly*. Chicago: University of Chicago Press.

Halliday, Terence C., and Bruce G. Carruthers (1990) "The state, professions and legal change: reform of the English insolvency act, 1977–1986," Paper Presented to the World Congress of Sociology, Madrid, August 13–17, 1990.

Hamilton, Robert W. (1978) "The role of nongovernmental standards in the development of mandatory standards affecting safety or health," 56 *Texas Law Review* 1329–1484.

Handler, Joel F. (1978) *Law and the Search for Community*. New York: Academic Press.

Handler, Joel F. (1986) *The Conditions of Discretion: Automony, Community, Bureaucracy*. New York: Russell Sage Foundation.

Handler, Joel F. (1988) "Dependent people, the state and the modern/postmodern search for the dialogic community," 35 *UCLA Law Review* 999–1113.

Handler, Joel F. (1989) "Community care for the frail elderly: A theory of empowerment." Los Angeles: University of California Los Angeles.

Handler, Joel F. (1990) *Social Movements and the Legal System: A Theory of Law Reform and Social Change*. Philadelphia: University of Pennsylvania Press.

Harris, Richard A., and Sidney M. Milkis (1989) *The Politics of Regulatory Change: A Tale of Two Cities*. New York: Oxford University Press.

Hart, Keith (1988) "Kinship, contract and trust: The economic organization of migrants in an African city slum," in D. Gambetta (ed.) *Trust: Making and Breaking Cooperative Relations*. Oxford: Blackwell.

Hawkins, Keith (1984) *Environment and Enforcement: Regulation and the Social Definition of Pollution*. Oxford: Clarendon.

Heckman, James, and Kenneth Wolpin (1976) "Does the contract compliance program work? An analysis of Chicago data," 29 *Industrial and Labor Relations Review* 544–564.

Herlihy, Edward D., and Theodore A. Levine (1976) "Corporate crisis: The overseas payment problem," 8 *Law and Policy in International Business* 547–629.

Hindess, Barry (1982) "Power, interests, and the outcomes of struggles," 6 *Sociology* 498–511.

Hindess, Barry (1988) *Choice, Rationality and Social Theory*. London: Unwin Hyman.

Hirschman, Albert O. (1984) "Against parsimony: Three easy ways of complicating some categories of economic discourse," 74 *American Economic Review* 88–96.

Hoffman, M. L. (1970) "Moral development," in P. H. Mussen (ed.) *Carmichael's Manual of Child Psychology*. New York: Wiley.

Hoffman, M. L. (1983) "Affective and cognitive processes in moral internalization," in E. T. Higgins, D. N. Ruble, and W. W. Hartup (eds.) *Social Cognition and Social Development*. New York: Cambridge University Press.

Hughes, Richard, and Robert Brewin (1979) *The Tranquilizing of America*. New York: Harcourt Brace Jovanovich.

Jost, Timothy (1983) "The joint commission of accreditation of hospitals: Private regulation of health care and the public interest," 24 *Boston College Law Review* 835–923.

Jost, Timothy (1988) "The necessary and proper role of regulation to assure the quality of health care," 25 *Houston Law Review* 525–598.

Kagan, Robert A. (1978) *Regulatory Justice: Implementing a Wage-Price Freeze*. New York: Russell Sage Foundation.

Kagan, Robert A., and John T. Scholz (1984) "The criminology of the corporation and regulatory enforcement strategies," in K. Hawkins and J. Thomas (eds.) *Enforcing Regulation*. Boston: Kluwer-Nijhoff.

Kaiser, Karl, George Leber, Alvis Mertes, and Franz-Josef Schulze (1985) "Nuclear weapons and the preservation of peace," in Fred Holroyd (ed.) *Thinking About Nuclear Weapons: Analyses and Prescriptions*. London: Groom Helm.

Katz, Robert N. (1976) "Industry self-regulation: A viable alternative to government regulation," in R. Katz (ed.) *Protecting Consumer Interests*. Cambridge, Mass.: Ballinger.

Kaufman, Herbert (1960) *The Forest Ranger: A Study in Administrative Behavior*. Baltimore: John Hopkins Press.

Keane, John (1988) *Democracy and Civil Society*. London: Verso.

Keillor, Garrison (1985) *Lake Wobegon Days*. New York: Viking Penguin.

Kolko, Gabriel (1965) *Railroads and Regulation, 1877–1916*. Princeton: Princeton University Press.

Krattenmaker, Thomas, and Steve Salop (1986) "Anti-competitive exclusion: Raising rivals' costs to achieve power over price," 96 *Yale Law Journal* 209–293.

Lampert, Nick (1985) *Whistle-Blowing in the Soviet Union*. New York: Schocken Books.

Langbein, Laura, and Cornelius M. Kerwin (1985) "Implementation, negotiation and compliance in environmental and safety regulation," 47 *Journal of Politics* 854–880.

Lansky, Melvin R. (1984) "Violence, shame and the family," 5 *International Journal of Family Psychiatry* 21–40.

Latané, Bibb, and John M. Darley (1970) *The Unresponsive Bystander: Why Doesn't He Help?* Englewood Cliffs, N.J.: Prentice-Hall.

Lepper, M. R. (1973) "Dissonance, self-perception and honesty in children," 25 *Journal of Personality and Social Psychology* 65–74.

Lepper, M. R. (1981) "Intrinsic and extrinsic motivation in children: Detrimental effects of superfluous social controls," in W. A. Collins (ed.) *Aspects of the Development of Competence: The Minnesota Symposium on Child Psychology*, Vol. 14. Hillsdale, N.J.: Erlbaum.

Lepper, M. R. (1983) "Social control processes, attributions of motivation and the internalization of social values," in E. T. Higgins, D. N. Ruble, and W. W. Hartup (eds.) *Social Cognition and Social Development: A Sociocultural Perspective*. New York: Cambridge University Press.

Lepper, M. R., and D. Greene (1978) *The Hidden Costs of Reward*. Hillsdale, N.J.: Erlbaum.

Levi, Margaret (1987) *Of Rules and Revenue*. Berkeley: University of California Press.

Levi, Michael (1987) *Regulating Fraud: White-Collar Crime and the Criminal Process*. London: Travistock.

Lewis-Beck, Michael S., and John R. Alford (1980) "Can government regulate safety: The coal mine example," 74 *American Political Science Review* 745–756.

Lorenz, Edward H. (1988) "Neither friends nor strangers: Informal networks of subcontracting in French industry," in D. Gambetta (ed.) *Trust: Making and Breaking Cooperative Relations*. Oxford: Blackwell.

Lowi, Theodore (1969) *The End of Liberalism: Ideology, Policy and the Crisis of Public Authority*. New York: Norton.

Luhmann, Niklas (1979) *Trust and Power*. Chichester: Wiley.

Macaulay, Stuart (1963) "Non-contractual relations in business: A preliminary study," 28 *American Sociological Review* 55–67.

MacAvoy, Paul A. (1965) *The Economic Effects of Regulation: The Trunk-Line Railroad*

Cartels and the Interstate Commerce Commission before 1900. Cambridge, Mass.: MIT Press.

Macey, Jonathan (1986) "Promoting public-regarding legislation through statutory interpretation: An interest group model," 86 *Columbia Law Review* 223–268.

Mann, Kenneth (1985) *Defending White Collar Crime.* New Haven: University Press.

Manning, Peter K. (1989) "The limits of knowledge: The role of information in regulation," in Keith Hawkins and John Thomas (eds.) *Making Regulatory Policy.* Pittsburgh: University of Pittsburgh Press.

Marcus, Alfred A. (1980) *Promise and Performance: Choosing and Implementing an Environmental Policy.* Westport, Conn.: Greenwood.

McChesny, Fred (1987) "Rent extraction and rent creation in the economic theory of regulation," 16 *Journal of Legal Studies* 101–118.

McCloy, John J. (1976) *The Great Oil Spill.* New York: Chelsea House.

McFarland, Andrew S. (1976) *Public Interest Lobbies: Decision Making on Energy.* Washington D.C.: American Enterprise Institute.

Mearsheimer, John S. (1983) *Conventional Deterrence.* Ithaca: Cornell University Press.

Meidinger, Errol (1986) "Regulatory culture: A theoretical outline," 9 *Law and Policy* 355–386.

Meidinger, Errol (1987) "Regulatory culture and democratic theory," Working Paper, Baldy Center for Law and Social Policy, State University of New York, Buffalo.

Meiners, Roger E., and Bruce Yandle (1989) *Regulation and the Reagan Era.* New York: Holmes and Meier.

Melnick, R. Shep (1983) *Regulation and the Courts: The Case of the Clean Air Act.* Washington D.C.: Brookings Institution.

Mendeloff, John (1979) *An Economic and Political Analysis of Occupational Safety and Health Policy.* Cambridge: MIT Press.

Menkel-Meadow, Carrie (1984) "Toward another view of legal negotiation: The structure of problem solving," 31 *UCLA Law Review* 754–842.

Michelman, Frank (1988) "Law's Republic," 97 *Yale Law Journal* 1493–1537.

Michels, Robert (1915) *Political Parties.* Glencoe: Free Press.

Mileti, Dennis S., David F. Gillespie, and D. Stanley Eitzen (1979) "Structure and decision making in corporate organizations," 63 *Sociology and Social Research* 723–744.

Milgram, Stanley (1974) *Obedience to Authority: An Experimental View.* New York: Harper Colophon Books.

Mills, C. Wright (1940) "Situated actions and vocabularies of motive," 5 *American Sociological Review* 904–913.

Moore, Charles A. (1987) "Taming the giant corporation: Some cautionary remarks on the deterrability of corporate crime," 33 *Crime and Delinquency* 379–402.

Moran, A. J. (1986) "The business regulation review unit," 13 *Canberra Bulletin of Public Administration* 283–287.

Nader, Laura, and Claire Nader (1985) "A wide angle on regulation: An anthropological perspective," in R. G. Noll (ed.) *Regulatory Policies of the Social Sciences.* Berkeley: University of California Press.

Neustadt, Richard M. (1980) "The administration's regulatory reform program: An overview," 32 *Administrative Law Review* 129–159.

Noble, Charles (1986) *Liberalism at Work: The Rise and Fall of OSHA.* Philadelphia: Temple University Press.

Nonet, Philipe, and Philip Selznick (1978) *Law and Society in Transition: Toward Responsive Law.* New York: Harper & Row.

Olson, Johan P. (1981) "Integrated organizational participation in government," in P. C.

Nystrom and W. H. Starbuck (eds.) *Handbook of Organizational Design*, Vol. 2. Oxford: Oxford University Press.

Olson, Mancur (1965) *The Logic of Collective Action*. Cambridge: Harvard University Press.

Orland, Leonard, and H. R. Tyler Jr. (1987) *Corporate Crime Law Enforcement in America*. New York: Practising Law Institute.

Osborne, D. R. (1976) "Cartel problems," 66 *American Economic Review* 835–844.

Osgood, Charles E. (1985) "The GRIT strategy," in F. Holroyd (ed.) *Thinking About Nuclear Weapons: Analyses and Prescriptions*. London: Groom Helm.

Page, Alan C. (1980) "Self regulation and codes of practice," *Journal of Business Law* 24–31.

Page, Alan C. (1987) "Financial services: The self-regulatory alternative," in Robert Baldwin and Christopher McCrudden (eds.) *Regulation and Public Law*. London: Weidenfeld and Nicolson.

Pantich, Leo (1979) "The development of corporatism in liberal democracies," in P. C. Schmitter and G. Lehmbruch (eds.) *Trends Toward Corporatist Intermediation*. Beverly Hills: Sage.

Pantich, Leo, (1980) "Recent theorizations of corporatism: Reflections on a growth industry," 31 *British Journal of Sociology* 159–187.

Parke, R. D. (1969) "Effectiveness of punishment as an interaction of intensity, timing, agent nurturance and cognitive structuring," 40 *Child Development* 213–235.

Peltzman, Sam (1980) "The growth of government," 23 *Journal of Law and Economics* 209–287.

Pengilley, Warren (1989) "Competition, law and voluntary codes of self-regulation," Paper to Trade Practices Workshop, Broadbeach, Queensland.

Pettit, Philip (1988) "The consequentialist can recognize rights," 38 *Philosophical Quarterly* 42–55.

Pettit, Philip (1989) "The freedom of the city: A republican ideal," in A. Hamlin and P. Pettit (eds.) *The Good Polity*. Oxford: Blackwell.

Pettit, Philip, and Geoffrey Brennan (1986) "Restrictive consequentialism," 65 *Australasian Journal of Philosophy* 438–55.

Pittman, Thane S., Eugenia E. Cooper, and Timothy W. Smith (1977) "Attribution of causality and the overjustification effect," 3 *Personality and Social Psychology Bulletin* 280–283.

Porter, Michael E. (1990) *The Competitive Advantage of Nations*. London: Macmillan.

Posner, Richard A. (1969) "Oligopoly and the antitrust law: A suggested approach," 21 *Stanford Law Review* 1562–1606.

Posner, Richard A. (1976) *Antitrust Law: An Economic Perspective*. Chicago: University of Chicago Press.

Posner, Richard A. (1986) *Economic Analysis of Law*. Boston: Little, Brown.

Powe, Lucas A. Jr. (1987) *American Broadcasting and the First Amendment*. Berkeley: University of California Press.

President's Commission on Coal (1980) *The Acceptable Replacement of Imported Oil with Coal*. Washington D.C.: Government Printing Office.

Quirk, Paul J. (1981) *Industry Influence in Federal Regulatory Agencies*. Princeton: Princeton University Press.

Quirk, Paul J. (1989) "The cooperative resolution of policy conflict," *American Political Science Review* 905–921.

Rasmussen, Eric (1989) *Games and Information*. New York: Blackwell.

Rawls, John (1973) *A Theory of Justice*. London: Oxford University Press.

Reed, Jean D. (1980) "Corporate self-investigations under the foreign corrupt practices act," 47 *University of Chicago Law Review* 803–823.

Rees, Joseph (1988) *Reforming the Workplace: A Study of Self-Regulation in Occupational Safety*. Philadelphia: University of Pennsylvania Press.

Reichman, Nancy (1988) "Risk, trust and regulation: Control and crisis in financial markets," Paper to the Annual Meeting of the American Sociological Association, Atlanta, Georgia.

Reinganum, Jennifer (1985) "Innovation and industry evolution," 100 *Quarterly Journal of Economics* 81–99.

Reiss, Albert J. (1980) "The policing of organizational life," Paper to International Seminar on "Management and the Control of Police Organizations," Nijenrode, Netherlands.

Reiss, Albert J. (1984) "Selecting strategies of social control over organizational life," in K. Hawkins and J. Thomas (eds.) *Enforcing Regulation*. Boston: Kluwer-Nijhoff.

Riordan, Michael H., and David E. Sappington (1989) "Second sourcing," 20 *Rand Journal of Economics* 41–58.

Rogers, Joel (1989) "The limits of legal liberalism: Implementation and empowerment in administrative regulation," Paper to Law and Society Association Annual Meeting, Madison, Wisconsin.

Rogers, Joel (1990) "Divide and conquer: Further 'reflections on the distinctive character of American labor laws'," 1 *Wisconsin Law Review* 1–147.

Romano Richard E. (1991) "When excessive consumption is rational," 81 *American Economic Review* 553–564.

Romano, Roberta (1985) "Law as a product: Some pieces of the incorporation puzzle," 1 *Journal of Law, Economics and Organization* 225–283.

Ronalds, Chris (1989) *I'm Still An Individual: A Blueprint for the Rights of Residents in Nursing Homes and Hostels*. Canberra: Department of Community Services and Health.

Rose-Ackerman, Susan (1988) "Progressive law and economics—and the new administrative law," 98 *Yale Law Journal* 341–368.

Rotenberg, Julio, and Garth Saloner (1986) "A Supergame—theoretic model of price wars during booms," 76 *American Economics Review* 390–407.

Rushton, Philippe (1980) *Altruism, Socialization and Society*. Englewood Cliffs, N.J.: Prentice-Hall.

Sarat, Austin, and William L. F. Felstiner (1988) "Law and social relations: Vocabularies of motive in lawyer/client interaction," 22 *Law and Society Review* 101–133.

Scheff, Thomas J. (1989) *Microsociology: Discourse, Emotion and Social Structure*. Chicago: University of Chicago Press.

Schelling, Thomas C. (1966) *Arms and Influence*. New Haven: Yale University Press.

Schelling, Thomas C. (1974) "Command and control," in J. W. McKie (ed.) *Social Responsibility and the Business Predicament*. Washington, D.C.: Brookings Institution.

Scherer, Frederick M. (1980) *Industrial Market Structure and Economic Performance* (2nd ed.). Chicago: Rand McNally.

Schmitter, Phillippe C. (1979) "Still the century of corporatism?" in P. C. Schmitter and G. Lehmbrush (eds.) *Trends Toward Corporatist Intermediation*. Beverly Hills: Sage.

Scholz, John T. (1984a) "Deterrence, cooperation and the ecology of regulatory enforcement," 18 *Law and Society Review* 179–224.

Scholz, John T. (1984b) "Voluntary compliance and regulatory policy," 6 *Law and Policy* 385–404.

Scholz, John T. (1991) "Cooperative regulatory enforcement and the politics of administrative effectiveness," 85 *American Political Science Review* 115–136.

Scholz, John T., and F. H. Wei (1986) "Regulatory enforcement in a federalist system," 80 *American Political Science Review* 1249–1270.

Schwartzman, David, (1976) *Innovation in the Pharmaceutical Industry.* Baltimore: John Hopkins University Press.

Sciulli, David (1988) "Foundations of societal constitutionalism: Principles from the concepts of communicative action and procedural legality," 39 *British Journal of Sociology* 377–408.

Shapiro, Martin (1988) *Who Guards the Guardians? Judicial Control of Administration.* Athens: University of Georgia Press.

Shapiro, Susan (1987) "The social control of impersonal trust," 93 *American Journal of Sociology* 623–658.

Shapo, Marshall S. (1987) *Cases and Materials on Tort and Compensation.* St. Paul: West.

Shleifer, Andrei (1985) "A theory of yardstick competition," 16 *Rand Journal of Economics* 319–327.

Sigler, Jay A., and Joseph E. Murphy (1988) *Interactive Corporate Compliance: An Alternative to Regulatory Compulsion.* Westport, Conn.: Quorum.

Silbey, Susan S. (1984) "The consequences of responsive regulation," in K. Hawkins and J. Thomas (eds.) *Enforcing Regulation.* Boston: Kluwer-Mijhoff.

Simon, Herbert A. (1982) *Models of Bounded Rationality.* Cambridge: MIT Press.

Simpson, Antony E. (1977) *The Literature of Police Corruption.* New York: John Jay Press.

Solomon, Lewis D., and Nancy Nowak (1980) "Managerial restructuring: Prospects for a new regulatory tool," 56 *Notre Dame Lawyer* 120–140.

Sommer, A. A. Jr. (1977) "The impact of the SEC on corporate governance," 41 *Law and Contemporary Problems* 115–145.

Spence, Michael (1975) "Monopoly, quality of regulation," 6 *Bell Journal of Economics* 417–429.

Stalans, Loretta J., Karyl A. Kinsey, and Kent W. Smith (1990) "Talking about tax compliance: The role of complexity, legitimacy and effort." Paper to Law and Society Association Meeting, San Francisco.

Stenning, Philip C., Clifford D. Shearing, Susan Addario, and Mary G. Condon (1990) "Controlling interests: Two conceptions of order in regulating a financial market," in W. L. Friedland (ed.) *Securing Compliance.* Toronto: University of Toronto Press.

Stewart, Joseph, James E. Anderson, and Zona Taylor (1982) "Presidential and congressional support for 'independent' regulatory commissions: Implications of the budgetary process," 35 *Western Political Quarterly* 319–326.

Stewart, Richard B. (1981) "Regulation, innovation and administrative law: A conceptual framework," 69 *California Law Review* 1256–1377.

Stewart, Richard B. (1983) "Regulation in the liberal state: The role of non-commodity values," 92 *Yale Law Journal* 1537–1590.

Stigler, George J. (1964) "A theory of oligopoly," 72 *Journal of Political Economy* 44–61.

Stigler, George J. (1971) "The theory of economic regulation," 2 *Bell Journal of Economics and Management Science* 3–21.

Stone, Christopher D. (1975) *Where the Law Ends: The Social Control of Corporate Behavior.* New York: Harper & Row.

Stone, Christopher D. (1980) "The place of enterprise liability in the control of corporate conduct," 90 *Yale Law Journal* 1–77.

Streeck, Wolfgang, Peter Seglow, and Pat Wallace (1981) "Competition and monopoly in interest representation: A comparative analysis of trade union structure in the railway industries of Great Britain and West Germany," 2 *Organizational Studies* 307–330.

Streeck, Wolfgang, and Phillipe Schmitter (1985) "Community, market, state and associations? The prospective contribution of interest governance to social order," in W. Streek and P. Schmitter (eds.) *Private Interest Government*. Beverly Hills: Sage Publications.

Sullivan, Kathleen M. (1988) "Rainbow republicanism," 97 *Yale Law Journal* 1713–1723.

Sunstein Cass (1988) "Beyond the republican revival," 97 *Yale Law Journal* 1539–1590.

Sunstein Cass (1990) *After the Rights Revolution: Reconceiving the Regulatory State.* Cambridge, Mass.: Harvard University Press.

Sutton, Adam, and Ron Wild (1978) "Corporate crime and social structure," in Paul R. Wilson and John Braithwaite (eds.) *Two Faces of Deviance*. Brisbane: University of Queensland Press.

Swedish Institute (1988) *Monograph on News Media*. Stockholm: Swedish Institute.

Tay, Alice Erh-Soon (1990) "Communist visions, Communist realities and the role of law," 17 *Journal of Law and Society* 155–169.

Taylor, Michael J. (1976) *Anarchy and Cooperation*. London: Wiley.

Tirole, J. (1988) *The Theory of Industrial Organization*. Cambridge: MIT Press.

Tramontozzi, Paul N., and Kenneth W. Chilton (1987) *U.S. Regulatory Agencies Under Reagan 1960–1988*. St. Louis: Center for the Study of American Business, Washington University.

Tribe, Laurence (1988) *American Constitutional Law*. Mineola: Foundation Press.

Tyler, Tom R. (1990) *Why People Obey the Law*. New Haven: Yale University Press.

Unger, Roberto M. (1987) *False Necessity*. Cambridge: Cambridge University Press.

United Nations Commission on Transnational Corporations (1977) "International standards of accounting and reporting," Agenda Item 9(b), U.N. Doc. E/C.10/33.

United States Congress (1989) "Untie the elderly: Quality care without restraints," Serial No. 101-H, Washington D.C.: U.S. Government Printing Office.

Van Maanen, John and Stephen R. Barley (1985) "Cultural organization: Fragments of a theory," in P. J. Frost, L. F. Moore, M. R. Lewis, C. Lundberg and J. Martin (eds.) *Organizational Culture*. Beverly Hills: Sage.

Vickers, John and George Yarrow (1991) "Economic perspectives on privatazation," 5 *Journal of Economic Perspectives* 111–132.

Victor, Bart, and John B. Cullen (1988) "The occupational bases of ethical work climates," 33 *Administrative Science Quarterly* 101–125.

Viscusi, W., and R. J. Zeckhauser (1979) "Optimal standards with incomplete enforcement," 27 *Public Policy* 437–456.

Vogel, David (1986) *National Styles of Regulation: Environmental Policy in Great Britain and the United States*. Ithaca: Cornell University Press.

Vroom, Victor H. (1969) "Industrial social psychology," *The Handbook of Social Psychology*, (2nd Ed.) Volume V, 196–268. Reading, Mass.: Addison-Wesley.

Walker, Jack L. (1983) "The origin and maintenance of interest groups in America," 77 *American Political Science Review* 390–406.

Wardell, William M. (1979) "The impact of regulation on new drug development," in Robert I. Chien (ed.) *Issues in Pharmaceutical Economics*. Lexington, Mass.: Lexington Books.

Weidenbaum, Murray L. (1979) *The Future of Business Regulation*. New York: Amacom.

Wells, Joseph T. (1988) "Banking's bleak forecast," 2 *The White Paper* 2–4.

Wilkins, Leslie (1964) *Social Deviance*. London: Travistock.

Williamson, Oliver E. (1990) *Antitrust Economics: Mergers Contracts and Strategic Behavior*. Oxford: Basil Blackwell.

Willmott, Hugh C. (1985) "Setting accounting standards in the U.K.: The emergence of private accounting bodies and their role in the regulation of public accounting practice," in W. Streek and P. D. Schmitter (eds.) *Private Interest Government.* Beverly Hills: Sage.

Winter, Gerd (1985) "Bartering rationality in regulation," 19 *Law and Society Review* 219–250.

World Almanac and Book of Facts (1990) New York: Newspaper Enterprise Association.

Yeager, Peter (1990) "Realms of reason: Notes on the division of moral labor in corporate behavior," Paper to Edwin Sutherland Conference on White-Collar Crime, Indiana University.

Zahn-Waxler, C. Z., M. R. Radke-Yarrow, and R. A. King (1979) "Child rearing and children's prosocial initiations towards victims in distress," 50 *Child Development* 319–330.

Zartman, I. William, and Maureen R. Berman (1982) *The Practical Negotiator.* New Haven: Yale University Press.

INDEX

Abolafia, M. Y., 163n.3
Abrams, K., 164n.12
Abreu, D., 43
Accommodation, 91–92
Accountability, 114, 115
Accounting standards, corporate, 109
Ackerman, T. A., 56, 174n.11
Adams, J., 13
Affirmative action, 141
Agencies, regulatory, 6, 19, 36, 44, 46, 87, 96, 115, 118, 120, 123, 127, 132, 137; administration of, 10–11
Agriculture Department, 9
Air Navigation Act, 174n.15
Airline industry, 139, 147, 150, 151, 175n.45, 177n.2
Alford, J. R., 107
American Council on Hospital Standards, 8
American Pharmaceutical Manufacturing Association, 176n.50
Amsterdam, A. G., 174n.12
Anderson, F. R., 38
Andreen, W. L., 8
Antitrust regulation, 9, 12, 15, 16, 149, 150, 179n.25
Arendt, H., 97
Arrow, K. J., 85, 86
Asquith, L., 172n.40
Association of Future Brokers and Dealers, 102
Association of the British Pharmaceutical Manufacturing Industries, 176
Associational order, 14, 16
AT & T, 153, 178n.9
Australian Automotive Industry Authority, 100
Australian Broadcasting Tribunal, 40, 46
Australian Conservation Foundation, 159
Australian Consumers' Association, 15
Australian Council of Trade Unions (ACTU), 76, 170n.28
Australian Federation of Consumer Organizations, 84, 100, 166n.3
Australian Retailers Association, 102
Australian Trade Practices Commission (TPC), 15, 16, 102, 163nn.4, 6
Aviation industry. *See* Airline industry

Axelrod, R., 21, 26, 29, 42, 55, 56, 60, 62, 63, 70, 74, 98, 167nn.9, 10, 12, 168n.19
Ayres, I., 62, 108, 137, 139, 147, 150–52, 166n.2, 178n.12, 179n.31, 180n.41

Baar, E., 59, 170n.35, 171n.35
Bailey, E., 166n.2
Bain, J., 133
Bardach, E., 20, 25, 26, 42, 56, 68, 118, 129
Barley, S. R., 93
Barron, J., 152
Barry Wright Corp. v. IIT Grinnell Corp., 140, 144, 178n.16
Barzel, Y., 142
Base-point pricing, 177n.7
Basic v. Levinson, 174n.8
"Battle of the Sexes" game, 171n.39
Baumol, W. J., 57, 177n.6
Bechtel plan, 176n.51
Bellah, R. N., 13
Bendor, J., 170n.29
Benign big gun agencies: 40–41, 51, 165n.13; theory, 47, 50, 155
Bentsen, L., Senator, 8
Berman, M. R., 88
Bernstein, M. H., 81
Bernstein, R., 97, 99
Berry, J. M., 12
Black, D., 55
Bocock, R., 79
Boggiano, A. K., 49, 50
Bollinger, L. C., 152, 153, 180n.41
Bowles, C., 26
Bowles, S., 75
Boyd, R., 168n.12
Boyer, B., 10, 76, 83, 167n.6
Braithwaite, J.: agencies, regulatory, 11, 22, 38, 40, 55–56, 74, 86, 102, 164n.11, 169n.23, 170n.30; antitrust regulation, 15; coal mining industry, 22, 26, 34, 112, 117, 122, 127; community, 13, 98; compliance, 20, 35, 46, 81; consumer protection, 15; forgiveness, 51; law, 171n.37, 174n.14; nursing home industry, 27–30, 31, 50, 90, 112, 127, 170n.32; phar-

Printed in the United Kingdom
by Lightning Source UK Ltd.
136147UK00002B/119/A